THE
MIRROR
OF

THE
MIRROR
OF

A Rediscovery of True Love & Human Sexuality
within a Happy Marriage & Family

Joachim Chu Chee-Kong

 **World Scientific**

NEW JERSEY · LONDON · SINGAPORE · BEIJING · SHANGHAI · HONG KONG · TAIPEI · CHENNAI

Published by

World Scientific Publishing Co. Pte. Ltd.
5 Toh Tuck Link, Singapore 596224
USA office: 27 Warren Street, Suite 401-402, Hackensack, NJ 07601
UK office: 57 Shelton Street, Covent Garden, London WC2H 9HE

Library of Congress Cataloging-in-Publication Data
Chu, Joachim Chee-Kong.
   The mirror of love : a rediscovery of true love and human sexuality within a happy marriage and family / Joachim Chu Chee-Kong.
      pages cm
   ISBN 978-9814556736
   1. Marriage. 2. Marital quality. 3. Love. 4. Sex. 5. Families. I. Title.
   HQ734.C556 2014
   306.81--dc23

2013050112

British Library Cataloguing-in-Publication Data
A catalogue record for this book is available from the British Library.

In-house Editor: Lum Pui Yee

Typeset by Stallion Press
Email: enquiries@stallionpress.com

Printed in Singapore

Preface

A loving relation that is founded on excessive "self-love" is likely be short lived, while a loving relation that is focused on "love for others," respect and equality would bring dignity to such a relation and is likely to be fruitful and long lasting. The internal struggle between "self-love" and the "love for others" forms the fundamental essence of the two opposing forces in this book on "Mirror of Love." To speak about love and marriage would draw attention; if I choose to speak about human sexuality, it would turn heads. In reality, to speak about human sexuality, either in public or private venue, is naturally a daunting challenge. The subject is so vast and diverse that deliberations on it would often expose contradictory thoughts and differing ideologies prevalent in our modern society.

When we take a look into the mirror of love, do we see a reflection of our portrait in "self-love," or do we see a reflection of our portrait in "love for others"? When I contemplate what "self-love" is, and what it consequently may bring, I can think of: pride, selfishness, impatience, greed, laziness, self-gratification and self-satisfaction, hatred, envy, anger, and a disposition of treating others as an object of selfish desire and pleasure. Whereas when I contemplate what "love for others" is, and what it consequently may bring; I can think of charity, understanding, patience, joy, forgiveness, kindness, diligence, self-mastery, meekness and a disposition of treating others as equal human beings, with dignity.

In the crossroad of human dignity, new ideologies promulgate and equate happiness to mere pleasure, reducing genuine human love and sexuality to the level of animal mating. If the basis of marriage were sex and the sexual pleasure that it brings with it, then it is a huge misunderstanding. When the first thrill is gone after several years into marriage, the couple would probably feel that the marriage bond does not exist any longer. "The pleasure associated with love, or what is today called sex, is the frosting on the cake; its purpose is to make us love the cake, not to ignore it." (Fulton Sheen) The mentality of wanting only the frost — the pleasurable — and not the cake; finds its roots in the confusion with the essence of true love. What some people love is not the person, but the experience and the pleasure derived from being in love. "One of the greatest illusions of lovers is to believe that the intensity of their sexual attraction is the guarantee of the perpetuity of their love." (Fulton Sheen)

To write a book on human passion and sexuality has never come across my mind in my entire adult life, simply because I thought I would never have the interest to do so as an investor and business executive. However, my inspiration to say something about the subject came alive in recent years, from witnessing the immense sufferings resulting from marital failures and broken families, of people and children who I personally know. It is not difficult to see the level of psychological trauma in separation of couples and its devastating emotional effects onto children of divorced family; and other tragic happenings as a consequence of failure in marital love and commitment. The morality of human sexuality within marriage between husband and wife should be founded on genuine self-giving love. It is essential for youngsters to realize before entering into marital commitment that love is primarily in the *will*, not in the emotion, or the sexual organ.

"Mirror of Love" consists of both theories and practical discussions. It draws references and quotations from educators and philosophers, particularly from one of the greatest theologians and philosophers of our time, blessed John Paul II from whom I have the opportunity to learn so much and influenced by his teachings in "Personalism" and the social doctrine about the rights and duties of individuals and society. Readers may find some of the discussions and quotations of his teachings in the following chapters. This book does not intend to contradict anyone, or his or her action or lifestyle, nor is it to address the issues only to those who think that they might be committing errors in their relationships. Based on many contradictory voices and comments, this book intends to enlighten with insights from the perspective of "To love is to will the good of another." It intends to clarify and to encourage, especially to young persons and married couples who are seeking a point of reference in order to lead a joyful and committed loving relation in marriage in accordance with what the nature presents.

This book is written from the perspective of a husband and father, in layman language. The readers will find a short memoir of my family history and my work life in different chapters, and some real life examples are used to enhance the discussion. This book does not merely aim at addressing fellow Catholic Christians, but it also aims to address all married couples, parents and educators, young and matured persons, believers and non-believers, of different cultural backgrounds, who have interest in seeking the ultimate answer for happiness, and the truth about human love and sexuality within the context of a happy marriage. I have tried to compile all the relevant information, material and experience, with examples of my own, to the best of my knowledge based on studies, research, questions, feedback and comments of people from all "walks of life" of different cultures, over last two decades.

During and after writing this book, I must say that I have benefited substantially from the richness and the immensity of the subject. It gives me great joy to share the knowledge and experience surrounding this important area of marital love and human passion and sexuality with readers. My emotion articulates the sense, in a thought: if only we, ordinary people, men and women, young and old, were to understand a tiny fraction of the meaning of the original design of human passion and sexuality; our world would not have been in such a mess as it is today; and as well as in the past.

I like to give special thanks to my beloved wife of over 30 years who has stood by me as my great companion and genuine friend, and for her patience in supporting me in writing this book in the last several years. I like to give my special tributes to my parents, and friends who have inspired me to write my very first book, 'thank you' to them all.

Contents

Chapter 1

Take a Closer Look

During a family trip to visit our sons who were then studying in United Kingdom, my wife and I had a chance to meet up with some of our old friends living there. In our conversation, a topic such as "rich and famous of today's world" came up. Our English lady-friend said to us while sipping her tea after a delicious lunch with her husband: "The properties price in London has gone crazily expensive nowadays, don't you think so?" Her husband followed: "You know a house was recently sold for over a-hundred-million pounds, who can afford that kind of money?" Indeed, there was a transaction in the premium housing market in Central London which was considered the most expensive property sold in the country at the time, by a foreign investor. Our lady-friend continued: "Now some wealthy people can afford a luxurious life comparable to the nobles, it is absolutely amazing, isn't it?" After a moment of these words, the husband continued: "It is unbelievable, how could anyone get to that level of wealth in the first place?" True enough, today some individuals have accumulated such great wealth and resources that enables them a life truly as luxurious as, if not more than, the nobles, the kings and queens of the present day could afford.

Rarely has our human race possessed such an abundance of wealth, and resources as it does today, some individuals possess economic power that is comparable to, if not more than, a nation; their power can reach far beyond their home turf. Yet, we see a huge proportion of the world's population still tormented by hunger and poverty, and countless numbers of people and families suffer from illiteracy — the most basic needs such as, a roof for shelter, and food

1

that is so essential to lead a dignified living, are missing. Although the world of today has a vivid awareness of its unity and solidarity, conflicts occur between neighboring countries and are on the rise between races and cultures promulgated by opposing forces and ideologies. It is obvious that political, social, economic, racial and ideological disputes are continuing bitterly in various parts of the world. At the same time, we are witnessing a true cultural and social transformation, a phenomenon that has its repercussions on our physical and spiritual life as a whole. As happens in any type of growth, it brings certain growing pain along with it. Such transformation and changes have brought about serious difficulties and consequences to our human race. On the one hand, man extends his power in every direction, in technology, in advancing scientific research, progress and development, in medical arena, in aerospace technology, in advanced military technology that could wipe out a nation and its citizen in matter of seconds, etc. On the other hand, man does not always succeed in subjecting these fruits of power and development to his own conscience. It seems the more he strives along the path of this transformation and changes, the more he would probe profoundly into the deeper recesses of his own mind and conscience, he frequently appears to be more uncertain of himself, at a loss for direction and his purpose amid advancement and progress.

What if, I had chosen to review and to emphasize, not the kind of evils which the nature brings forth into the world; such as earthquake, tsunami, calamities, windstorm and hurricanes; but those kind of evils which man inflicts on one another; such as ravages and devastations brought about by wars and greed, and by selfish individuals who possess dominant power and resources? Along with these conflicts and disputes came the peril of war, or so called, pre-emptive wars justified by humanitarian propaganda in the world political arena of some advanced cultures to eradicate Weapon of Mass Destruction (WMD) in weak countries. It does not take a knowledge of rocket science to understand that "war", no matter how justifiable it may appear in the parliaments and congress of these countries of advanced development, as well as in the eyes of the general public, war reduces everything — people and structures — to ashes. As a result, millions and millions of innocent people are killed or injured, children lost their parents, and/or parents lost their beloved children, hospital and schools collapsed, city streets and roads were filled with shells and appeared fragmented, homes and families were destroyed, and the dreams of its citizens were shattered. Thousands and thousands of innocent people turned victims of unjustifiable wars overnight, due to arrogance, greed of the aggressor(s). To those who remain alive have suffered from their tremendous loss of everything, their loved ones, their home shelter, their future dreams and hope, but most of all, their dignity of being part of the mankind being trampled by fellow human beings, as if their life and dignity are expendable. Who could possibly be benefitted most from these wars? Without much speculation, it is rather obvious that the benefactors could possibly be the weaponry manufacturers, military suppliers, warzone contractors and logistic supply-chain companies and their securities personnel, and some unknown and unidentifiable individuals behind the scene.

People wearing a badge of human rights who crave for more freedom under the umbrella of the "so-called democracy" have become the dominant slogan of the new millennium where the individual rights challenge traditional values and culture of our global society. Homosexuals and transsexuals who crave for their rights to marriage and family; human trafficking and sex trades, a huge-divide between the immensely wealthy on the one side and extreme poverty on the other that are unable to survive due to the absence of the most basic needs in many parts of the world are some of the examples of this social phenomenon we experience in today's world. Freedom and creative power are valuable assets of human being, when such powerful assets are utilized for good intentions, many people are likely to benefit from the fruits. On the contrary, when human freedom and creativity are used for an unjust cause, to achieving a selfish purpose; consequently, only a limited few would benefit, while the majority would almost be destined to suffer. The global financial tsunami that swept across the world in the recent years echoes this phenomenon; creative ideas orchestrated by some brilliant minds to achieve a selfish objective that only benefit a limited few while causing pain and sufferings to the majority, this brilliant and selfish act is indeed a sign of degradation of our human race!

In social life, we experience constant tension in meeting people's expectation of us, or of what we imagine them to be; and this could become an overwhelming burden amongst the citizens of our society. I recall an interesting incidence that happened over 15 years ago in a cruise trip to Alaska which began from Canada that I had brought my mother along with my wife. As my dad died quite early in the late seventies, I took it as personal responsibility to look after my mother with great care and love. On a night of formal dinner on the cruise where all the guests were supposedly to dress themselves up as to a dancing ball, fleshy-long nightgowns for the ladies and tuxedo and dark suits for the men were seen everywhere. We were sharing a table with two other couples as the dinner started with lovely live-music in the background; we were having a nice time while drinking the champagne prior to the gourmet dinner. After some courtesy handshakes, hello and hello, and initial friendly gestures, one of the ladies in black gown who shared our dinner table asked: "How nice to have met you, where are you from?" I replied politely. And she continued to ask: "Is it your first time to Alaska?" I replied with a yes. Her husband started: "Oh, this is our third time to this lovely place, we enjoy every bit of it." He was joined by another couple who said it was their second trip to Alaska. Then the lady in black asked: "Have you ever been to North America before?" All this while, their four pairs of eyes were beaming onto the dresses of my wife, and my mother, and onto my dark suits, and my hands and wrists as I did not wear a tuxedo, as if they were searching for something more glamorous than our simple outfit. I reluctantly but politely replied to these two couples: "Yes, we have been to your great country before." And they continued with a smile: "where and which city?" Then, I patiently replied again: "Oh, quite a few cities, such as ABC cities on the east coast and XYZ cities on the west coast."

After the subsequent "machine-gun" type of questions, we finally had a quiet time at our dinner, for a while. Then, the topic of children

"Where do they go to school? Is the school any good? How much do you pay for the school fees? etc." came alive in the midst of our dinner. Then my wife and I tried to explain the education system in Hong Kong and Asia and that our children were at their summer school in the United Kingdom sponsored by a former teacher-friend of ours as we were on the cruise trip. We noticed that these couples had very little idea of what is going on in other parts of the world outside the USA. Some do not even know where Hong Kong is, while asking questions "Is Hong Kong part of Japan?" indicating how innocent some of these local tourists are. At one conversation regarding television in the USA, we referred to one of our favorite program host C. Rose in Bloomberg television, these couples in the cruise did not know who this host was, and explained that they did not watch this particular channel in USA.

When these two couples on the cruise learned our experience in continental Europe and United Kingdom and our professional and personal networks; they were awed by the fact we were so well informed about things. Their enthusiasm of the questions started to slow down and we began to have a normal conversation when the deserts were served. After showing my mother back to her cabin, my wife and I went for walk on the level below the main deck of the cruise, a track for jogging; I asked my wife if she enjoyed the dinner. She replied: "Yes, very much. I could feel the intensity of the four pair of eyes beaming on me at the dinner table." We had a good laugh, and we enjoyed the rest of the cruise in different islands of Alaska.

The incidence in the cruise has reminded me how much the ideology of materialism gets into the social culture. At times, we are inclined to look at a person for his possessions; the car he drives, his house, the clothes and handbag that his girl friend wears, the blinks and diamond that she wears, and focus on how glamorous she looks; while we seem to lose sight of "who the person he or she really is." The true quality of the person, behind the glamorous outfit, clothes and suits, blinks and branded goods, are often missed out as if quality of the person is not significant. We shall discuss this phenomenon later in the book.

In the last several decades, our human race has experienced profound rapid changes that have spread around the world at very high speed, reaching a new stage in history with some distinctive achievements. Early in my career, I was working with a multi-national food and beverage company that had three main worldwide businesses in food and beverage: "Cola and juice", "Pizza and Chicken" restaurant chains, and "snack and chips" packaged-snack food, etc. In the early 70's, the pizza business had experienced major failure in the Chinese dominated city that resulted closing of tens of pizza outlets with the rationale that the Chinese did not like the taste of "cheese" and that they only drank tea, not the cola drinks. Then, when the cola business took off and became popular in China from the late 70's to 90's and beyond; the idea of re-launching pizza restaurants flashed in the minds of some top executives of the company. However, they believed a puzzle was yet to be resolved, "Will the Chinese be ready for the taste of cheese again?" With the help of some of my colleagues, I had become an advisor to the people of the pizza branch while they planned to forge ahead with their business plan. True enough, today we can find variety of pizza outlets and restaurants that serve cheese of various kinds and gourmets in many cities in Hong Kong, China and Asia. In a short span of two decades, the "taste of cheese" and soft drinks market have been opened up in a 1.3 billion people country. Paradoxically, I am not prepared to discuss the business opportunity, nor its future; rather I simply borrow the above scenario as an example to point out the "speed of change" that a product as minute as pizza — a tiny aspect of our society — has experienced in such a short period of time. This change in habit is relatively minor in comparison with the change of moral values driven by ideologies that were introduced in the several decades of the last century. To name a few: "To work hard, and to play hard", "Do as you wish anytime, anywhere...!" "Retire as early as you can, and do what you like", "Homosexual and gender preference is human rights", and "Do whatever you want as long as no one gets hurt", etc.

In recent years, a family trip that took me to the country-side farm has given me a rare chance to refresh my insights of how beautiful the nature is — the day begins with the sun rise and ends with sun set, the appearance of the moon and stars at nights, everything is in such a good order. The cycle of nature happens in such a regular and consistent manner, and yet so quietly without much noise of any kind. Things in nature work in such a harmonious way that brings us the necessary amount of oxygen in the air, the right temperature that fits human habitat and the right amount of sunlight, and vegetation and animals for human survival, the earth rotates in perfect harmony with the universe without any external help, or interference from our human invention. Nevertheless, "Influenced by such a variety of complexities, many of our contemporaries are kept from accurately identifying permanent values and adjusting them properly to fresh discoveries. As a result, buffeted between hope and anxiety and pressing one another with questions about the present course of events, they are burdened with uneasiness. This same course of events leads men to look for answers; indeed, it forces them to do so." (*Gaudium Et Spes*, no. 4) It is obvious that human being has brought about his own frustration, unhappiness and mischief; a sad consequence of misusing his power. Happy index is commonly used to measure the extent of happiness in a person's life in today's society. The finding interestingly indicates that the happy index tends to be lower in well-developed societies than among people in poorer regions.

Change in Family Structure

While the industrial and commercial segments of society are gradually under transformation in the last decades, some nations have prospered in economic affluence, while radically transforming their social conditions and behavior through technological advancement and modernization. Likewise in the last century or so, massive migration was evident as younger generations left their rural and agricultural life for urbanized city life that resulted in the growth and proliferation of urban society presenting new opportunities to its new inhabitants. "By this very circumstance, the traditional local communities such as families, clans, tribes, villages, various groups and associations stemming from social contacts, experience more thorough changes every day." (*Gaudium et Spes*, no. 4) Consequently, the family structure has also undergone drastic transformation from larger-sized families in a clan society, to the recently emerged, isolated and unitized smaller families, living in urban society, in high-rise buildings, apartment blocks, likens organized boxes. As for the family, dissonance results from population, economic and social pressures, from difficulties that arise between succeeding generations, and from new social relationships between men and women in search of a better and happier life. "Nevertheless, brotherly dialogue among men does not reach its perfection on the level of technical progress, but on the deeper level of interpersonal relationships." (*Gaudium et Spes*, no. 23) One of the salient features of the modern world is the growing interdependence of fellow human beings on one another, a development promoted chiefly by modern technological advancement.

Families in modern societies have been under profound pressure amid rapid changes that have affected our values and culture, in particular, of young people when we look at how many young people are brought up in highly urbanized societies, where excessive comfort is provided in almost every aspect of their life. Their already pristine and comfortable lives are further eased by latest home appliances coupled with domestic helpers who make the house chores a much simpler task, yet we are looking at a phenomenon that we have not seen before in the distant history of mankind. How can we expect responsibility and commitment from these young people, when they have never been asked to be responsible for simple tasks at home during their upbringing? This reminds me a true story which lingers in my mind for a number of years now. In the summer month of July, my friend, Rene, had brought his family, wife and two teenage children to join a summer camp at the suburbs of Hong Kong. One of his friends requested Rene to take along their only teenage daughter, Betty, so that she would be able to spend a week of healthy summer holiday with Rene's family. Rene, after consulting with his wife, agreed to take Betty along with his family. In the summer camp, meals were normally self-service operations, similar to cafeteria or canteen of a college. During supper time one evening, everyone lined up at the food counter to get their respective meal that included Rene, his wife and their two children, except Betty who chose to remain in her seat at the table. Almost everyone finished in the line, Rene's clan too returned to their table with trays of food and drinks, when they saw Betty was still sitting at her seat unmoved. Then Rene's wife, asked: "Betty, are you not hungry? There are only a few people now in the line, you can get your food now." The tiny teenage girl, Betty looked up and replied: "At home, my helpers would serve me every meal and snacks anytime I like." She continued: "I don't know how to get my food from the counter, can anyone help me?" Even though in her teens, Betty is almost as tall as my friend Rene, but her behavior was similar to a child of three years old. She has acquired physical attributes matching her teenage built, but her corresponding human maturity lacks behind so much that her behavior is absolutely not compatible to her age. If this situation of Betty continues for the next few years into her full womanhood at 20 years, we would probably expect even more personality mismatches and other possible moral problems of serious nature springing out.

In the absence of knowledge and awareness that it is only individual efforts that enables us to acquire things, the youth of today will have very little, or no idea of what it takes to be a human being, or the necessary values that are required in order to deal with their family, friends, colleagues, neighbors and society. We are living in a society founded on little, or no fixed moral principles, where the benchmark of absolute moral certainty, the criteria and ability to differentiate right from wrong, is becoming blur, as though moral principles that supposedly govern and guide human behavior frailly hangs on a pendulum that swings from one side to the other depending on the mood of a certain individual, or the society as a whole. Many people believe that as long as the social conduct and behavior of its citizens are not criminal or anti-social, then nothing else really matters, or be considered wrong; while anything can be right depending on the feeling and choices of each individual. If young people are not taught any objective moral values and human virtues by their families or society, then everything seems to be relative that subjects to personal desire or whims.

In today's society, owing to changes in social structure and family structure, the educational system heavily leans on academic excellence while neglecting the most fundamental values of what it takes to be truly human. Many of us have the impression that the modern world has a strong tendency to violence, where this present situation inevitably produces plenty of "technically-capable barbarians". Such a society inevitably generates a large number of irresponsible people. When people in general are irresponsible and selfish, the chances of these people, young and old, turning to violence would definitely multiply. The first and the most extreme physical violence that I can think of is obviously when a mother would decide to kill her own baby, in an abortion, for whatever reason. While seemingly relevant reasons are given to justify this horrific act, however, there will be no peace in the heart of this individual woman for the rest of her life, if not sooner than later. This lack of peace could propagate directly or indirectly through certain form of violence widespread in society: crimes in the micro-environment; and in a macro environment, wars and killing in the battle fields between disagreeing nations or cultures. To legalize abortion is to legalize violence, and to promote individual and social irresponsibility; thus promotes further disorder, both individual and collective.

What has Gone Wrong with Marriage?

Back in the 1950s, when I was still a child, I recall from my mother that people then regarded contraception as unnatural, and divorce was an exceptional phenomenon, while abortion was an indescribable evil and criminal offense in the eyes of people. Nevertheless, the picture looks very different today. Contraception, divorce and abortion are commonly accepted and endorsed by the legislations in many developed countries, where millions of people have accepted these as the lifestyle of the modern world. Quite a number of people are prepared to identify these phenomena as signs of progress of our time.

Progress is a fine word, but progress does not necessarily mean advancing in any direction "blindly". Progress should rather mean advancing towards a goal, that is towards something that man, human being, positively wishes to attain, and thus towards something good in relation to his destiny.

Few people would deny that man's objective in life is to find his ultimate happiness. However, it is questionable that our modern society is progressing towards greater happiness or not. Very often, people pursue happiness in an individualistic and selfish way. For example, when a man says to a lady at a hotel lounge, after meeting her for 30 minutes, that he is very fond of her and he "likes" her very much and wants to take the relation to a more intimate level, it is highly probable what he really means is to obtain sexual pleasure from the relationship as soon as he possibly can. Many people equate finding true happiness with seeking pleasure. In this case, the relationship that ensues would have a minimal component of true and committed loving relationship.

For some people today, children are to marriage as accessories are to cars: the "optional extras". That also explains the increase in cohabitation while abandoning marriage commitment for life and marital fidelity. The rationale behind not wanting children in marriage has many facets, but fundamentally it is due to the ideology of individualism "I am a free person, and I can choose to do whatever I want" which finds its origin in materialism. This translates effectively into a terminology or slogan of "human rights" in our modern society so often being misconstrued to give a twisted meaning for the selfish cry of depicting "human rights" to "to do whatever you desire, without any boundary!" — such as "pleasure without responsibility".

Recently, I came across a movie title that resembles the slogan: "Love with no-strings attached" while finalizing this chapter. There are many more movies produced based on this phenomenon. When we look closer at the issue and its consequence, this ideology masked with freedom and democracy intuitively promotes a bourgeois and irresponsible lifestyle that eventually gives rise to contraceptive mentality that translates into a propaganda: "Enjoy sexual pleasure without strings attached." The possible problem related to contraception and its effect on young people and families will be discussed in the later chapters of this book. The propaganda by media promotes values contrary to marital commitment between spouses, encourages an individualistic lifestyle in pursuing a mistaken notion of personal freedom, sex with no commitment.

Divorce marks the final collapse for two people in love and their final rejection of an ideal and dream of happiness on which they had embarked one, five, 10 or 20 years earlier. That dream was the dream of a happy marriage. Whichever way we look at the problem, every divorce is a sign of failure. Some people argue in favor of divorce; however, practically no one says that divorce is a good thing; at most, they will argue that it is a lesser evil: it is obviously a myth that to get divorced is a lesser evil than to remain bound by a failed marriage. Each individual case is different, no one should generalize the issue since it cannot resolve the root of each individual problem. However, in principle, many people still believe that marriage and family should stay intact and should be protected from breaking down regardless of culture and geographical differences.

Difficulties of Modern Family

There is a vivid awareness of personal freedom and great attention to the quality of interpersonal relationships in marriage; such as to promote the dignity of women-wife, responsible parenthood and education of children. We also notice there is awareness of the need to develop closer relationship within the family members for reciprocal and mutual support of their spiritual and material needs, and the rediscovery of self-giving love between spouses, and their responsibility toward each other, and proper education and development in intellectual, physical, psychobiological, spiritual capability of their children in the building of a just society. However, on the other hand, there are also signs indicating a declining awareness of fundamental values of family, matrimonial love and upbringing and education of children of good character. Confusing ideology that promotes a pleasure-seeking lifestyle affects the integrity of spousal love and their marital commitment in the family; and eventual serious misconception of the role fatherhood and motherhood springs forth. There are also signs of growing number of divorces, teenage unwanted pregnancies that frequent recourse to sterilization, contraceptive and abortion; the rise of cohabitation as a socially acceptable lifestyle; and the homosexuals outcry their rights to "family" in adopting other people's children. These negative phenomena almost certainly find its root of a misconstrued slogan of human rights and freedom. In the third world countries where the birthrate is relatively high, families often lack the means necessary for survival, such as food, work, housing, education, medicine and homes which are the most fundamental human rights and freedom. Whereas, in the wealthier countries where the birthrate is relatively low, immersed in excessive prosperity and the consumerism mentality which is paradoxically fused with a certain anguish and uncertainty about the future, married couples are deprived of the generosity and courage to have more children. Thus, new life is often subconsciously perceived not as a blessing, but as threat to the freedom of the couples from which they shall have to defend themselves.

The historical situation in which family finds itself an intertwining relationship between light and darkness, and that history is not simply a fixed progression towards what is always better, but rather it demonstrates that it requires our effort, as human beings, to struggle between freedom and responsibility which is mutually conflicting, and yet mutually complementary. This reminds me of the expression of conflict between two loves: "the love of God to the point of disregarding self, and the love of self to the point of disregarding God" of St. Augustine. Incidentally, this echoes the essence of "Self-love" as opposed to "Love for others" in "Mirror of Love".

The Local Scene

In the past several decades, political, economic and social changes have taken place in Hong Kong, exerting great influence and bringing about a series of new phenomena, as well as problems to the local communities and families. After the confirmation of the reversion of Hong Kong to Chinese sovereignty in 1997 by the Sino–British Joint Declaration (initialed in 1984), there had been an upsurge in emigration, with a significant number of Hong Kong residents moving overseas. On the other hand, the reality of Hong Kong residents getting married on the Mainland led to the influx of tens of thousands of Mainland women (and children) to Hong Kong. This has definitely put pressure on Hong Kong's educational, medical and social services, as well as in her labor market, particularly in the non-skilled labor sectors. After the reunification of Hong Kong with China, a lot of emigrants decided to return to Hong Kong and be integrated once more into our local society. Due to this, the labor situation which has been experiencing keen competition since the economic-monetary crisis of 1997, has become more and more difficult. This keen competition in the labor market has in turn intensified the conflicts between local residents and the new arrivals from the Mainland.

Since the opening up and economic liberalization of Mainland China in the beginning of the 1980's, the local manufacturing industries have been moving northwards to China, so the local economic development has concentrated mainly in the financial and services sectors. Due to this social and economic restructuring, many non-skilled, middle-aged workers have to face the pressure brought on by salary cuts and unemployment. Simultaneously, Hong Kong residents from different walks of life have started to work and live on the Mainland for longer periods, leading to the separation of family members and the phenomenon of "virtual single-parent families". The long separation from spouses not only weakens their relationships and impedes their communication, but also makes the supportive function of the family ineffective.

In my years of dealing with families and couples, from different walks of life, different cultures and backgrounds through professional and social contacts, I can say that most of them are decent and good people who are busy in pursuing their life's goals, particularly material well being for themselves and their families. The situation is particularly challenging due to the high living standards and relatively expensive housing and ineffective social safety net; quite often both spouses have to work for long hours in order to pay the bills and maintain a home in a relatively small flat. Often, due to work reasons, husbands have to travel to other countries or to Mainland China, leaving their spouses and children unattended over long periods of time. Frequent travel away from home renders family unity a very challenging task — it adversely affects conjugal intimacy and parents–children relationship. When this situation is prolonged over an extended period, children get used to the absence of their father or mother, spouses get used to living alone without the presence of their better halves, often producing many unwarranted family problems which could eventually become social problems; such as, infidelity in marriages that produces unhappy children, lack of family harmony, youth problems, drugs, child abuse, premarital sex, contraceptive and abortion. Children from unhappy or broken families easily become the object of pleasure of the predators.

Education of children and parenthood are quite often left in the hands of teachers and schools, or at times in the hands of the domestic helper. Moreover, the traditional Chinese ideal of academic excellence continues to hold sway even in the modern world. Academic excellence is often equated with economic success: "scholar certificates open the door to wealth". Education has, therefore, become a means to be successful, to get rich and to acquire power. This has spawned intense competition in examinations, thus relegating to second place moral, intellectual, emotional and developmental education that constitutes holistic education and development. Living in such an intensely competitive environment, many people are ruled by the survival instinct where the stronger and the better prevails. Families subject to this social and environment pressure have to struggle to survive and make a living, with a tendency to become materialistic. In addition, under the influence of mass media, families do not always remain immune from the obscuring of certain fundamental values, nor set themselves up as the critical conscience of family culture and as active agents in the building of an authentic family humanism.

Along with economic development and the implementation of general education, the traditional concepts about love and sex have become more vague, while premarital sex, cohabitation and trial marriages have become more socially acceptable. According to a survey of young people in Hong Kong, 75% of students were not opposed to premarital sex. It is obvious that the new generation accepts the idea that if a man and a woman have mutual affection, then they may establish a sexual relationship either by living together or remaining single but with multiple partners. Marriage is no longer regarded as the permit to start sexual relations, nor is it considered an "inevitable" choice, since the number of people who choose to stay single is on the rise. This is due to their unwillingness to forge a long-term marital commitment, or to a lack of confidence in the relationship, or love of an individualistic life style. This also explains why cohabitation is on the rise. Nowadays, men and women tend to postpone to tie the knots and to raise children until the later years of their life. According to a government survey of local families in 2000, the median age for first marriage was 30.0 for a man and 27.3 for a woman.

Another phenomenon is that as a result of economic development, the average family enjoys better and more comfortable living than previous generations. Many parents tend to over-protect their children as a sign of affection, pampering children with lots of material goods and comforts and depriving them of the necessary hardships in life that had made parents what they are today. According to a study made by the Yang Memorial Methodist Social Service in September 2000, children were not only being well looked after by their parents and provided far beyond what is reasonable, but often, even what the children ought to do for themselves as a matter of responsibility was done for them by their parents. Parents were also over-tolerant of their children's misbehavior. Consequently, our children lack self-confidence, have less respect for authority or concern for others, are more selfish and easily get angry and often become withdrawn due to a lack of interpersonal skills.

Some very common examples are teenage students who still ask their domestic helpers carry the school bags for them or do their household chores for them. These children never need to lift a finger to get something to eat or sleep — everything is "well taken care of". In fact, that excessive care has produced many youngsters who do not know how to care for others, or what love really means. Most young people or even adults of this generation believe love is to get what one wants or whatever is pleasurable to him or her: "never mind how others feel, as long as I feel good and satisfied, that is good enough... that is my love for the person."

During the past few years, another serious family problem has been extra-marital affairs.

Marital Incompatibility?

Apart from asking for mutual care, the greater majority of couples also expect intimacy, meaningful communication and a loving sexual relationship. Though couples are expecting more from their marriage, many couples still spend most of their time and effort in their work, struggle with limited means in raising and educating their children. Quite often, couples distribute these tasks separately for the sake of convenient and efficiency; the husband focuses on working and bringing home the money while the wife takes total responsibility of rearing the children and the family. After several years into their marriage, the couple tend to forget each other's needs, and thus genuine dialogue and mutual communication is neglected, love, care and intimacy which are necessary and proper to a married couple is often missing. Sooner than later these couples would start drifting apart as the mutual love that they initially shared starts deteriorating between them.

Since a large number of husbands work or travel frequently to the Mainland or overseas over long periods, marital relations gradually crumble due to extended separation. This factor accounts for their temptations in seeking compensation outside their marriage, due to their loneliness and dissatisfaction in their married life and most of all due to their misconception of true marital love. As a result, these men — husbands to their wives, father to their children — start pursuing illicit pleasure from relations with opposite sex and mistresses. Indeed, many people no longer cherish the values of marital fidelity, but instead focus their attention on mere sensual excitement and pleasure seeking lifestyle. Statistics of Caritas shows that a considerable number of people, men or women, who are involved in extra-marital affairs are in their mid-40s, but the trend indicates that the age group is getting younger. According to the recent figure from a field data of The Hong Kong Catholic Marriage Advisory Council, approximately 68% of married couples who have approached the Council for marriage counseling have either decided, or are seriously considering separation as the ultimate solution. And amongst this group, 55% say the reason for separation or divorce is incompatibility of character after several years of marriage, while 45% of the people cite marital infidelity as the cause.

Mass Media Overdose

While information technology has been developing at a tremendous pace, social structures, the family, and ethical ideals are now very different from that of the past. Thanks to advanced technology, the standard of living has improved substantially. However, as far as interpersonal relationships are concerned, people are drifting further apart. More often, people communicate through cellular phones or Short Message Service (SMS) and Multimedia Message Service (MMS), through e-mail or other forms of electronic applications, through different types of social networking in computer and mobile devices etc. Thus, personal face-to-face interactive dialogue and communication is diminishing drastically, real personal dialogue is replaced by electronic images and digitized sound tracks, strangers talking to strangers hidden behind the screens.

Mass media and communication play a dominant role in many people's lives. In the olden days, it was a box sitting in the living room that invaded the privacy of a family, but nowadays, it is small electronic device that everyone carries around wherever he or she goes, to the bedroom, classroom and bathroom. At times, people may carry more than one of these devices. During a business convention dinner, I saw a middle-aged businessman carrying four mobile devices at one time: two mobile phones and two reading devices. It is now quite common to see young children — even those of kindergarten age — tiny little creatures, carrying one of these smart electronic devices hanging from their neck. This shows how communication and media play a vital role in our life: family, work and society. The media, through this tiny mobile device, has a power that can affect the moods of thousands and thousands people in a split of a second. While it does give an almost instant report of news from many thousand miles away, it could bring families together and at the same time it could connect your child with strangers; it can also paint a gloomy picture of family and marriage through various forms of entertainment that twists the idea of true and genuine love in family. There are many such entertainment programs on TV showing multiple love affairs in a law firm, or a café or in the operating theater in hospital. There is even a program series on the sexual affairs of a group of desperate housewives. The percentage of gossip and paparazzi in the media are on the rise in many places. Some fashion shows and music videos display brutal scenes of sexually-arousing programs blended with adult entertainment and these are easily accessible to young children through the internet. Pornographic live-shows or cyber sex are easily accessible through different mediums of internet connections. I have recently observed a documentary report on the murder of a young man in his early 20s who was "innocently" involved in a triangular cyber-sex affair between a teenage girl and a handsome young marine. When the true story was revealed, it appeared that the teenage girl was faked by a mother of 46 years of age, while the young marine was faked by a ex-marine of 50 years. What a pathetic incidence, yet it only reflects the tip of an ice berg. Science and technology have indeed brought major achievements and benefits to our daily lives to enhance our communication, information, education and entertainment; however, it has also brought along much unwarranted damage to family and children.

Print media such as newspapers, magazines and even comic books, probably due to pressure of achieving high sales targets, regularly report news of a highly salacious or violent nature. Quite often, human rights and democracy are being used as slogans or labels for the underlying ideologies in promoting materialism, individualism and hedonism. This bombardment of massive propaganda by the media is corrupting the moral values of the citizenry. Eventually, the viewers and readers — men, women, children and the general public — are led to believe that human sexuality is mainly for pleasure, that marital commitment is a subjective value that can be discarded. Gradually, this phenomenon becomes a socially accepted behavior; it subconsciously becomes a sign of progress, and this idea slowly permeates into the lives of many people in the modern society. As the family is the basic element of society, so long as we face all family and marriage problems squarely and tackle them in earnestness, we can surely make a crucial contribution to fostering social harmony as a whole.

New and more efficient media in social communications set off chain reactions that allow the swiftest and widest possible circulation of styles of thought and feeling. A change in attitudes and human structures frequently calls accepted values into question, especially among young people, who have grown impatient on more than one occasion, and indeed become rebels in their distress. Aware of their own influence in the society, they want a part in it sooner. This frequently causes parents and educators to experience greater difficulties day by day in discharging their tasks.

Violence in Sexuality

"Sex, if untamed, is man's most unruly and explosive instinct" and it does not easily let itself be subordinated to any control. Once the sexual impulse is aroused, it wants immediate satisfaction, and it wants it on its own terms, as an end in itself.

Family violence is yet another problem seriously affecting the family. The increase in cases of violence against married women is alarming. A few couple-lovers, for various reasons, have been killed in their household by their partners before committing suicide; the crime of passion seems to have become more frequent and intensified. Rape is one of the most brutal and violent expressions of this selfishness that occurs globally, in some countries women are portrayed as tools for sexual satisfaction, rather than being respected as an equal member in our society. Uncontrolled sexual desire tends to run wild, it is destructive. This "lack of respect and love for life" is indeed a cause of concern. It destroys human love, for love and selfishness are mutual enemies. It is inevitable that the extreme form of physical violence is abortion. It is the murder of an innocent child. Abortion is a direct action that terminates the pregnancy before viability, i.e. the fetus is unable to live outside the maternal womb, so that if there is any interference with its normal growth and development, or is expelled, the little creature — a living human baby — will certainly die.

Abortion Information

- Year 1920–2006 estimated global abortions at 929,000,000
- Estimated current global monthly average of abortion is 1,202,000
- Between 1975 & 2004, the number of abortions reported in Hong Kong had increased by almost 30%. The reported abortion as a percentage of pregnancy was 1.2 in 1975; whereas the trends increased and peaked at 28.3% in year 2000. It is a quite a substantial increase in 25 years period. (see Table 1.1 and Fig. 1.1)

Table 1.1. Abortion in Hong Kong

Year	Live Births	Abortions, Reported	Abortion %*
1975	79,759	1,000	1.2%
1980	85,290	9,400	9.9%
1985	76,126	15,400	16.8%
1990	67,731	21,000	23.7%
1995	68,637	25,363	27.0%
2000	54,134	21,375	28.3%
2004	49,796	15,880	24.2%

Abortion % is abortions as percentage of pregnancies (excluding fetal deaths/miscarriages).

Historical abortion statistics, Hong Kong — Complied by Wm. Robert Johnston, last updated 18th February 2006.

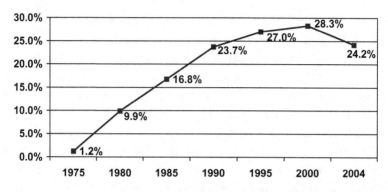

Fig. 1.1.   Hong Kong: Abortion Statistics 1975–2004

Mother's Choice — Statistics 2005–06

- Mother's Choice has reached out to more than 25,000 pregnant girls and women since its establishment in 1987.
- Mother's Choice website has received well over 55 million hits since it was launched in June 2001.
- Mother's Choice website receives on average 1,000 visitors per day.
- On average, 25,000 students are challenged each year to think about their choices and values before making decisions about sex.

Problems with Our Youth?

One of the many difficulties parents encounter today is to give children an adequate preparation for adult life, particularly with regard to education in the true meaning of sexuality. There are many reasons for this difficulty. In the past, even when the family did not educate their children about sex, the culture was such that it provided respect for fundamental human values that served to protect the younger generation from corruption. In the greater part of society, both in developed and developing countries, the decline in tradition and cultural values has left children deprived of consistent and positive guidance, while parents find themselves unprepared to provide adequate answers to the challenge. Quite often, we see that society and mass media provide depersonalized, recreational and often pessimistic ideas of sex. Moreover, this information is influenced by distorted concepts of freedom, in an environment that lacks basic values of life, human love and family.

Then for some good reasons, schools actively take up the role in promoting and conducting sex education programs, directly or indirectly taking the place of the parents in this regard. Most times, sex education provided by educational institutions mainly focus on safe sex, the detailed process of how to avoid pregnancy with the mere intention of keeping the energetic teenagers "out-of trouble". At times, the situation could be worse than many parents can imagine. In reality, this so-called sex education involves displaying the actual sex scene through video or photographs followed by discussion amongst students and teachers. This type of sex education not only fails to serve the original purpose of proper understanding of human sexuality, but also arouses unnecessary sexual curiosity among teenagers and gives a misleading idea that sex is only for pleasure, excitement and play, thus ultimately leading to a deformation of consciences. Some smart parents do spend time to research on the school and its views on sex education to see whether some of the vital elements of human sexuality are missing in the sex education program promoted by the school; elements such as, mutual love and respect, commitment and responsibility in a loving relationship. Many parents treat this as one of the most important criteria for school selection years before the time of enrolment. In other cases, parents have given up their duty in this field, or have agreed to delegate it to others, because of the difficulty of the topic and their own lack of knowledge and preparation as responsible parents.

In such situations, many parents find themselves quite helpless and yet it seems there is no one to turn to for support and guidance. Parents therefore must be prepared to know and understand human love and sexuality in order to anticipate the growing needs of their children especially from pre-teenage years, i.e. as early as from 8 to 9 years old, to impart proper values on sexuality in a natural manner. They need not enter into the specific process and details of the sexual act — this is unnecessary — but focus on the scientific process of the fusion between sperm and egg during conception. They can also speak about the moral principles behind human sexuality within marriage.

The Missing Link

- Parents only begin to realize the need to discuss human love and sexuality with their child when he reaches the teenage years or when they see their children encounter problems. It might be a bit late, but not too late.
- Often parents find it very difficult to start the conversation on sex: how and where to begin?
- When the child is 3–10 yrs of age, parents think it is too early to discuss the topic with them.
- When the child reaches the pre-teens age of 9–11 yrs, parents are normally unprepared and too embarrassed to talk about it.
- When children reach the teenage years, parents tend to ignore it psychologically as it is difficult to start with the hope that "they will know as they grow-up".
- At the end, the child grows into the teenage period with absolutely no proper idea of what sexuality is. Thanks to the mass media, his own curiosity and stories from the peers add more confusion in his or her young mind.
- And the price to pay could be quite high.

Parents need to know the fundamental truth about human love and sexuality ahead in order to anticipate their children's needs and the way to impart proper formation necessary for the children while they are growing up. Sooner or later they will realize the importance of loving their children with good examples and of themselves as effective role models within the family.

Internet Generation

Internet wave sweeps across nations and cultures that sees no navigation boundaries. In the early 90s, my career had experienced a twist that involved me with a European multinational corporation in electronics industry. During those years, the capability of telecommunication in technology as well as its reach, to communicate in business and between people was far behind what it is today. The most common means of communication was telephone or IDD for overseas, but mainly between telephone sets, mobile phone was a huge black tower with a thick and long antenna sticking out to the sky in its first generation model. Voice and data communication were independent from each other; there was no email or SMS as such back in those days; video conferences had to be specially organized through the satellite communication, and it was a very expensive means of conducting a teleconference meeting across oceans. Then internet technology exploded in the mid-90s setting a huge shock primarily to the telecommunication industry; almost as much as a wave comparable to Apollo landed on the moon in 1969, if I may say. Later on, the shock wave of internet and its capability continued to awe the telecommunication experts and ordinary users of the immensity of its power and reach for many years that followed.

People at the time had great hope and projection of what this technology could bring; one was the idea of paperless office, another was easier and more efficient communication between people across the continents thus enhancing efficiency in work place, another was fewer business travels compensated by the better and cheaper solution of teleconferences where people would have more time to think, to analyze and establish more interpersonal communication such as with friends and family; with the promise of the "internet technology will do the rest..!", etc.

However, the projected benefits of enhancing family and interpersonal exchange of internet technology seems to be broken today as people are busier by the day, if not by the hour. We have become more dependent in the what the screen can bring, internet-based communication has brought about overwhelming "solutions" to enhance our daily life that we all, directly or indirectly, end up more dependent on our mobile devices. The form of communication has changed so much that some people do not necessarily step out of their homes, or their so-called living-quarters to "achieve" what he or she needs to do during the day; video-on-demand and news are easily available in a matter of minutes, if not seconds, half-way across the world, on-line shopping or investment can be done over the web, or booking an air-ticket is just a key-punch away.

Internet-based social networks that bring about virtuous images of people and data are becoming popular and getting popular through different application software for work and entertainment. This change brought about by internet is seen as progress and development that enhances work efficiency and people's lives, however, it has repercussions; people become addicted and are unhappy without it, the boundary between real world and virtuous reality is getting unclear, and it has become a tool for perpetrators in various forms of crime of theft, pedophilia, sex abuse, financial fraud, etc.

Man's painful search for an ideal and better world, without a corresponding spiritual advancement, has proved to be a failure in the history. Differences and conflicts crop up between races and various social orders, and between variety of cultures and civilizations; between wealthy nations and those which are less influential and less powerful, between international institutions craving for peace, and those that are ambitious to propagate their own ideology through means of force. We see single-polar diplomacy, as well as individual and collective greed that exist, particularly of pre-emptive warfare led by some developed nations; and the realm of the global financial system that has destroyed precious lives and families. We obviously could see this in the global economic and financial tsunami that has swept across continents in the recent years, and wars that resulted in destruction of livelihood of millions of people and families.

When we take a closer look at the world that we all live in today, at times it tarnishes many of the good works of so many good and heroic people. We can see disturbing consequences of divorce on the rise, of broken families caused by infidelity, ignorance, selfishness and lack of genuine selfless love within marriages and other reasons such as bourgeois lifestyle that focuses on pleasure-seeking in our modern society. We see man–man lovers or woman–woman lovers claiming to be the gender-of-the-third kind; there are increasing number of homosexual individuals craving for their rights for family and adopting other's people children, we see growing population of pedophiles in every corner of the world, the abuse of women and children and the international sex trade and human trafficking are relentlessly increasing. These situations have produced painful experiences and anxiety to the affected people.

To Land a Helping Hand

Yet, the power and strength of the institution of marriage and family can also be seen time and again, despite the difficulties, where profound changes in modern society reveal the true character of this marriage institution in one way or another that produces so much fruit and goodness. A teenage boy who took his normal trail in the city street was stopped by a scene; he noticed an aged woman, with her bended-body, was pushing a wooden cart loaded with garbage sacks on a drizzling winter evening. This teenager was moved by the scene and the aged woman. He emptied his pocket and gave the money to help this aged woman. A moment later, he realized that he had given away his own bus fare, and he had no choice but to walk home under the drizzling rain on a cold winter night.

It is encouraging to see that there are people in different parts of the world with great hearts and empathy who are willing to live as true human beings, to have necessary sobriety and solidarity, with commitment and responsibility, are willing to bare some sacrifices to do good and be helpful to others. Never before have we needed more desperately young people with these qualities in our society as we do today; this is only made possible through family and responsible parenthood in education and character formation of their children. Such youngsters practice and enjoy true and self-giving love within marriage, toward their loved ones, spouses and children, in raising a large and happy family. One of my best friends in Spain has 16 children, all of them are successful, the last count I have received from my friend was years ago when he was grandfather to over 30 grandchildren. My friend used to tell me many lovely stories about his family and children and the intensity of his happy family life whenever we met or traveled together. One example is the family meals that he usually conducts at home that serve over 30 people in two sittings. When I asked him how he could possibly remember all the 30-plus names of his grandchildren, he revealed to me that he has a little notebook that he carries around that records all the names of his grandchildren so that whenever he meets them, he would greet them by their names, individually. Whenever I relate to someone the story of my Spanish friend, I always have to add automatically with anticipation of the next question: "yes, 16 children; yes, with one wife".

In the summer of 2006, I took my own family to a holiday trip in Spain. In the mountainous country side, we resided in a summer chalet of a nearby village where my Spanish friend also spends his summer vacation with his family and friends. The idea of summer vacation homes for families was started some 40 years ago in a small village near the Pyrenees, at the border between Spain and southern France; now these have become sizeable holiday homes that can house over 100 families at any one time through out the year. My friend was so kind to take us through a *"paella* cooking competition"* (Spanish fried-rice) among some 50 families with children of all ages on a hot summer evening. It was such a wonderful experience for my wife. Our teenage children enjoyed the warmth of their presence, the joy and active family life, especially after the *paella* dinner competition on the lawn in an open garden, we had the chance to witness how my friend, as a proud grandpa, enjoyed distributing ice-cream lollipops to a long-line of beautiful little girls and boys, one after another, very orderly and yet vibrant and energetic; and a bit naughty as well. I felt so proud and happy for him.

Another example I can think of is a large family in the United States of a relatively young couple with 18 children in a single marriage. The whole family takes dinner at home in one long table. The father takes care of the laundry with some of his children displaying several washing machines just to show the scale of the task for such a large and happy family. The members of the family play different musical instruments to form a small orchestra. Everyone learns to share and help everyone else. They also learn to do household chores: preparing meals, washing clothes and dishes, making beds or shopping for food and grocery. The older ones watch over the little ones on behalf of the parents etc. But most of all, what one can observe from these large families is that their children learn to give a bit of themselves in order that others can live better from their early years.

The good news is that many people seem to be aware of the key to neutralize the "culture of death" in our society is by doing a lot of good; to drown the evil with abundance of good. Our hope is in our children — our future generations. However, mere hope and doing nothing will render us emptiness in the future, we all need to act, and act swiftly. We need to provide good and solid education to form our children, as much as, if not more than, the nutrients for a healthy life; by focusing on food for "the mind" rather than merely food for the stomach. To re-establish a just society (justice) and solidarity (charity) is an undeniable expression of love for others, a prerequisite of fostering two key human virtues of *Fortitude* and *Temperance,* the disposition of being not-fearful and self-mastery that will play a vital role in understanding and practicing genuine love and human sexuality.

In this chapter, we have discussed the current situation and problems of our society in relation to human love and sexuality. In the next chapter, we shall examine the root of the problem of this very important subject.

Chapter 2

Knowing the Origin

At their wedding anniversary, a woman asked her husband: "Are you happy, my dear?" and he nodded and said: "Yes, I am; but!" The question "Are you happy?" Makes me think,…and think deeper!" For a person to be happy is a natural tendency. It is probably as natural, if not more than, as to have a good-night-sleep, or to fill a hungry stomach. I believe every sane individual wants to be happy, in fact, most people crave for finding his or her own happiness, and have probably fixed "in search for happiness" as their goal in life. However, a different perception of happiness exists today in our society; happiness could equate to wealth, or comfort, pleasure or just simply being lazy — enabling oneself to do nothing. At times, people project a different perception of happiness as to having acquired certain state of wealth, or a certain state of mind, or an achievement, or certain social status, or the ability to do whatever he or she desires, or want, at any time and anywhere.

Man to Hope for Happiness

True happiness is generated from true love. Genuine human love can only be found in the self-giving love of a mother toward her child, and self-donation of love between spouses within a marriage, genuine love between father and son, and among brother and sister in a family, and to be found in genuine friendship. When we give ourselves to others, when we place others' needs over our wants, that is the beginning of genuine love. Genuine love between a married couple is not and cannot be based merely on material satisfaction and pleasure. True love is when married couple selflessly surrenders to each other even when it involves inconvenience and some sacrifice from one of spouses, or both. On the contrary, when man in the modern society begins to forget God and the hope of eternity, his heart centers on earthly and material things that would seemingly satisfy his thirst for merely material happiness and pleasure. He forgets how to give himself.

Different people choose different means to acquire whatever they believe to be happy, and quite often the general perception amongst the citizen of the global village equates happiness to mere pleasure and comfort; as if genuine happiness can only be found on the feeling of the pleasurable or comfort, "If there is no pleasure, I won't be happy." A similar analogy of the perception equates human love to sexual pleasure; as it plainly says: "No sexual pleasure, no love." The issue becomes obvious in a common dialogue amongst teenagers, when a teenage boy who wants to have sex with a teenage girl soon after their first few hours of acquaintance, would say: "If you love me, you will make love with me, or you should do this or that, otherwise, you don't really love me!" The ideology of "pleasure first" finds its origin from "materialism", this has shaped one of the most serious phenomenon of moral culture in our contemporary society; to treat fellow human beings as objects to achieve certain purpose, to use love as an instrument for sex, to place material things above human dignity and his spirit.

Mirror of Love

The struggle between "love of self", or self-love and the "love for others" forms the fundamental essence of the two opposing forces in this book "Mirror of Love." When looking in a mirror, do we see a reflection of our portrait of "self-love", or do we see a reflection of a portrait of "love for others"? When we contemplate what "self-love" is, and what it might consequently bring, I can think of: self-centeredness, pride, impatience, covetousness, laziness, self-gratification, hatred, envy, self-satisfaction, anger, selfishness and a disposition of treating others as objects in obtaining our selfish desire; our satisfaction or pleasure. Whereas, when we contemplate what "love for others" is, and what it might consequently bring, I can think of charity, understanding, patience, joy, forgiveness, kindness, diligence, self-mastery, meekness and a disposition of treating others as true human beings. The phrase "I love you" is probably one of the most frivolous carelessly used and often misused expressions by many people. Genuine love is an act of the will, not merely an emotional expression and sweet words.

It is not difficult to see that the incorrect perception of human love and sexuality is widespread, however, there are many facets that cause the problem. One of the fundamental causes is the ignorance and absence of knowledge of the 4-letter word — LOVE. "Love is to will the good of another person." We shall discuss this notion of love in more detail in the following chapters. Precisely due to the unclear notion of genuine human love amongst the citizens of our society, young and old, the residual love that remains is the inordinate love of self. When we look at the media today, the news headlines are almost dominated by "crimes of passion" of different kinds, from celebrities to ordinary people of all walks of life. The escalating numbers of domestic violence, indecent assaults on women in public transportation and malls, child abuse, drug use by teenagers and sex-related crimes, abortion and rape, increase in the number of pedophiles and other violent crimes of sexual nature are some of the examples of problems of this nature. Furthermore, we see increase in the number of divorces and induced singled-parent families. One can imagine the effect on children growing up without either a father or mother; and again, the number of the related tragic happenings is growing by the day. There is an outcry over: What has gone wrong with our society? Why are we seeing so much crime arising out of passion, and failure in marriage?" We shall examine the problems, analyze them and try to bring reasonable answers to light. Considering how important and widespread the problems are, and how difficult the subject matter may seem, we should undoubtedly anticipate it is even more difficult to practice and live up to the promises of true happiness and the dignity of man. I believe it worth our try to uncover this seeming mysterious mask of human passion and sexuality.

In my view, mere reasons cannot explain everything about human love and sexuality from a purely anthropological perspective. In search of true and original meaning of conjugal unity in marriage, marital commitment is founded on a covenant, which is neither a contract that stipulates the role and duty between party **A** and party **B**, nor merely an agreement that binds commitment of the parties involved. In my opinion, one of the fundamental confusion about human passion and sexuality, second to the ignorance in understanding "love", finds its root in separation of love from sex. A lady whom my wife and I met in a cruise trip once said to us: "To have sex with your loved one, my husband, is good. But sometimes, you can also have sex without love, I think that's a different kind of sex...!" Human sexuality is the most intimate expression of this mutual self-giving love between married couples. Unconditional love makes human sexuality truly human. The mutual self-giving love of the spouses involves unconditional surrender of their personhood to each other; a mutual gift in exchange between spouses. The marital covenant is thus "one plus one is equal to ONE", a bigger one" through communion of persons where unconditional self-donation love of the spouses makes it possible.

In the past, people had a pretty clear idea of what marriage and family are, though they might not be able to write down in detail a comprehensive definition of what marriage and family are, they would have said "marriage is between a man and a woman in love for as long as they live" while family is a logical development of extending this spousal love to bring forth their fruits — their children — to establishing a family. However, today the picture is quite different, there are different camps of thoughts about these two fundamental structures of our human society — marriage and family — along with plenty of confusion and debate around their significance and functions. In search of this understanding from one of the most ancient book of revelation, we find the following scripts that give resonance to our discussion earlier:

The original passage reads: "God created man in his own image; in the image of God he created him; male and female he created them." (Genesis 1:27, Navarre Bible) Subsequently, "Therefore, a man leaves his father and his mother and cleaves to his wife, and they become one flesh." We shall notice an even more explicit meaning "leaves and cleaves... they become one flesh." The normative meaning is interesting, "So they are no longer two but one flesh. What therefore God has joined together, let not man put asunder." (Genesis 2:24, Navarre Bible) I could anticipate that not all readers may share my view, but I would like to request the patience of the readers to read through these pages and chapters with an open mind, as the subject matter is far too important to be ignored due to different camps of thoughts and beliefs. The excerpt "let not man put asunder" is decisive that sets the principle of unity and indissolubility of marriage as the very content described in the most ancient revelation that willfully resonates our discussion.

During the talk with the Pharisees, who asked Jesus the question about the indissolubility of marriage, Jesus Christ referred twice to the "beginning." The talk took place in the following way: "And Pharisees came up to him and tested him by asking, 'Is it lawful to divorce one's wife for any cause?' He answered, 'Have you not read that he who made them from the *beginning* made them male and female, and said, 'For this reason, a man shall leave his father and mother and be joined to his wife, and the two shall become one flesh.' So they are no longer two but one flesh. What therefore God has joined together, let not man put asunder.' They said to him, 'Why then did Moses command one to give a certificate of divorce, and to put her away?' He said to them, 'For your hardness of heart Moses allowed you to divorce your wives, but from the *beginning* it was not so.' (Mt 19:3–9, also Mk 10:2–9, Navarre Bible). Thus, it shows the *beginning* was twice referred to. "Have you not read that the Creator from the beginning made them male and female...?" (Mt 19:4, Navarre Bible). This *beginning* is considered as the first account of man's creation is of theological nature that defines man in a dimension of being and of existence (*esse*). The second account of man's creation by its nature a different character that links to original innocence, original happiness and the first fall.

The first human being was a "man" and was named Adam, but from the moment of the creation of the first woman, they began to be called "man" and "woman," because the woman was taken from the man. "And the rib which the Lord had taken from the man he made into a woman and brought her to the man; then the man said: 'This at last is bone of my bones and flesh of my flesh; she shall be called woman, because she was taken out of man'" (Genesis 2:22–23, Navarre Bible). It is also significant that the "beginning" was not only linked with the mystery of creation of man, but also led us to the note man's primitive innocence, and of original sin. Noting the scene, it essentially reveals two different states of human nature: the state of integral nature and the state of fallen nature. Or perhaps, we can say between two states comprising *man's original innocence* and his *sinfulness*. Evidently, it has a fundamental significance for the theology of man and for the theology of the body.

Man's Original Solitude

The starting point of this discussion is given directly by the following words "It is not good that man (Male) should be alone; I will make him a helper that would be fit for him" (Genesis 2:18, Navarre Bible). It is significant that the first man — Adam — was defined as "male" only after the creation of the first woman. When we speak about solitude, it is in reference to the solitude of "man" as such, and not just to that of the male. Nevertheless, the complete context of that solitude of which Genesis 2:18 speaks can convince us that it is a question here of the solitude of "man" (male and female) and not just of the solitude of man the male, caused by the lack of woman. Therefore, it seems that this solitude has two meanings: one derived from man's very nature, that is, from his humanity, and the other derived from the male–female relationship. The understanding of the meaning of man's original solitude emphasizes, over and above, the philosophical interpretation of person; "Person is defined as *Individual* substance of rational nature." (St. Thomas Aquinas) Though we will further discuss human persons more substantially in a later chapter on "Marriage as Communion of Persons", here I would like to note the understanding and relationship between the meaning of solitude and human person as "an individual substance." For example, a 7-year old boy, against the advice of his parents, played football in the living room and broke a precious vase. His parents on return home asked: "Who did it?" The boy found himself trembling and answered with fear and embarrassment: "I did it." This echoes the philosophical interpretation, "I, the person, in my solitude, individually and wholly, is responsible for my own action." From the very beginning of human existence, it was revealed to man and woman, that over and above the vocation of marriage, there is another vocation, namely, that of renouncing marriage, in view of the kingdom of heaven. With this vocation, a truth was highlighted about the human person. If a man or a woman is capable of making a gift of himself or herself for the kingdom of heaven, then the vocation of renouncing marriage for the sake of kingdom of heaven proves to be valid, and perhaps even more, shows that there is the freedom of the gift in the human body. It intuitively means that this body of ours possesses a full nuptial meaning.

Man's Original Innocence and Happiness

In dwelling on the mystery of man's original state and the awareness of the meaning of the body which I am trying to highlight through an analysis of the existence of man from the very beginning, reveals the peculiarity of his original innocence. Interior innocence as purity of heart made it impossible for a person to be reduced by another to the level of a mere object, a means to an end, for pleasure or for whatever purpose. To grasp the meaning of this original innocence "the man and his wife were both naked, and were not ashamed", expresses this innocence in the reciprocal experience of the body. The fact that they were not ashamed means that they were united by an awareness of the gift with the clear notion of innocence for each other. They were mutually conscious of the nuptial meaning of their bodies, in which the freedom of the gift is expressed and all the interior richness of the person. In the mystery of creation, man attains this free-gift in the mutual acceptance of what makes them male and female.

In the narrative of creation, the woman was certainly not merely an object for the man. They both remained in front of each other in all the fullness of their objectivity as creatures. However, after committing the original sin, this whole situation changed. The view that only the nakedness makes woman an object for man, or vice versa, is a source of shame. The mere fact that they were not ashamed means that the woman was not an "object" for the man, nor he an object for her. Original happiness explains to us of the beginning of man, who emerged from love and initiated love that happened in an irrevocable way, despite the subsequent sin and death. Happiness is fundamentally rooted in love. Original happiness can also be understood as the original and beatifying immunity from shame as the result of love which directs·us toward the mystery of man's original innocence, in the mystery of his existence, prior to his knowledge of good and evil. The fact that man existed in his original innocence and happiness, before breaking the first covenant with his Creator, belongs to the fullness of the mystery of creation. This is the primary reason and foundation of human being's original innocence and happiness.

This mutual complementary experience finds its root in the interior freedom of the gift of oneself to the other, united above all with original innocence. Only love creates the good, communion of persons begins, in which both man and woman meet and give themselves to each other in the fullness of their personhood. It is precisely in the perspective of man's existence that marital love is continually renewed by means of procreation; sexuality founded on mutual self-giving love within marriage accounts for more than the sex act itself. Through this mutual self-giving love, the married man and woman are continuously perfected through every positive occurrence in marriage which in turn enriches the husband and wife as persons within marriage.

I can think of the story of my friend to help illustrate our discussion on mutual help between married couple. A man, let us call him Robert, who was raised from a broken family, married a female friend of my wife and I, let us call her Anna. After several years into their marriage, they have several children and Robert became quite successful in business. His frequent travels coupled with the resurrection of his embedded longing for his bachelor life, Robert began to drift away from his family, enjoying his bachelor travels and social drinks at bars after work hours. He often missed his family dinners, arrived home late and friends suspected that Robert may possibly be seeing another woman. After some intervention, Anna began to see the problem, she started to dress up a bit and made herself look as good and attractive as during their courtship, and she began to explore with friends on how to make the family home neat and orderly, comfortable, more attractive, and more welcoming, while she took up classes on gourmet cooking. This effort of Anna proved to be effective as Robert became curious of what was going on at home and was enamored by his wife's new looks and beauty; then they started to engage in regular dialogues and exchanged their feelings and concerns, likes and dislikes. They began to revisit fond memories of their courtship and began to re-open their hearts. Anna facilitated in establishing a relationship between the father and children that eventually strengthened Robert's bond with his sons and daughters, while they mutually discussed how to redirect their lives together. Hand-in-hand they strived to make their daily family life more enjoyable as a common objective. In the process, Robert became a more concerned father as he realized the joy of having his loved ones — lovely children and his kind and beautiful wife — around him whenever he needed them, and he also realized that they all needed each other in the journey of this common life. Robert considered himself lucky to have found his family again and began to see how stupid he was unable to see this earlier. One evening out in a walk with his wife Anna under moonlight, Robert confessed that he has never had such a great feeling as a responsible dad and a loving husband as he simply never knew how to be one before. Anna successfully helped her husband, Robert, to rediscover the values and joys of his fatherhood and the role as a husband through her self-giving love. As she says "I marry you in order to love you, and to will the good of you, my dear husband"; while Anna became more attractive, physically and emotionally, founded on her mature womanhood of greater love that enhanced each other's life. Mutually, they become better persons and hopefully they shall grow old together.

The Original (Nakedness) Sin

As mentioned earlier, two states of human nature have been revealed: the state of integral nature and the state of fallen nature. These are two states of *man's original innocence* and that of his *sinfulness*. For the sake of discussion; if the original man — Adam — had not lost his original innocence and happiness through the first fall i.e. the original sin, we probably would not have had the opportunity to see and experience the consequence of the shattered human nature — the disorder of human passion and sexuality.

The first fall of the man and the woman is linked with the mysterious tree "tree of the knowledge of good and evil" (Genesis 2:17, Navarre Bible). The man who gathers the fruit of the "tree of knowledge of good and evil" makes, at the same time, a fundamental choice. He carries it out against the will of the Creator, by accepting the motivation suggested by the tempter: "You will not die. For the Creator knows that when you eat of it your eyes will be opened, and you will be like Him, knowing good and evil." And true enough, their eyes were indeed opened, "...and they knew that they were naked, and they sewed fig leaves together and made themselves aprons" (Genesis 3:7, Navarre Bible). We shall analyze these words which describe the mutual shame of the man and the woman as a symptom of the fall; while at that moment, their shame reaches its deepest level and seems to shake the foundations of their existence. "And they heard the sound of the Lord God walking in the garden in the cool of the day, and the man and his wife hid themselves from the presence of the Lord God among the trees of the garden" (Genesis 3:8, Navarre Bible). The reason and necessity of hiding themselves indicates that they were deeply ashamed before each other, they hid their bodies with leaves. Then the Lord called the man and said: "Where are you?" and he replied: "I heard the sound of you in the garden, and I was afraid, because I was naked and I hid myself" (Genesis 3:9–10, Navarre Bible). Then the Creator asks: "Who told you that you were naked? Have you eaten of the tree of which I commanded you not to eat?" (Genesis 3:11, Navarre Bible) We should focus on two sequential situations: the first situation of original innocence, in which the first man was outside the sphere of the knowledge of good and evil, until the moment when he transgressed the Creator's prohibition and ate the fruit of the tree of knowledge. The second situation, however, was after having disobeyed the Creator's command at the temptation of the evil spirit in a form of a serpent, the man understood and recognized immediately the fruit of "the tree of good and evil" which determined the state of human sinfulness, in contrast to the state of primitive innocence.

After the original sin was committed, man and woman have lost the grace of original innocence. The discovery of the nuptial meaning of their sexuality will cease to be for them a simple reality of the revelation and grace. However, it is believed that this nuptial meaning will remain as a commitment given to man as a gift from the Creator, inscribed in the depths of the human heart, at a distant echo of original innocence to be regained with "great effort", through human and spiritual effort. Through authentic human love and the spousal self-surrender of their personhood in conjugal love, man will be able to rediscover the true nuptial meaning of the body. Through the veil of shame, man will continually rediscover himself as the guardian of the mystery of his sexuality in the freedom of the gift; and by striving in "great effort" he will be able to defend his own inclination toward sin in treating another human being as an object of pleasure.

Disorder in Human Passion

As a consequence of the fall of man and the original sin, fundamental disorder in human passion not only destroys the purity of heart, but also induces man with a strong inclination to do things that are contrary to fundamental good.

Lust is a disorder of man who merely uses sex as an instrument of satisfaction of his or her own desire. It is an obsessive desire to use another person's body, or image, for satisfaction of his sexual fantasy and desires, thus it violates human dignity of the persons involved. A lustful person acts and lives like an addict, similar to an alcoholic who cannot control his desire for his next drinks, who has little or no control of his passion and sensual wants particularly in sexual desires. Lust damages personality and human integrity, it dehumanizes the person and his/her victims, and destroys human relationships. Lust is a counterfeit of love and destroys genuine love which characterizes self-giving in the marital union.

The Origin of Lust

Let us recall the following words "'You shall not commit adultery.' But I say to you that anyone who looks at a woman lustfully has already committed adultery with her in his heart" (Mt 5:27–28, Navarre Bible). Adultery, to which the aforesaid commandment refers, means a breach of the unity by means of which a man and a woman, only as husband and wife, can unite so closely as to be with "one flesh." A man commits adultery if he unites in the same way with a woman who is not his wife. Similarly, the woman commits adultery if she unites in this way with a man who is not her husband. Then it must be clarified that "adultery in the heart" committed by the man when he "looks at a woman lustfully", means a definite interior act. Here we are talking about interior act such as a thought, a desire or the intention of a person.

Let us say, if a person contemplates a desire or intention of a violent act toward his business partner, as long as he does not actually commit the act, he is unlikely to be incriminated by the court of law, because his desire or intention remains invisible and unknown to the law enforcer due to the fact that it is an interior act still within his mind. Unless otherwise he chooses to materialize his thought into action, then it becomes an evidence of his pre-meditated violent action caught in the act. Nevertheless, purity of heart, guided by the moral principle that guides human thoughts and action, has clarified that "looking at a woman lustfully" is considered a sin of "adultery in the heart". It concerns a desire directed by a man toward a woman who is not his wife, in order to unite with her as if she were his wife. A desire or intention, which is an interior act, is normally expressed by means of a sense of thought, or imagination, a look or reflection of a memory. With today's technology, similar crimes of passion could be extended to pornography, lustful dialogues through social-networking, such as "cyber sex" through the internet connectivity of mobile devices, laptop computers, etc.

A Cyber-Sex Mother

A recent video documentary came to my attention; a triangular cybersex affair happened on the social web where a 20 year old young man was murdered due to the envy of another man. However, the stunning part of the story is the central character of this triangular cybersex affair, the attractive young woman in her late teens with whom the two men were in competition of her "love and sex", was impersonated by a middle aged woman, who was the mother of this pretty teenage girl. This middle-aged mother had been impersonating her own daughter by posting the photos of her 18 year old daughter in her own social-web in order to conduct cybersex with men other than her own husband who was unaware of the malicious acts of his wife in compromising the safety of their only teenage daughter for her perverted sexual fantasy. When the true identity of falsely-projected image of the middle-aged woman was finally revealed after the murder, not only did her husband and her 18 year old daughter found the act of this middle-aged woman, a wife and a mother, shocking and disgusting, even the detectives who were involved in the investigation found themselves amazed and puzzled in disbelief. How could a mother betray her own daughter as such, as the primary role of the mother is to protect her own child? Indeed, lust untamed obsession of sexual desire and fantasy, can drive a person to insanity.

Lust has three different forms: "For all that is in the world, the lust of the flesh and the lust of the eyes and pride of life (1 John 2:16–17, Navarre Bible). Through corruption in this world, man turns his back on Love, on his Creator, he casts Him out of his heart and at the same time, he detaches his heart and almost cuts it off from what is of the Creator, therefore, what remains in him "is of the world." Though we can say "man turns his back on his Creator and casting Him out of his heart" was the phenomenon of the past, of the first batch of human of the creation. However, when we look closely at the near history of mankind until the present times; the act of casting out the Creator from the hearts of man seems to have reappeared in the last centuries and in the past generations, and is still continuing today. I find the following quotation from the most ancient book of revelation particularly relevant to this discussion: "For while professing to be wise, they have become fools, and they have changed the glory of the incorruptible God into an image made like to corruptible man and to birds and four-footed beasts and creeping things." As a consequence of the man turning away from his Creator, the truth; all forms of corruption and the different forms of lust promulgate in the life of man, as discussed earlier: "For all that is in the world, the lust of the flesh and the lust of the eyes and pride of life."

One of the key disorders of human beings as a consequence of the original sin is the opposing forces of *spirit* and *flesh* that contradict each other constantly. "The desires of the flesh are against the Spirit, and the desires of the Spirit are against the flesh" (Galatians 5:17, Navarre Bible). Let us continue the discussion through a relevant quotation with strong and decisive words that resonate the mystery of man's fallen nature after the original sin. "Therefore, God has given them up to shameless lusts; for their women have exchanged the natural use for that which is against nature, and in like manner the men also, having abandoned the natural use of the women, have burned their lusts one toward another, men with men doing shameless things and receiving in themselves the fitting recompense of their perversity, ...being filled with iniquity, malice, immorality, wickedness full of envy, murder, contention, deceit...and not only do they do these things, but they applaud others doing them." (Romans 1:22–32, Navarre Bible) These words uttered some 2000 years ago remain a shocking resemblance to what is happening to our society today. I could almost hear an outcry of disenchantment from a close distant: "So what if we cast the Creator out of our heart? So what if we are lustful persons, what is the big deal?" "And what is the relevance to our today's world?" Yes, I can appreciate the straightforwardness of the comment, and the honesty of some people to speak out from their hearts. However, let us drop these opposing thoughts of disagreement out the window for a moment and try to look at this issue from a new perspective.

A logical way to identify the true cause of a complicated issue is to analyze its effect, the resulting consequence. In this case, lust in its three forms: the lust of the flesh, and the lust of the eyes, and pride of life; lures the man away from the love of the Creator. The inordinate human passion of lust of flesh, lust of the eyes and pride of life is consequently likened to a parasite living in the deepest recess of our shattered human nature. When we take a closer look into the world and see what are most radical problems of our world today, we are likely to find that most of the crimes originate, directly or indirectly, from man's inordinate love for passion and sexuality. I would not disagree if someone says crimes of passion take up major sum of all the crimes together, the growing population of pedophilia and sexual exploitation of young children boys and girls, particularly in some southern Asian countries for the purpose of sexual pleasure and torture across the different continents. Recent news uncovered the devious act of pedophiles imprisoning their abducted young girls for 10, 20 years in the underground cells of their homes, where sexual abuse and torture were a daily event. Upon hearing news of this nature, one can really howl with anger; "How could any human person commit such an inhuman act to fellow human beings, treating young innocent girls worse than animals?"

The list seems to be endless; sex slave and human trafficking controlled by organized crime is getting serious by the day in some developed countries. While I was organizing these thoughts on the piles of my notes, I noticed a local news headline about a middle age pedophile suspect caught by the police with video clips and pictures of children's sexual acts with grown ups, and scenes of sexual torture of young girls and boys in his computer, the evidence presented in the court was overwhelming number of 700,000 video clips and photos. Pedophiles and rapists tend to share their "successful stories" or trophies with each other across the world. Though the Interpol is working hard with local law enforcement agencies that aim to resolve the crimes locally and internationally, this problem is undoubtedly getting serious. Why is the effort rendered unnoticeable?

If anyone says that the reason for all these is due to faster growing population of pedophiles than in the past, I would accept the explanation without hesitation. However, our puzzle remains unresolved as of why human beings get to this magnitude of degradation? Of sexual exploitation of the minor, boys and girls, sex slave and torture of their "preys" and all the horrendous crimes of this nature that we see happening in different parts of the world, everyday!. Similar crimes of passion in gang rape, abortion, sex abuse of women at home, at work and in public area are obviously increasing. Extramarital affairs among men–women as well as homosexual and heterosexual affairs, and crimes of passion in homicides and suicides dominate the news headlines. The scene is really getting ugly. The parasite of lust that lives in the deepest recess of human nature has to be removed, and wounds should be cleansed. The opposing force of lust is purity of heart; we shall discuss further on this in the chapter on chastity.

It is, therefore, essential for young couples prior to their marriage to understand the original cause of the disorder of human passion. The misunderstanding and misuse of the power of human sexuality and its consequence has such an extensive effect to our humanity — men and women, family and children, and our society at large in the past, present and in the coming future. The logical reason is that our society has broken away from the full truth about what the original meaning to be a human being, and from the truth about what man and woman really are as human persons. Thus, this explains why many people in different societies cannot comprehend the real meaning of the gift of person in marriage and responsible love at the service of fatherhood and motherhood, the true meaning of human sexuality of procreation and education of children.

What Constitutes a Family?

What constitutes a family? This question attracts much debate especially nowadays amongst different interest groups in the modern society, and also amongst the pro-homosexual activists. The fundamental elements that make a family are a man and a woman brought together by their mutual love and commitment for life. The primary end of this marital union is the procreation and education of children; without education or upbringing of the children as the ultimate purpose, it would be like animal-mating. A temporary — marital — union would not guarantee this commitment in the upbringing of children, therefore, the union has to be for life. The mutual love and friendship of husband and wife must be for the good sake of the children, otherwise it will not be a sustainable love and friendship between the married couple. That is why every sexual act which deliberately deprives its function of generating new life (e.g. contraceptive mentality and its negative consequence will be discussed in the later chapters) goes directly against the common good of the family. Family is most basic community in civil society, a "natural" domestic society since it is natural for men and women to love one another and be willfully committed to each other. Family is a natural school where everyone learns to love and be loved, to learn and practice the common good appropriate to human nature. To understand the nature of marriage, it is essential to look at the difference between man and animal; to see the distinctive features in human beings. Essential as it is, due to the focus on the common good of the family — the children — our human species is propagated within marriage, because only within a marriage between a loving and committed couple, a male and a female, can the children be properly brought up to the common good of the society. Therefore, the *unity* and *indissolubility* of marriage is the only means to serve the common good of the family, the well being of the children, and certainly to ultimately serve the common good of the society at large.

Today, marriage as an institution is undergoing a severe challenge and attack, amid the culture of materialism and pursuance of pleasure permeating the society where young men and women are raised from families with little formation and lack knowledge of what true and self-giving love is. The wellness and happiness of families is threatened by selfishness of members due to the absence of commitment and genuine love, but also by external influences such as the ideologies of materialism and consumerism. Marriage seems to have gone wrong for modern men and women. They seem uncertain and even disillusioned about it, as is evident from the upsurge of broken families caused by divorce in many developed and developing societies all over the world. Yet the excellence of marriage as an institution has not been reflected with equal brilliance, since polygamy and one-night-stands, the plague of divorce, the so-called free love, and other disfigurement in passion and sexuality have the obscuring effect. In addition, marital love is too often profaned by excessive self-love between two married individuals, the worship of pleasure and illicit practices that tarnish the true meaning and the essence of human sexuality within marriage.

Because children are the natural fruits of marital love of the married couple, parents have the natural obligation to educate the children; thus they are the first and primary educators of their own children. The duty of educating children in the family is essentially important and parenting cannot be substituted by anyone. It is the obligation of the parents to create an environment and atmosphere in the family of love, sincerity and simplicity that enables an integrated education of human virtues primarily through the examples of the parents. The relationships in the family should be natural and simple where every member would learn to love and accept each other for who he or she is. Love within the family should not be founded on what the child could do, or perform, or how pleasing she/he may be; but by the very nature of who he is — being a member of the family.

A child born into a family that cares and loves all its members, is well loved, cared and accepted by the parents and siblings for who he/she is, because each child is an unrepeatable gift to the family. This unconditional love and acceptance within the family provides foundation for overall personal development of the child, in particular, the necessary sense of security and self-esteem that a child needs for his development to maturity.

When a child is born in a family that does not accept him for who he is, then this child would grow only to believe in himself and none other; he would strive very hard to demonstrate how good he is, and how well he does things in order to prove his worth. It is highly probable that this child will dedicate his energy of his entire life to show others his capability and performance so people may recognize his worth in the organization he works, in the environment where he lives, by and large in the society where he belongs. It is pity to observe that such phenomenon does exist in our contemporary society so much so that the value of a person rests only on what he/she can perform, but not on who the person really is. Thus, a healthy upbringing in the family says it all; the acceptance of a child with unlimited love in family constitutes the fundamental values in character building that would help in shaping the personality of the growing child that would remain with him for the great part of his life.

Some Useful Definitions

Though readers may find the following list of relationships too simplistic, some may find it useful for a quick reference. To suit different needs of various readers, I have decided to write a few lines to list down some of the thoughts and questions from couples who I got to know personally while conducting courses on Family Enrichment.

Erotic (Sexual) Desires arise from our intuitive awareness of the nuptial meaning of the body; the procreative power and the associating pleasurable experience that brings with it. Though it is an integral part of human passion, it can lead to lustful desires, and therefore, would need to be tempered and controlled. Just like anger is a normal human passion, it can be destructive when escalated, and therefore, it needs to be under control. The loving desire of making the marital spouse happy and open to life in a sexual relationship within marriage is fundamentally different from the erotic sexual desires that aim only at using another person as an instrument to quench a selfish sexual desire, for self-gratification and/or self-satisfaction.

Infatuation is a type of emotion that involves physical attraction of sensuous nature, or sexual feeling for another person. It is an emotion and obsessive want of another person for sensuous desire "Look at the muscular young man, he is totally infatuated with the bikini girls on the beach." Infatuation mainly refers to physical and sexual attraction "I am infatuated by your beauty, I am crazy about you", it is not true love but is often confused with the notion of what love really means. On the contrary, it is good for a man to say decisively: "I really love you, I want to marry you. I will never hurt you; and I will refrain from any action that might hurt you in any way I might be capable of." Due to the nature of the embedded sensuous and sexual nature in infatuation, it is quite often lustful.

Lust is a counterfeit of love and it destroys true love, a serious vice of human passion. It is an obsessive desire to use another person physical — sexual — body to satisfy his own sexual fantasy and desires, thus it violates the human dignity of the persons involved. A lustful person acts and lives like an addict, or alcoholic, who has minimum ability to control his passion and sensual cravings particularly in sexual desires. Lust damages personality, friendships and human integrity, it dehumanizes the person and also his/her victims. A person can be lustful toward another person even without any physical contact; through memory, imagination, spoken words, texting or through video image in front of the electronic screen such as in the cyber sex. Lust, like an addicted person, often leaves a lasting scar onto the life of the lustful person even long after his or her inordinate lustful life has been corrected. It is like a sore wound that needs to be cleansed and corrected through repetitive good tasks and achieving self-mastery to eradicate this embedded bad habit of lust.

Friendship is a natural phenomenon among human beings who have a natural need to live in a social environment, to build friendships and human relationships based on trust, care and affection. There are various levels of proximity in friendships, from being a mere acquaintance to an ordinary friend and to a personal friend. Friendship also exists between colleagues, superior and subordinates, between members of a social circle and club, certainly friendship between father and son, mother and daughter, and friendship between spouses as well. I once heard a mature woman said: "In my marriage, I have a healthy and handsome husband, a responsible father of my children, a loving fiancé, a confident, a mentor, a trusting advisor and a great friend. This person is my beloved husband whom I have been married for 40 years...!"

Family consists of a male-husband and female-wife who willfully consent to their mutual marital commitment; to love one another for life and to share of oneself with the spouse through mutual self-donation within marriage. "I want to marry you in order to make you happy," a marriage opens a new life, where children will be the natural fruits of this loving and committed relation. While the spouses shall gradually assume their respective roles of fatherhood and motherhood in the process of begetting children, they will acquire their responsibility to education and upbringing of children as a natural consequence within a family.

Courtship usually refers to a stage in a couple's falling-in-love relationship where they are seriously contemplating a lasting relationship, marriage. It is commonly expected that the courting relationship of this to-be married couple is usually exclusive: "I have only you in my heart while I am learning more about you"; exclusivity is not the same, and as strictly as, in the marital bond, however, it entails that this to-be-married couple should not be seeing or courting another person at the same time.

Spousal relationship is the only relationship that is best described as "two-in-one flesh" communion of persons consummated through selfless love, mutual respect and sexual manifestation that opens to new life. Marriage is the only proper context for a responsible and committed human sexual relationship that provides a stable environment for children to grow in all aspects. Family is a natural springboard of fostering healthy, upright, intelligent and responsible young individuals of good character.

A Glimpse of Human Freedom

Never before has man enjoyed his freedom as he does now, yet at the same time new forms of social and psychological slavery emerge. What comes to my mind is the slavery of materialism, and slavery of sensuality; where vanity of luxurious lifestyle and branded goods overwhelmingly "dominate" the lives of many people of our age. Not too long ago, it was on the news that a young teenage boy was found dead in the street, and according to the police reports in the following days, it was believed that the teenager was killed and stabbed several times in the body and his famous branded sports jacket and his pair of running shoes were missing. The boy was robbed and killed for his famous branded goods of sportswear. While ideology of sensuality infiltrates almost every aspect of our daily life as evident in the popularity of spas; paparazzi of the rich and famous, sensational news dominates the headlines. More variety of choices over a wide range of options to own, or to possess become the dominant perception of freedom.

Nowadays, nearly everyone I encounter seems to be talking about freedom: Freedom of choice, freedom of speech, freedom of thoughts and freedom to vote, yet more freedom is demanded by teenagers. Parents are concerned when they see the extent of freedom the youth of today enjoy and yet it seems the youth is not satisfied. Adolescents constantly demand more and more freedom, even younger children are beginning to talk about it. Adolescents have a strong tendency to assert independence from their parents; this is normal and it is even necessary as part of their upbringing. Sooner than later, they will become independent with the ending years of their teenage between 17 and 19 years depending on the variance of maturity of teenage boy and girl. It is seen to be a genuine need for parents to explore the concept of freedom during the upbringing of their children. Quite often, freedom could be an ambiguous watershed and a potential cause of misunderstanding between the teenagers and parents. Normally, the tensions between parents and teenagers arise from an imbalanced view of freedom between unclear notion of freedom and responsibility.

Parents will soon realize they would not be able to avoid talking about freedom in the family and to rationalize freedom in a practical sense with their teenage children, or even with children younger than the teenage. Some interesting questions are "What is human freedom?" What benchmarks could be used to justify true human freedom in dealing with children's curiosity and demands later on in their lives? How would we understand it and apply it in our daily family life? We shall try to discuss what human freedom is in the context of a family, and how it would affect the happiness and the success of our children's life.

It is essential to be aware that true freedom is not merely allowing anyone to choose whatever he or she likes to do. To make it easy to understand the notion of freedom for teenage children, I suggest we use a series of questions and examples related to daily lives that would help us visualize a better picture of what true human freedom really entails:

1. A 6 year old child asks permission of his mother, "Can I play Lego with Anthony, (a boy from the neighborhood) after finishing my homework?" Does this child exercise his freedom by asking his mother's permission?
2. A 4 year old boy, after watching TV program (e.g. Spiderman), wants to dress up like him — imitate Spiderman to fly out the window of his 10-story apartment. Does he exercise his own freedom…, and in a right way?

3. A 8 year old girl happily tells her mother the daily schedule she tries to follow: time to do homework, playtime after work, time to use her computer and time to bath and the choice of her pajama etc. and the mother rejects and asks the daughter to alter all timetable according to her own (mother) wish. Whose freedom is at stake?

4. Freedom of choice: Some drug addicted young men comment that they have as much right in ingesting drugs as others have in smoking cigarettes and drinking alcohol. How would we qualify this statement and conclude a rational answer? Would we certify attempts to "drink and drive" as sane decisions? Are these right choices of freedom, if not, why not?

5. Similarly, a teenage girl said to a friend that she has the right to dress up "fashionably" — as tiny a dress as probably a swimming suit — to disco or party, following the slogan of "dress to impress"; and not return home until morning. Can this really be called personal freedom?

6. The idea of hard work as part of the essence of human being has gone out of fashion. Works seems to be equated with merely making money, even the notion of work as service has been largely replaced by idea of "Act for money." Only a minority could experience the joy of doing things on their own initiative by serving others or the society.

7. A postman says to himself: "Since my work is so hard and my salary is low, I will deliver mails slowly as I please, anyhow no one notices me." Is this a right attitude of exercise own freedom?

8. A father and a son argue about the son's homosexual friend, the son says his friend has the right to live his life the way he likes. Why do people always discriminate against such "less-privileged" people? What would be your argument?

9. A mother complains that tending to housework and educating children are difficult tasks and that life is boring. She says to herself "I am not going to cook for them; and I am going to dedicate my rest-time on computer games six hours a day and everyday! I don't care if they have food to eat, or not."

10. A father says, "I am the main money earner of the family and my job is tough and my life is hard. Therefore, I need to entertain myself: have dinners and entertainment with business associates/ and friends every night" etc. The question is can this incidence be called exercising of personal freedom?

The above examples reflect the exercise of personal freedom at different situations at different age groups in life, from toddler to teenage and beyond, consequences vary from less serious to quite serious, in terms of different levels of moral responsibility and the proximity of physical danger. The above examples help to set the framework of what true freedom is. It is clearer than ever from the above examples that 'freedom and responsibility' must co-exist, they are like two sides of the same coin, "If you are not responsible, someone will definitely suffer"; we can find this from examples 1, 6 and 9. If freedom results in the loss of responsibility, the victim could very well be the person himself, or a member in the family, or anyone else, as given in examples 1, 5, 7 and 8. True human freedom is to choose knowingly the good and to do the right thing according to the moral principle that governs human thoughts and action. These examples aim to stimulate the thoughts of readers of what is morally correct, what criteria govern our human acts and the importance to choose and to do the right thing. The 10 examples also intend to reflect and highlight the moral virtues of temperance, fortitude, justice and prudence. Examples 2 and 3 were chosen to highlight the cause and effect of the possibility of parents choosing to place unnecessary restrictions on their child, it could cast an incorrect perception of freedom in the mind of the child. If parents choose to place restrictions on all aspects in the family life, i.e. irrespective of the level of seriousness and its moral implication; a child would not be able to distinguish what is morally wrong verses a simple error. The child grows up mistakenly believing there is no freedom in the family, and parents can choose to do whatever they want to do irrespective of whether the act or decision is right or not. This unnecessary interference in a simple free choice by the parents could become the confusion and an act of injustice to the child concerned. Thus, it could very well be the root cause of rebelliousness of the teenage child and the conflict builds up between the child and parents.

A child's upbringing involves the risk of letting him or her to commit mistakes, after all, he cannot hold on to his parents' hands forever. Someday he will have to stand on his own and take responsibility for his own actions. The challenge, of course, is whether parents can instill the proper notion of true human freedom into the children's heart and mind, so that when they reach the age of responsibility, say pre-teenage period and beyond, they would be in a position to knowingly choose and to do the right thing in life, and choose to do good. One thing is quite clear, the two extremes of the pendulum effect between freedom and control is in itself a contradiction, the two extremes of the contradiction signals a potential conflict of what the teenage youth wants as opposed to what the parents want gaining in control. The pendulum effect presents a substantial challenge in balancing between letting the child to try out his freedom, or not letting the child to do what he wants to do. Some parents will even go to the extent to protect the child away from any so-called "social contamination" by sheltering the child in a "green house" environment which initially seems to be free from outside influence. This type of parental protection of greenhouse effect will most likely be short-lived when the child begins to see, from his classmates and friends, the difference of family values and practices. The pre-teenage youth would likely to become more rebellious against his parents when this parental protection of greenhouse effect is being used in the child's upbringing. It is fundamentally essential to help youngsters to understand that true human *freedom* and *responsibility* go hand-in-hand and must co-exist. True freedom is to choose to do good knowingly, and do the right thing according to the moral principle that governs our human behavior; our thoughts and action. I am a free person, and I can only be as free as a human being is possibly can.

Rules of Life

It is not difficult to observe that there are certain rules and laws that regulate our planet in a systematic way of the nature; from natural rotation of the earth to Newton Law of Gravity, from daily sunrise and sunset to rain-and-water cycle. The lightning in a thunder storm could probably kill a person who chooses to stand right next to a tall pole on a rainy night. These are not just laws of physics or chemistry that we learn from textbooks, they are also realities of the nature of human life; we human beings have the capacity to learn the reality through observation of the nature. When thousands and thousands of flying insects suddenly appear in the sky, we know that a low pressure is nearing and a rain-storm is anticipated. Life has its rules, and if these rules are not respected and observed, the consequences can be quite serious. Freedom and happiness are not always mutually exclusive and they are not under our possession either in absolute terms. There are certain conditions imposed by reality of the nature to which all living beings, including human beings, are subjected to. We begin to see the negative effects of a suffered nature in recent global warming, rising of the sea-level, melting away of glaciers in the north and south poles, relentless killing of whales and sharks for human gourmet and epidemics presumably caused by genetic alteration of crops and cattle, etc. I can hear an outcry of "I want my nature back, a pure nature in its original form." One of the conditions is that we respect the rules of life prescribed by the nature. People who are not aware of these rules, or some people that have decided to break the rules without knowing the truth and the consequences, will soon discover that their ignorance would cost them dearly.

Interior Freedom

Human freedom is not merely a freedom of choice, for someone to choose his likes over his dislikes. Many people think that the greater the range of choices, the greater is the freedom they have, while many people measure freedom by the range of options they have. People logically want to choose the destination of their vacation, the number of children they want to have, the teachers of their children, the color of their car, their favorite restaurant for a gourmet dining experience. In the reality of life, there are essential things for which we do not have choice at all, for example; we are not able to choose our parents, our blood types and our natural gender as well. As discussed earlier, genuine love is to will the good of another person. When a wife willingly chooses to join her husband to watch a detective-action movie that she does not like but because it is her husband's favorite type of movie, she buys the tickets and tries to enjoy the movie; this wife has exercised her interior freedom to choose what appears to be good for her beloved, over her own favorite. Or of a father who did not hesitate for a second to run into a burning house to save his baby girl when the family house was hit by the debris of a plane crash. He forgot his own safety and decided to make a move to save. This father did not only demonstrate his courage driven by his charity-love for his baby child, but also, he made a willful consent of his interior freedom for the good of his offspring.

Like most men, I naturally do not enjoy shopping or window-shopping. When I was young, I would just go into a shop and if I spotted a merchandise that I wanted, I would buy it and leave; a simple operation. After nearly 30 years into our marriage, I have developed a new habit of accompanying my wife for window-shopping. At the beginning, I held my breath and followed the footsteps of my wife, quite slowly, I gradually learnt to count the steps and my pulses "1001, 1002 and 1....!" as we strode slowly on the path winding from one part of the shop to the next, at times, little "progress" was made, so to speak. Through this exercise, I have learned to train up my patience in the last decades, but today my patience is still underscored.

Nowadays, shopping at malls has changed so much similar to so many other transformations that we see around us. I soon came to realize that shopping at the malls could be a self-gratifying experience that gives you a taste of sensuous feeling with exotic scent, comforted by the cool and ever-flowing air-conditioning, accompanied by ambience music and attractive lightings. I guess the ultimate intention of this enhanced "shopping experience" is an attempt to lure the shoppers like us to spend a few more hundred dollars to buying things that we might forget in a few days time; fortunately these "tricks" do not work on me, and neither my beloved wife. In order to become truly free, a person is often being called to decide what he or she does not actually need.

A mother freely chooses to give up her supper in order to feed her hungry children. I recall a scene on the news, when a middle aged man realized that a drunken woman had fallen into the sea on a cold winter night. Without much thinking he dived into the freezing water and swam for minutes before he saved this woman who was in coma when rescued. By endangering his own life to save the drunken woman, he demonstrated his free decision thinking driven by his interior freedom to will the good of this woman by saving her life. Being truly free also means consenting to do what we do not like in order to serve a good cause, and for the good of others.

Conclusion

Though many of our contemporary citizens are gratified by the scientific discoveries, and the extraordinary power reached beyond boundaries, however, anxious questions are raised about the current trends in the world — global climatic change, drastic shift in the ecological balance on our planet, global warming, and rising of the sea level at an alarming rate; and our growing anxiety about the role of man in the global arena; about the meaning of his individual and collective efforts in life purpose, development, relevant social and political order, and about the ultimate destiny of humanity.

As a consequence of the fall of man and the original sin, fundamental disorder is induced not only in human passion that destroys the purity of heart, but it also induces man with a strong inclination to do things that are contrary to fundamental good. We are led to see the disorder of human passion as a consequence of the original sin which does not necessarily limit human beings to the corruption of the flesh — fornication, impurity, licentiousness, drunkenness, carousing" which are corruption of the flesh and of sensual nature — but it could also lead us to the corruption of the spirit. There are other sins that could be attributed to a carnal and sensual character, such as: "idolatry, sorcery, enmity, strife, jealousy, anger, selfishness, dissension, party spirit, envy..." (Galatians 5:20–21, Navarre Bible) If we examine this phenomenon closely, we would be inclined to call all these attributes listed here as corruption of the spirit, rather than corruption of the flesh. Not without reason we might have noticed in these sins the effects of the lust of the eyes and pride of life; rather than merely the effects of the lust of the flesh. In reality, one corruption leads to another, moral corruption of human being is contagious, if our eyes sin and betray us followed by the corruption of the flesh, we can be rest-assured that other sins of the spirit and carnal nature will soon follow.

Human sexuality involves not just the body but the whole person, yet conjugal sexuality can never be reduced to a mere biological exchange. Precisely because of this mutual self-giving of spouses of their personhood, as man and woman, of their love in marriage, matrimony begins with "two souls in one body" and it seeks to become "one soul and one body." That is why the ultimate purpose of marriage cannot merely be motivated by the sexual passion engendered merely by physical attraction.

We can visualize the reason — if marriage is not lived in and within the spiritual context, it makes the spouses fall into degradation of animal mating. To a certain extent, it reduces married love to a tool for satisfying sexual need as an end itself that damages the very specific common good of marriage: *procreation and education* of children. Perpetuity of a loving commitment in marriage between spouses finds its root in self-giving love. When a wife truly loves her husband, she consents to will the good of her husband by making him good and happy, to understand his needs and concern, his physical and spiritual well being, making him good and healthy. She will try her best to make their home comfortable and welcoming, bright and cheerful, by making herself good looking and attractive as much as she can, and by making him happy. Whereas, man-husband should strive to learn the manifestation of the self-giving love from his wife, with daily refresh and love commitment. In both scenarios, the wife and husband are to exercise their respective interior freedom to will the better — good of the other. "I love you and will make you good and happy." With interior freedom as the door hinge, the door of marriage opens to mirror of love that reflects an image of true love, "Love for others"; the genuine self-giving love between spouses.

Chapter 3

Love in Marriage

During a recent lunch appointment, I met with an old friend whom I had not seen for over a decade. After our mutual greetings, he said to me: "I am a free man!" I asked him: "What do you mean?" And he continued; "You know Sarah and I are separated,...we have divorced three months ago." After a quiet moment, he nodded: "Well, we still like each other as before, just that our lives are so different now." My friend probably realized that I was still recovering from the shocking news, he continued: "Look, nowadays divorces are so common, please don't be so shocked, I am not the only one" as if he was trying to convince me that everything is fine and life as usual. My friend had been married to Sarah for 25 years, they have three children, and I knew them soon after their wedding. Of course, I was in shock. After pondering for minutes, I came to realize what my friend has said is quite true; the shocking reality of the escalating numbers of failure in marriage that happens is just phenomenal, and it happens almost everywhere, abroad and at home.

Not only is the number of divorces increasing, but also the problems of separated couples and families and the residual effect onto the children are getting worse by the day. It is quite horrifying to see that the traditional values of a family and marital commitment have deteriorated so much and so fast, in such a short time; lacking a sense of urgency and awareness of its problems has blurred the lens of our today society to the fact that the collapse in marriage in great numbers, is propagating to an immense social problem in every corner of our global village.

A field survey report that I came across from a marriage counseling organization indicates there are two main reasons for marital failure: character conflict and marital infidelity. These are indeed very strong reasons, but if we dig deeper into the problem, it appears that there are some other fundamental reasons as well. The most common missing part is the ignorance in understanding what spousal love is, it often begins with lack of mutual respect between the married couple and letting their love and care age with time. When marital love is not strongly founded on self-giving love, true friendship and loving commitment, then self-complacency and self-love is allowed to promulgate in the marital relationship. One misunderstanding builds on perception when unresolved and will keep piling up over time, with the slightest spark of temperament that seemingly coming from no where, will become a scourging fire of anger that consumes the entire marriage. It is unfortunate to find that most of the divorced couples have little idea of what the true marital love really is.

Genuine human love entails self-giving, to love others selflessly, rather than merely getting what one desires from the receiving end. Millions of people of our modern society, young and old, believe that to love is more or less equating to finding pleasure; to take something pleasurable out from another entity, be it a pet, a car or a glass of wine, or having a delicious meal in an ambient and romantic environment. Quite often, a sensuous spa treatment or a casual relationship with another person is taken as pleasurable love! The perception of sensuous pleasure in relation to love has been one of the root causes of this misunderstanding of genuine human love. As if, it resonates in the minds of many people "if there is no pleasure, there is no love."

"Man cannot live without love. He would remain incomprehensible of himself, his life would be senseless, if love is not revealed to him, if he does not encounter love, if he does not experience it and make it his own, if he does not participate intimately in it." This four letter word "Love" is often over simplified, misunderstood and misused by many people; and yet it bears such a deep meaning and transcendental value since the very beginning of human history. Quite often, people equate human love to a purely physical and emotional satisfaction. When a teenage male says to a female "I love you," in fact most probably what he really means is "I want you, I want something from you that would give me pleasure". This attitude of love almost translates that love is an "effective and convenient" means to satisfy one's emotional need and sexual satisfaction. What some people love is not the person but the experience and passion of being in love.

"Love is primarily in the Will, not in emotion or the glands." (Fulton Sheen) The male animal is attracted to female animal, but a human personality is attracted to another human personality. The attraction among animals is physiological, the attractions among human beings is psychological, physiological and spiritual; as human beings possess something fundamentally different from beast, this 'something' is the composition of body and spirit fused together into an inseparable form since the time of the Creation. In a more fashionable terminology, we may call human a hybrid of material and spiritual being. Thus, there is no such thing as giving the body without giving the soul. Sex separated from personality, is not a human act, thus does — should — not exist in human beings.

In our modern society, it is quite common to see that genuine human love is being degraded to a level as a tool for self-gratification and sexual-satisfaction. It is even more tragic to see that this incorrect perception about human love is being brought into marriage, at times from the disoriented teenage life that has a high possibility to further corrupt the marital relationship between couple. Love is primarily in the will: "I love you because I wanted to give myself to you, and to do my best to take great care of you; and to make you happy for the rest of your life."

One of the greatest illusions of human love is the perception of the longevity of loving experience and the loving relationship depends merely on the intensity of the sexual attraction between the couple. As soon as the physical sexual attraction dies down, or not as strong as it used to be, the couple claims that they no longer love each other, or one spouse has "outgrown" another "in different aspects in life" that they are no longer compatible with each other anymore. I came to know about the expression "outgrown my husband" from a documentary program series where a married couple, with eight children, divorced as consequence of this outgrown effect.

This seemingly reasonable excuse is a clear sign that humans, as rational beings, see the need for justifying his or her irrational behavior when they commit a mistake, and knowingly make a wrong decision. This is an example of self-centeredness that leads to extreme selfishness. In this case, the person has never loved the other person in the first place, he only loved the experience of being in love which is absolute contrary to what we will be discussing further about self-giving love, or self-donating love in a marriage as a communion of persons, in the next chapter. Thus, it is essential for young adults to know and understand the fundamentals of human love that love should primarily be in the will as early as possible, long before their courtship; and before their pondering an immature decision to get married; as opposed to the socially-accepted perception of marriage being a license granted to a couple to open the doors of the world of sexuality. Marriage founded on sexual passion only lasts as long as the animal passion lasts; after two to three years into this passionate love, the relationship starts to age and the loving fire goes dim, the usual physical passion is lost between the couple; they want to separate or divorce appears imminent.

Phases of Love

Though readers may be fully aware of the different phases of love, considering various backgrounds of readers, I believe it is good to bring the subject matter on the table, to some it may be a quick review, and to some others it may be a new beginning in their quest of knowledge. It is essential for young men and women to understand and realize that human love is not a mere emotional act, based on feeling and senses, before they start their dating the opposite sex or prepare to enter into any serious love affairs or marital commitment with their beloved. In fact, it is even better for young children to see and learn genuine human love from the parents, through their daily lives, within the family. The patience and kindness toward each other in the most ordinary daily life, the humility to say sorry when in wrong and to forgive each other; the generosity and sharing practiced at home, the solidarity toward less fortunate people, enduring love in face of difficulty between the husband and wife, the dialogue and willingness to listen to each other is the best education of love to the children when growing up.

It might be useful to re-visit the concept of human love in three stages even though it may be familiar to some people. To review and learn with repetitions in knowledge and practices is one of the sure ways to gain perfection; the logic of repetition of good habits builds strong human virtues.

Phase 1. Love of Desire (Love of the Senses)

It is more a sensation rather than a feeling, it is a tendency to seek and enjoy the sensation that is derived from sensuous pleasure. Love of desire is similar to a five year old kid that sees an ice-cream sign on his way back home and cannot help but display his eagerness to obtain his want — the delicious ice-cream cone. Love of desire is nothing wrong essentially, in fact it can be good; as Fulton Sheen said: 'The pleasure associated with love, or what is today called "Sex" is the frosting on the cake; its purpose is to make us love the cake, not ignore it.' However, if love of the senses is not regulated to the right order: merely seeking the frost on the cake but not the cake; it can cause much harm to the individual concerned, to married couples, families and society at large.

Passionate Love

When a teenage person is immersed in frantic romance, he is actually entering into some kind of illusion. His teenage hormones would keep him jumping up and down; weird body moves and compulsive phone calls at strange hours; serenading in the rain; yelling from rooftops; singing and dancing in the bathroom, waiting at school gate just for a glimpse of the beloved. All these out of place behavior looks much like some kind of mental illness to the rest of the world, a kind of madness, but to those who are in love, it makes perfect sense. When falling in love, the person is overwhelming, he or she seems to be out of control and irrational. When we have a chance to witness this strange behavior of our teenage children in their first love, at time it is quite astonishing and inexplicable. This phenomenon actually takes place in this very unromantic part of our bodies called the brain.

New York Times had published an article in a May 2005 about a group of neuroscientists that had carried out a project study on human brain in relationship to its emotions. The study involved analyzing 2500 brain images from college students who were in their first weeks or months of new love. The selected students were asked to look at the pictures of their beloved while an MRI (Magnetic Resonance Imaging) machine scanned their brains. The researchers then compared the images with others taken while the students were asked to look at pictures of a normal acquaintance. This study was conducted by Dr. H. Fisher, an anthropologist at Rutgers University in New Jersey, Dr. Arthur Aron, a psychologist at the State University of New York, and Dr. L. Brown a professor of neurology of Albert Einstein College of Medicine.

Just like the muscular tissue, the brain needs more blood when it is active and is used more; and less blood when it is inactive or is used less. The MRI machine is a huge cylindrical scanning machine that measures blood flow in and from the brain. Scanning the brain in an MRI shows areas that are more active and working harder than the rest; and areas that are inactive. The results illustrate an interesting phenomenon of human brain when the person is in love.

An area of our brain — reward center — "lights up" when it is emotionally stimulated such as when a person is falling in love, when a mother breast-feeds her new-born baby, or when a fellow engages in winning an electronic game competition. Such lit areas in our brain indicate the person is in love and emotionally high and the system produces the brain hormones. These hormones are responsible for the ability to bond, form attachments, and establish trust between people (see Fig 3.1).

Some areas of the brain are turned off when people fall in love while those areas of the brain that are used in judgment go dim! Basically what happens is when a person falls in love, he or she temporarily loses his/her function of common sense in judgment. That is the reason for sensible people to behave a bit insane when falling in love, they often do not listen to advice of others relating to the love relationship and are often referred by some people as: "He's *crazily* in love." Perhaps this is the reason why one can go on and on without eating or sleeping, and would feel sad or possibly in tears when encountering difficulties in the relationship or when breaking up with the beloved. When a person is immersed in love, he or she is easily pre-occupied, her emotion is impulsive, often distracted as her mind is filled with the images of romance; the moon becomes colorful and everything seems to be beautiful. We see teenager in love would often

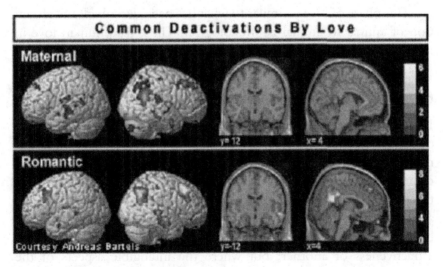

Fig. 3.1. The Human Brain in Relation to Love

smile to oneself, acting as if he or she is a bit crazy, giving a dozen calls to the beloved in an hour, or engage in endless phone calls until mid-night, etc. This passionate love is merely the beginning of an attraction mainly found on physical attraction, this is not what true love is.

In the post-modern society, people are trapped in this stage of love and clearly the effect is that of treating other human beings as though they were objects for pleasure or exchange for something material. This is practically the enculturation of thinking aloud: "If I no longer could obtain the sensation of physical attraction, of pleasure, I'll have to look for someone else — something else — who can give it to me." People are being treated as instruments to satisfy the selfish desire for pleasure; rather than to be loved for who they really are; people are being pursued for what he/she can produce in quantity or quality i.e. a measurable phenomenon of the efficiency and effectiveness syndrome. As a consequence, human love is degraded as a means to an end, a journey of pleasure seeking, an interchangeable relationship for satisfying own selfish desire; and human being has become an object of the pleasurable.

This phase of love is similar to what has been described: the attraction of animal to animal is physiological. Thus, true human love in marriage exceeds far beyond this phase "love of desire."

Phase 2. Love of Appreciation (Love of the Heart)

In this phase, a person discovers the beauty of the character and personality of another person. It is similar to the emotional feeling and recognition of events such as the beautiful sunrise or sunset, or the overwhelming emotion when hearing a lovely piece of classical music that could uplift our mind and body. Love that is felt from genuine appreciation of noticing and appreciating the inner beauty of his or her beloved is not merely derived from the physical appearance or the attractiveness of another; but where the intangible aspects of the person, such as some aspects of the personality: honesty, responsibility, charity and sincerity, etc are revealed and appreciated. This phase of love is similar to what we have mentioned in the early chapter: the attraction among human beings is psychological, physiological and intellectual, however, true love that motivates a person to love another genuinely for the good of that person founded on principle of self-giving shall be considered in the next levels of love.

Phase 3. Love of Benevolence (Love of the Will)

Genuine love is primarily in the will — a will to love another, over and above the physical attraction of the superficial beauty of a person and which grows beyond the underlying essence of the personality and character of the beloved. To better describe the love of benevolence is the selfless love of a mother; in numerous cases we see in real life, many mothers readily and willingly give up their own lives for the protection of her children. She loves her child so much that she wants to give the child a life by bringing her to the world, and she loves the child to the point of death by keeping her alive. Love of benevolence enables a person to love another without any expectation of a return, or reward, a self-giving love purely to will the good of the beloved. "I love you and want you to be good, happy and healthy, no matter how difficult it may seem."

The following is a story that helps illustrate love of benevolence of a mother. In early 60's when life was not as prosperous as today, and was filled with poverty and constraint of material resources, a mother made it a habit of giving fillet of the entire fish to her husband and children during family dinners with the excuse that she liked the bones and leftovers in the dishes. The consistency of the mother was so convincing that her children eventually believed that their mother really liked the fish-bones and leftovers, until they discovered later on in their lives the truth of sacrifice of their mother. The loving sacrifice of the mother has become the good of her children in their physical, psychological and spiritual aspects, realization of self-giving love symbolizes this Love of benevolence.

Love Within Marriage

When we apply this love of benevolence in marriage, it is the love of the will that decides to give oneself mutually and to one another in marriage, this constant falling in love of the will keeps loving relationship fresh and alive. Through communion of persons, spouses learn and practice mutual self-donation of their personhood that opens to new life. Genuine love demands a love of the good deeds as well as the faults of the beloved through daily renewal while recognizing with humility that no one is perfect and each has to struggle to become better each day and for the good of each other, and for the sake of children and family. A will that determines not only of what the present marital love may bring, but a love of the will that would enable the couple to forge ahead in continuing this mutual love of the will to the future; until the end of time.

Love of benevolence is primarily in the will that corresponds to what has been described earlier: the attraction between human beings is spiritual, psychological, physiological and intellectual. Marriage is the only human relationship where an unconditional truthful reciprocal self-giving love among spouses is made possible, the covenant of conjugal love freely and consciously chosen, whereby man and woman accept the intimate communion of love and life. This conjugal love also corresponds to the responsible fertility that directs to the generation of a new human life, and the upbringing and education of children.

Marriage as an institution is founded on mutual self-giving love between the spouses and involves unconditional surrender of their personhood to each other — a mutual gift in exchange between spouses. Thus, genuine spousal love is *Total* and *Exclusive*. The word total means totality and everything, "we are the only one", or entirety of my being. Unity between spouses is founded on the unconditional surrender of their personhood that makes the spousal love total: "My love, I give everything of myself and my being to you, physical and spiritual, for the love I have for you." Similarly, the wife does the same. Spousal love is also exclusive; exclusivity in spousal love is "I for you only, and you for me only" there is only "you and I" and nobody else in between. To those who share the Catholic faith, there is someone invisible in between, the Holy Spirit, who lives and continues to shed light and strength to the married couple throughout their entire marriage. In marital vow, the husband makes a consent to love the wife for life, and enable himself willfully and freely to share his personhood with her in this exclusive spousal union, and vice versa. Precisely because of this unity: exclusive, total and mutual self-giving of their personhood that gives rise of the indissolubility of the marital unity.

God created man in His own image and likeness, calling him to existence through love and He called him at the same time for love. He inscribed in the humanity of man and woman the vocation, with capacity and responsibility, of love and communion. Therefore, the sexual act where man and woman give themselves to one another is proper and exclusive to spouses, and is by no means only purely biological, but concerns the innermost being of the human person. Thus, self-giving marital love is integral and total.

It takes the integration of the three stages of love namely: love of desire, love of appreciation and the love of benevolence in marital love to be truly human. Marriage is realized in a truly human way in an integral part of the love where a man and woman commit themselves totally, the total physical and spiritual self-giving, to one another "until death do we part." It is a love which is total — that very special form of personal friendship in which husband and wife generously share everything, allowing no unreasonable exceptions and not thinking solely of their own convenience. Whoever really loves his spouse loves not only for what he receives, but loves that spouse for the spouse's own sake, content to be able to enrich the other with the gift of oneself.

Love in a marriage enables spouses to be faithful and exclusive of one other, until death. This is how husband and wife understood it on the day on which, fully aware of what they were doing, they freely vowed themselves to one another in marriage. Though this fidelity of husband and wife sometimes presents difficulties, no one has the right to assert that it is impossible; it is, on the contrary, always honorable and meritorious. The example of countless married couples proves not only that fidelity is in accord with the nature of marriage, but also that it is the source of profound and enduring happiness.

The fecundity of this marital love does not confine wholly to the loving interchange between husband and wife; it also contrives to go beyond this to bring new life into their lives. "Marriage and conjugal love are by their nature ordained toward the procreation and education of children. Children are really the supreme gift of marriage and contribute in the highest degree to their parents' welfare."

The Truth and Meaning of Human Sexuality

It is essential to know the true meaning of human sexuality within the framework of a genuine and rich anthropology. Since a human is made in the image and likeness of God, and God Himself is love, the meaning and aim of human existence is to lead a life in which the ultimate purpose is to love and be loved. Detached from this context, life would definitely lose its luster; in contrast, selfless love is full of vitality and creativity. Love is a gift of God, nourished by and expressed in the manifestation of human love in man and woman. In the plan of life, man and woman are called to love, which is a precious source for self-giving, in order to achieve their own self-realization and happiness. Man, as a physical and spiritual being, is capable loving with his soul and body in unity of the person. Therefore, sexuality is not something purely biological rather it involves the intimate nucleus of the person. The use of sex as a mere physical involvement has its own truth and reaches its full meaning when expressed as an act between a married man and his wife where the spouses give themselves to each other selflessly and for the purposes of achieving a unity of life together.

During our lifetime, love is exposed to the frailty brought about by original sin, a frailty experienced today in many socio-cultural contexts marked by very strong negative influences, at times deviant and traumatic. We have already talked about the Fall of man and the Original sin in Chapter 2. Therefore, the only way to accomplish the sacred mission of the union between the two sexes and procreation is for a man and a woman to give themselves to each other in a lifelong commitment to love and to bring forth and educate their children. A non-Christian is invited to adopt an open mind approach that begins to lead to realization of the truth, that is, with human effort and God's grace, the enduring love between a couple would ultimately triumph over whatever impacts and challenges marriage and family life might encounter.

Knowledge and Procreation

It is part of the nature when a man loves his wife and wants to surrender his personhood to her as she does the same within a conjugal covenant. In the mystery of creation, man and woman are mutual gifts to each other. The mutual gift of the person in marriage opens to the gift of a new life, a new human being, who is also a person in the likeness of his parents. This opens the great creative perspective, in which human existence is always renewed by means of procreation, is rooted in the consciousness of the nuptial meaning of the body, with its masculinity and femininity. Through the free and responsible cooperation of the married couple in transmitting the gift of human life; they share and participate in the love of the Creator and His power of creation in bringing new life through the fruit of their conjugal union. "Adam knew Eve his wife, and she conceived and bore Cain, saying, "I have begotten a man with the help of the Lord.' And again, she bore his brother Abel" (Gn 4:1–2, Navarre Bible). Nevertheless, it is significant that the situation in which husband and wife unite so closely as to become one flesh has been defined as "knowledge". The deepest essence of the reality of married life is communion of persons that results in procreation. In conjugal knowledge, the woman is given to the man, and he to her, since the body and sex directly enter the structure and the content of this knowledge. In this way, the reality of the conjugal union in which the man and the woman become one flesh contains a new and, in a way, definitive discovery of the meaning of the human body in its masculinity and femininity. A person can fully discover the true meaning of his existence and his ultimate happiness only by sincerely and selflessly giving himself. In conjugal union, any artificial contraceptive obstructs the true surrender of their personhood in the marital act. When a person willfully places an artificial barrier such as pill or condom, or diaphragm, with an intention to prevent conception in the act of conjugal love, the sexual act at this particular moment is no longer an act of "communion of persons." Contraceptive directly destroys the unity between spouses as it deliberately ruins the couple's potency of giving new life, which is a natural essence of openness in conjugal love. Consequently, the marital act becomes a selfish act of self-gratification and self-satisfaction "I want you to give me your body but not the rest of your personhood." This immediately reduces the supposedly self-giving spousal union to a selfish act of sexual desire satisfaction; the wife becomes the object of pleasure to the husband, or husband as an object to his wife. This selfish act destroys the nuptial meaning of human sexuality between the spouses.

Sex decides not only the somatic individuality of a person, but also his identity and personhood. The fruitfulness of conjugal love end solely in procreation of children, it also entails the concept of enriching the off-springs with moral, intellectual and spiritual fruitfulness through their active participation in the proper education and formation of their own children. The natural fertility and potency of the masculinity and femininity of the human body should be treated with respect and treasured by the spouses in order to serve the supreme self-donation of persons in spousal love and conjugal union. As opposed to the ideology of the current social culture of separating sex from the bodily person, "I want your body and your sexual appeal, never mind the rest of your personhood" and the socially acceptable norms of separate sex from true love, "Let's have fun and pleasure, never mind if there is love or not". The world that we live is filled with this notion that destroys human dignity and reduces conjugal union to animal mating; it shall continue to destroy the conscience and purity of hearts of our youth, our children and next generations to come, if we allow ourselves to sit still, and do nothing.

In giving life, parents cooperate with the creative power of God and receive the gift of a new responsibility — not only to feed their children and satisfy their materials and cultural and emotional needs, but above all to pass on to them the lived truth of the faith and to educate them the love of God and neighbor, this is the parents' first and the most important duty.

If it is true that by giving life parents share in God's creative work, it is also true that by raising their children they become sharers in his paternal and at the same time maternal way of education. In the framework of educating young people for self-realization and self-giving, the formation of chastity implies formation of cardinal virtues of temperance, fortitude, justice and prudence. Chastity is not to be understood as a repressive attitude, but rather as the purity, in heart and body, and temporary stewardship of a precious gift of love. Chastity is thus that "spiritual energy capable of defending love from the perils of selfishness and aggressiveness, and be able to advance it towards its full realization."

Some insights of True Love

Freedom: Husband and wife should love each other freely and complete, detached from any material cause, it is like possessing oneself and one's own future fully and giving oneself to another. That is why some people do not want to get married forever, cannot make their martial commitment, because they are not free to the extent of possessing themselves and their future; and thus incapable of committing to something that contravenes their freedom.

Love the shortcomings too: Husband and wife love each other for who they are, but not what they possess (have): beauty, physical appearance, tall or slim, wealthy or not so wealthy. "To be" and "to have" as life objective in children upbringing and developmental education will be discussed in later chapters. The couple shall naturally love the good qualities of his/her spouse, yet they need to learn to love each other's shortcomings as well. Gradually with patience, love and endurance the couple will learn to mutually help each other to improve their respective shortcomings as in the essence of communion of persons in the journey of marriage. Never form a judgment of the spouse based on what "I see, or even worse what I hear". Our observations and perceptions of certain human behavior are highly, very likely to be wrong perceptions.

"If you judge people, you have no time to love them" (Mother Teresa)

Integral and Total: The love of spouses is integral and total; I love the entire person of my wife and she loves me vice versa. This integral love has a crucial aspect that is very much overlooked nowadays: the intertwining relationship between will and emotional feeling. As in our human nature (unlike angelic or divine nature) the will is incapable of loving fully without the aid of the power of sentiments, of sensuality and of emotion. "Purity, which is love, cannot be separated from the essence of our faith, which is charity, a constant falling in love with God" (St. Josemaria, "For they shall see God" in Friends of God 186).

Therefore, as marriage advances in years, spouses in love should be more aware of their physical fitness and looks; e.g. the husband should probably watch for his growing belly and sloppiness, not-so-good habits of happy hours drinks after work or the number of the cans of beer on hot Saturday afternoons. And the wife should probably need to keep her habits intact as well as her physical conditions: physical appearance and fitness, the way she dresses and moves should aim to the best possible of human essence similar to that during their courtship.

Fruitfulness: True love is always exuberant, fertile, it is an overflowing of love that bring forth our off-springs, children. The natural and specific and the most characteristic course that distinguishes marital love from other human love is precisely the possibility of transmitting new life, of having children.

Daily effort to love: Every day is different in routine, therefore, begin every day anew by choosing to love our spouse every morning "she is my wife" or "he is my husband!" To do so, it may be necessary to return our mind to the past, of the courtship; the first date, the atmosphere, the color of the blouse or the shirt he or she wore; and the hairstyle then. "Nice memory flashes back, what made us laugh? Recalling the moments of joy with the children when young; to make the family photo albums easily available to look at and enjoy together". These tools will help our memories to reflect and recall the happy and memorable moment that seldom fail.

Every hug is an intimate act in which two bodily persons embrace each other for a few seconds is a good expression of love and understanding. Husband's affirmation of the good works and beauty of the wife; while the wife expresses a sense of appreciation for the care and protection of the husband could at time work wonders.

Observation with care: A look capable of noticing the smallest details, interests, the inner personal world of the spouse, whether in good spirit or when she or he is down due to physical tiredness or other cause, a joke or gesture corresponding to lighten up the spouse is definitely a sign of true love and care. It shows that the passionate love is not diminished with the passing of years but rather invigorated by a youthful look that does not know routine.

Giving-in, not giving-up. Husband and wife need to learn and to practice to give in to his or her own wants every now and then so that they both recognize equality in dignity and rights, in their sexuality and in their marital and family roles. Insistence on personal viewpoints or preferences of hobbies, food or movies, etc. can be disastrous in marital relationships. Quite often, the wife who is more inclined to give in to husband's preferences frequently and consistently, is the "victim" of this one-sided generosity; however over time, after a period of years, it could be a time bomb underlying in the marital relationship.

I am sorry: In family arguments or quarrels, there is no such thing who is absolutely right or wrong; the one who is more loving should start to say I'm sorry, then the other follows. If the spouse is in a bad mood, the other should strive to keep quiet, contemplate the goodness until the situation cools down, this could effectively reduce the possibility of a heated argument further. Never argue in front of your children, it symbolizes lack of unity between spouses, and children could easily mistakenly conclude that their father and mother do not love each other anymore.

To minimize disputes and quarrels between the couple, humility and sincerity are essential traits. They allow room for self-reflection and contemplation: "Why am I always angry at this certain point of discussion? Why am I convinced that I am always right and justified in any argument? As no one is perfect, why do I expect my wife to be one, and not myself to bend my preference, every now and then?" "One sincere resolution: to make the way lovable and easy for everyone else, since life already brings a lot of bitterness with it." (St. Josemaria Escriva, Furrow 63)

Starting from me: Each marriage is individual, theories and principles and advice are all meant to be good, however, a successful relationship depends on each person's willingness to change and to improve oneself in daily life. Only when a person contemplates in self-reflection, he realizes that the problem is still the same: "Yes, I am the problem... I don't know how to love and I am not capable of changing for better to make my wife and children happier." The question should be: do you want yourself and your spouse to be happy in your marriage? If yes, forget about yourself, put yourself and your wants on hold, and turn to your loved ones, get to know them and do things that please them and strive to make them happy. All it takes is to start from ME.

Conclusion

The potential of human is tremendous, particularly in the ability to acquire and communicate with notions, to learn new things, knowledge and skills. Through practices of these, he develops good habits that are gradually integrated into his being; then he could see changes within himself. These developed abilities and competencies are integrated into our being, as virtues based on repetition of good habits are integrated into our in-born personality; this struggle toward betterment is life-long journey, a clear sign of success in achieving our given potential. So husbands, be encouraged and be brave, we can all become better…if we want to be good desperately. I have learned the following story of enduring love between two loving individuals:

An aged lady asked her husband from her sickbed to bring an old wooden box that sat on top of the desk in the studies, the aged man took the box to the bed side; the husband opened the box and found a dozen or so beautiful knits, of different colors and shapes. He asked his wife: "What is this?" The wife explained softly: "Remember each time when we quarreled, I did not want to argue with you, so I silently went to the studies and made a knit each time. These are the collection of my knitting over the past 50 years." The husband was so embarrassed and yet began to feel a bit relaxed and thinking that there were only a several dozen knits over 50 years; "it's not too bad in 50 years!" Then as he removed the first layer of the knits, he found many rolls of money bills of hundreds underneath, curiously, he asked his wife what the money was. The wife answered briefly: "Oh, yes, this is the money I have saved up from selling most of the knitting work over the past years…! It is a lot of money there, you can use it anytime now and after I die." And the aged man burst into tears with remorse. This is a valid lesson of what genuine spousal love is.

In closing this chapter, I cannot think of any better way but to quote the following words "Love is patience and kind, love is not jealous or boastful; it is not arrogant or rude. Love does not insist on its own way; it is not irritable or resentful; it does not rejoice at wrong, but rejoices in the right. Love bears all things, believes all things, hopes all things and endures all things." (1 Cor, 13:4–7, Navarre Bible) Though these words apply to all aspects of human love, they are particularly true in marital love between husband and wife who have mutually consented at the beginning of their marriage to love each other unconditionally in marriage, and for life!

Chapter 4

Marriage as Communion of Persons

When I first encountered the phrase "communion of persons" some years ago, my initial response was probably like everyone else: intrigued and yet attracted by the depth of meaning of these three simple words. Driven by intuitive curiosity, I have started my search for the meaning of this simple terminology that has been articulated in various occasions by the late Pope Blessed John Paul II in many of his speeches, encyclicals and homilies, whose teaching and philosophy focus on personalism.

My search for the meaning likens an alcoholic who wants his next drinks, or as a greedy merchant who thirsts for his next million dollars profit. The engineering background in my early career facilitated the process of my search. In addition, my natural curiosity led me to investigate the fundamental knowledge of Christian philosophy which facilitates the search for the essential meaning of "communion of persons" in a systematic way. It likens peeling off the skins of an onion, layer by layer, one piece at a time, one after another...with patience. My search had begun with a simple question: "*what is a person*", that triggered a series of further questions such as "What it takes to be a person? What is the fundamental difference between a person and animal?" prior to giving further thought on the holistic notion of "communion of persons." The definition based on Christian philosophy says: "*Person* is defined as an *Individual Substance of Rational Nature*" and these lump of words seem to further complicate the meaning entirely. My search for the ultimate answer has been facilitated through a broadened hypothesis of grid and coordinates, and "business transformation system" of which inputs, processes and outputs are being measured and analyzed similar to a manufacturing plant.

A human being does not fully realize who he is and what he can become until he gives himself to others. It is only in giving, and by giving oneself to others that the human being gets to know the kind of person who he really is. This is resonated in management "You don't really get to know a person well until you start working with him/her for a period of time." In my years of management practices, I came to realize even though a manager scores very high marks in senior management training; in leadership attributes, 360 management profiling, the circle of influence, managing power distance and other tactics and skill sets, etc. one of the most effective ways to get to know a colleague is by working with him or her in order to know his/her characteristics and personality. The "truth about man" does not contradict, or differ from the Divine Law and the Law of the Nature, they are like two sides of the same coin, yet at different levels and essence. The truth about human person should be closely examined by the mere fact when we say a person is an individual substance of rational nature. *Nature* answers the question of *What we are*, *Person* answers the question of *Who we are*. Every being has a nature, but not every being is a person, only rational beings are persons. To elaborate further about human person, we do not normally ask of a stone or a flower "*who* is it?" But, the normal question should be directed as "what is it"? On the contrary, when a three year old daughter saw her mother greeting a neighbor at the shopping mall, the little girl asked her mother; "Mama, who is she?"

By our nature, then we are what we are, it follows that by our nature we do what we do. By our nature, we are human beings, and by our nature we perform what human beings are capable of. "Man is capable to work as naturally as bird is capable to fly." There are countless things normal humans can perform — walk, laugh, cry, talk, sleep and think, imagine, love, hate, analyze, communicate and to recall memory; and many more operations. All these and other things that we do are because as humans we have a nature that makes it possible. We are capable of doing and acting as our nature allows us to, but our nature also has its limitations. For example, as a human being, I simply cannot fly as naturally as a bird or eagle could fly, even though when I am equipped with modern technology of a flying machine similar to the rocket-man in the movie. Although my nature is the source of all my actions, my nature decides what kind of operations is possible for me, it is not my nature that does them. *I* do them, *I* the Person who does them.

Thus, both person and nature may be considered as source of actions, but in a different sense. In a more practical phenomenon, we can say that *we* operate according to our *nature*. Although we could see and understand the distinction between person and nature in us, it seems clearer than ever that one nature can only be possessed and operated by *one* individual. For example, if one day, a young man robbed a bank and was caught in the act by police; if he were to defend his act by telling the judge that his "nature" did the robbery, not he, the person who has committed the crime, his defense would sound ridiculous and groundless. It is because "action speaks louder than words"; unless this young man can produce very strong evident from the cross examination of psychologists to prove his insanity when committing the crime, he will unlikely be able to escape the incrimination by the court of law. Then this man will be sentenced to imprisonment due to his own act in the robbery. This young man, his person, individually, is responsible for his action.

A *person*, who is free and responsible, with intelligence and free-will, capable of knowing moral principle and understand what is good and evil, is therefore an ethical being. Perfection of being is Person, angel is person, and God is person, three persons in one divine nature — the Holy Trinity. Human being is also person, but far from being perfect due to the "shattered" human nature as a consequence of the Original Sin. A person, like you and I, is capable of profound relationship of knowledge and love with another person. A *person* with *human nature* is *integral* and *substantial*. The spiritual entity, soul, and the physical entity, body, are integrally fused together into one person; in a layman language, a person likens a hybrid living being that consists of soul and body, each cannot operate without the other and we call this being a "human person". Each person is unique, unrepeatable and substantial. Let us take the example of a new born baby boy, Austin. Through the love, care and the nurture of his parents, Austin grows healthier, bigger and taller by the day; yet he is still the same little fetus-person at the moment of his conception in the womb of his mother, and the same baby-person at his birth. Although the baby's external features, body size is changing and growing; in a split of a decade he will grow to his teenage; yet this teenager-person, is substantially the same person as Austin before and at the moment of his birth. The substance of Austin does not change from the time of his conception in the womb of his mother, only the accidents change. The substance of this teenage boy Austin is the same through out his life and beyond, thus Austin's personhood is substantial.

I Could Feel the Pain of My Son

An incidence of my friend, Jack, perhaps would better illustrate the integral aspect of soul and body of a person. Jack was traveling in a business trip to a country thousands of miles away from home. He once received a phone call from his wife in the middle of the night informing him that their four year old boy had met an accident in the playground and had broken his right forearm, in the same area of an old injury. Though the boy was hospitalized and under the care of several capable doctors, Jack was so terrified and worried upon hearing the unfortunate news of his son that his hands started to shake and sweat dripped from his forehead. Jack started to breathe heavily as his heartbeats increased and literally one could hear the heartbeats when standing next to him. Jack felt like a dagger pierced into his heart, his blood pressure shot up. Jack, as a human being, was capable of understanding and communicating abstract notion, analyzing complexity of a situation and recalling his memory of an old injury of his son even without his physical presence in the accident. Jack was able to share the intensity of the situation described by his wife and felt the pain of his loved ones. The accident of his four year old son acknowledged by

Jack in his mind, a notion which is intangible, was translated into his physical pain manifested through his shaking hands, faster heartbeats and heavier breathings, and then further into his anxiety and worries of the mind and spirit. A piece of news that came from thousand miles away had been converted into an image sense in the mind that caused effect in both physical and spiritual aspects. Such phenomenon in our physical–spiritual senses happens naturally that at times we do not even notice it.

An animal, in the absence of intelligence and free will, cannot communicate intangible notion or idea with another animal; or freely choose something over the other, but only acts based upon its created nature of instinct. Man, on the other hand, can communicate his thoughts, form general concepts and understand abstract notions. Only a human being is capable of analyzing, understanding and communicating *abstract notions* with one another, thinking about them, analyzing them, memorizing and recalling them when necessary. We cannot separate the human body from the human person. If we do so, we fall into a morally danger of dualism. A human body forms a unity with the person himself such that the way men and women treat each other's bodies determines their personality traits. For example, after watching a family movie together, father, mother and children would be talking about the story, or the characters in the movie, and communicating the twists and turns in the story and actions, or whether certain behavior is right or wrong and probably the father will ask the children what is the lesson learned, etc. After certain weeks or months, one of the children may ask her father if he remembered what one particular character said, etc. Recapping from the above, "Only human being is capable of analyzing, understanding and communicating *abstract notions* with one another, thinking about it, analyzing it, memorizing it and recalling it when necessary".

In considering human personhood, it is not difficult at all to understand that no human being should use another as a means towards an end, either as an object for pleasure, or even for the purpose of begetting children. The marital union between a male and female brings with it a tremendous power and responsibility for two persons who are involved. This personal union involving the power of procreation to give love and new life — begetting a baby — is considered a serious matter that must be treated with respect even when conducting a casual discussion. A personal sexual union is an expression of a human love and such a relation should receive proper respect and it is inappropriate to use it as a joke or a casual comment, especially in the public. It is important to discuss human sexuality between a man and a woman in the proper context of love and within marriage. This union of two persons is not just physical, but also emotional, psychological, willful, social, intellectual and spiritual.

The word 'sex' is frequently misused to refer to merely physical and sexual acts of males and females, or sexual intercourse. The culture of the contemporary society has promulgated and commercialized sexual experience to the extent it degrades human sexuality and likens it to mating between animals; while our teenagers are curious to discover this embedded potential of the human procreative power often stimulated by propaganda from the media. Due to inadequate understanding and lacking the ability to self-control, youngsters could face quite detrimental consequences. As their trusted examples and guides, parents can help them to see that intimate relationship between two individuals, a male and a female, is more than just a feeling.

Communion of Persons

Matrimony means one man committing himself to love his wife for life. The concept of marriage as communion of persons appears in Genesis: "This at last is bone of my bones and flesh of my flesh — she shall be called woman, because she was taken out of man" (Genesis 2:23, Navarre Bible). In this way, the man manifested for the first time joy and even exaltation, for which he had no reason before, owing to the absence of a human being like himself. Communion expresses more, with greater precision since it indicates precisely that "help" which is derived from the fact that a person exists "beside" another person as discussed in earlier chapter. Communion of persons could occur only in a "double solitude" of man and of woman, that is as their conjugal union distinguishes them from the world of living beings, which gives them both of being and existing in a special reciprocity. The concept of "help" also expresses this reciprocity in existence, which no other living being can ensure. The sexual union of the spouses is to express and enact their spousal surrender to each other and their spousal belonging to each other. Conjugal union cannot be fully understood from a purely biological viewpoint, subsequently, the most perfect form in which one human being makes a sincere gift of himself, or herself, to another human being occurs between a man and a woman in spousal love through mutual and reciprocal self-donation in physical and spiritual essence.

The two aspects of marriage as "communion of persons" of equal dignity and a common endeavor are: (1) it is a communion of persons equal in dignity and rights and (2) requires the collaboration of two persons complementary in their sexuality and in their marital and family roles. Husband and wife are both created in the image and likeness of God, each has the capacity for self-donation and the need for communion with one another. Both husband and wife are equal in their personal dignity and enjoy the rights appropriate to them both as human beings and as spouses. Precisely because they are equal in their personal dignity, they are meant to be friends, for one can be truly a friend only to one's equal. A human cannot be truly a friend of one's dog or cat, because he or she cannot share one's life in totality and essence with a non-human being, and any true friendship means that the friends share some, or equivalent aspect of their lives. But the friendship meant to exist between husband and wife as a communion of persons is a very special kind of friendship. Unlike other kinds of friendships and love, marital friendship is exclusive, because a particular man and a particular woman have freely consented to each other in their lives when they enter into their marital covenant.

Love in marriage is the mutual self-giving of the spouses in their personhood which is substantially present in the married couple. Sex is an intimate manifestation of love between a male and female, a communion of their personhood, thus sex is not merely a biological exchange. Human sexuality involves not just the body but the whole person; sexual act can never be reduced to a mere biological exchange, none the less for mere pleasure, or satisfying selfish desires. The husband loves and surrenders himself totally to his wife, while receives and accepts her completely; in the process, the wife does the same to her husband. Unconditional love between marital couple is what makes the sexual act truly human. "The husband should fulfill his duty toward his wife, and likewise the wife toward the husband. A wife does not have authority over her own body, but rather her husband, and similarly a husband does not have authority over his own body, but rather his wife." (1 Cor 7:3–4, Navarre Bible)

When conjugal act, an expression of marital love, is genuine and self-giving, it is *total* and *exclusive*, the couple capacitate themselves to become "one flesh" in the mutual self-giving of their personhood in the conjugal union. Unmarried male and female, such as cohabitants or one-night-stand relationship, even when they have mutually consented to sexual intercourse, will be unable to engage in the mutual self-donation of their personhood in the sexual act because they do not capacitate themselves to total and exclusive consent of the personhood in the sexual relationship. Marital friendship, thus, is a *unique* kind of friendship, where husbands and wives, as equal in their rights and dignity, are summoned to deepen throughout their lives the unique and exclusive friendship they established when they gave themselves irrevocably to one another in marriage. Saint Josemaria once distinguished the complementary roles of husbands and wives within the family by saying that "in a family, the mother is secretary of the interior...but leaves the position of secretary of the exterior affairs to the father."

These complementary differences among men and women are manifested in their social behavior, as numerous studies point out. As a whole, women tend to respond to situations wholly, with their minds, bodies, and emotions integrated, whereas men tend to respond in a more diffuse and differentiated manner. On the whole, women are more oriented toward caring for personal needs, whereas men, on the whole, are more inclined to formulate and pursue long-range goals and to reach objectives that they have set for themselves and his family. These major tendencies seem to correspond to natural capability where a man emphasizes differentiation, exteriority and future, while a woman has the natural ability to be integral and focuses interiority, and possesses the ability to handle complexities and people issues at ease.

It is obvious that the making of man and woman is very different, physically, emotionally and psychologically. Therefore, it is important to realize the essentials of this difference so that with refinement and anticipation, we can understand better our beloved in a systematic and intellectual manner.

The following Table 4.1 is an outline of the basic differences between men and women:

Table 4.1.   Different Attributes Between Men and Women

Men's Focus	Women's Focus
• Not a good listener	• A good listener.
• More self-focused.	• More focused about others well-being.
• Prefer and want more sex in relationship.	• Prefer and want more love in relationship.
• Talk about things or events.	• Talk about people.
• Like competition.	• Like and enjoy cooperation.
• More decisive, like to solve problems quickly.	• Like to talk about problems and take time for decisions.
• Don't mind conflict, power struggle and confrontation.	• Do not enjoy conflict and confrontation, tend to avoid.
• Concern of engulfment.	• Concern of abandonment.
• More sexually jealous & fear loss of control.	• Emotionally jealous and fear loss of commitment.
• More conscious of what to get.	• Willing and ready to give.
• Express quick anger and emotion.	• Tend to contain anger & emotion.
• Tend to identify with work/events.	• Tend to identify more with people.

By reading these attributes, we notice that how much men would need to learn from the opposite sex — our spouse. Making and sustaining friendship with the beloved: For example, when the mother changes a diaper, she spends a good deal of time talking to the baby, telling him or her how cute he or she is, etc., whereas the father ordinarily just wants to get the dirty diaper off and put the clean one on as quickly as possible and doesn't spend too much time chatting and playing with the baby child. Now let us consider how a wife and her husband complement each other as a mother and a father.

The Mystery of Woman — Motherhood and Man — Fatherhood

Procreation of children to family brings forth the roles of fatherhood and motherhood, consequently the self-giving of the marital couple grows and expounds beyond their spousal love for the well-being of their children. The constitution of woman is different, as obviously as compared to that of man, they are different even in the deepest bio-physiological determinants. Besides the external manifestation in the construction of a woman's body, maternity is manifested more substantially in the constitution of interiority; which is the inner potential of the female organism that serves the conception and begetting of a new human being. It is due to nature that woman, through her own body and sexuality, hides what constitutes the depth of her femininity. The consummation of marital union reaches the "objectivity" of the body of which man and woman are involved in their mutual knowledge that goes beyond being an object, as wife and husband are equal in dignity.

Procreation brings forth the man-husband and the woman-wife knowing each other reciprocally while a new life is potentially born through the spousal relationship. Therefore, this spousal relationship becomes a discovery, a discovery of each other in an unobtrusive manner, total and mutual donation of their mutual personhood. In this particular act of knowledge, through communion of femininity and masculinity among two human beings, is the discovery of mutual self-fulfillment in the gift — fatherhood and motherhood. Consequently, it is also a discovery of a new human being who originates from both of them and resembles the living image of the parents. From the moment of conception to the actual birth of the baby, the mother is fully aware of the mystery of creation, which is manifested in propagation of human generation. Motherhood is the fruit of the marital union between a man and woman that corresponds to the "union of the two in one flesh". This genuine spousal relationship is achieved in accordance with the original truth of the person only when the mutual self-giving love is not distorted by the desire of the man to become the 'master' of his wife, or by the woman remaining closed within her personhood.

Motherhood, during the period between the baby's conception and birth, is a bio-physiological and psychological process which is better understood in our days than in the past, and is subject of many detailed studies. Scientific analysis fully confirms that the very physical constitution of women naturally caters to motherhood, from conception, to pregnancy and giving birth, as a consequence of the marital union. Furthermore, motherhood also naturally corresponds to the psycho–physical structure of women. Motherhood also implies from the beginning a special openness to the new person. In this openness, in conceiving and giving birth to a child, the woman "discovers herself through sincere gift of self." The gift of inner readiness to accept the child and bring him/her into the world is linked to the marriage union and constitutes a special moment in the mutual self-giving by both the woman and the man.

Although husband and wife together are parents of the child, the woman's motherhood constitutes a special "part" in this shared parenthood, parenthood is more fully realized by the woman. From conception, pregnancy, to giving birth, woman-wife is the main bearer of this shared process of procreation that literally absorbs the energies from her body and soul. It is, therefore, important and necessary for the man-husband to realize that in their shared parenthood, he owes a special debt to the woman-wife. The husband, no matter how great his effort will be in the shared parenthood, remains "outside" the process of pregnancy and the baby's birth. In many aspects, the man-husband shall learn his own "fatherhood" from the woman-wife. Parents must involve themselves in the upbringing of their children: the maternal and paternal contribution; it is important to point out that that each of the paternal contribution and maternal contribution is different, and yet complementary to each other. Both parents' contribution in education and upbringing are decisive in laying the foundation for good character and development of a new human.

My Journey of Love

To me, marriage is a like a rare and highly valuable pearl that is so beautiful that whoever wants to discover it will sort after it. Man will spend enormous amount of resources and time to look for this rare pearl, and upon finding it, will spend his wealth to acquire it. After he has acquired it, he will use all his effort and power to keep it in good shape, to treasure it and to protect it, for as long as he lives. In reality, marriage is more than this valuable pearl. Marriage and family are naturally bonded in such a way that each cannot be separated from another, they are like two sides of the same coin. It is a pity that the essence of marriage and family is being so deeply misunderstood in our modern society. We have seen the evil caused by confusions in marriages and families, as discussed in the early chapters of the book, leads to majority of crimes related to passion and sexuality. Most of these crimes find its root in the ignorance of what true love is.

Genuine love is to will the good of another person. In the case of love between spouses in the family, I believe there is no free lunch, every married couple has to make a daily effort to renew and refresh their love for the spouse. Love is in the details, it does not allow carelessness and sloppiness, therefore, in exercising genuine love, spouses cannot afford to be complacent, or take the marital love for granted, especially after dozens of years into their marriage. The perpetuity of a happy marriage naturally exists through the procreation and propagation of children in a family; from which the selfless love between marital spouses would be expanded and extended to the fruits of their mutual love. I recall the thrill I experienced in my marriage and while we enjoyed the happiness of having each other and being together, however, the joy and excitement on the very morning when the nurse brought our first born baby into my arms, crying loudly, was beyond any description. I immediately realized that I had assumed a new role, besides being a husband to my wife; I was a father! At that particular moment, I looked down to this baby of ours, full of dark hair, and murmured: "Hi my son, my little baby. Don't be afraid, your daddy is here, holding you, loving you and don't you worry, I will take care of you." When our second child was born, I had the same thrill, while I was telling my wife that this little fellow had so little hair!"

My Journey of Love

I met my fiancé in a summer month of 1980, who became my wife years after. At the time, she was still studying her last year in Economics, London University while living with her mother, who visited her frequently there. I was working as a civil engineer then and we spent most of the summer seeing each other before she returned to London after the summer holiday for her last year of the degree course. My fiancé came home in December of the same year and on one occasion in summer we went out together on a boat trip with her three years old niece, lovely little girl, and I witnessed how she enjoyed being with her niece, talking, chatting and playing with her, and we had great fun. After then, we spent time together exchanging thoughts and views about life in general and quite often we talked about this little niece of her on various occasions whenever we went out together. This niece has now grown up to be a mother, she has a great profession and is now living with her first-born baby and husband in the United Kingdom.

In summer of 1981, I had decided to make a trip to visit several European countries including Rome. It was quite obvious that

I planned to start my European trip from London to see my fiancé. At that moment, I knew I was falling in love with her. From the depth of my heart, I was telling myself that I am in love this woman, my fiancé, and I wanted her to be my wife, and the mother of my children. Then a thought of "But how? Does she love me and will she marry me?" kept coming back to my head for sometime. I checked into a small bed and breakfast (B&B) hotel for two nights before starting the European tour. With the agreement and kindness of my future mother-in-law, the plan was to unload some of my luggage at the home of my fiancé in London so I could travel light in my onward trip. During the packing and unpacking of my luggage, my fiancé saw a stack of prayer cards of St. Josemaria Escriva that I had intended to bring to the crypt in Rome for his blessings and then bring them back to Hong Kong for use. The prayer cards were stacked up to about seven-inches thick, while my fiancé took one card to have a closer look and said: "I have seen this man." I stopped and said: "who?" and she continued' "This man in the picture, on the card!" I found myself speechless then. Later on, she explained to me that a few years back, she was invited to a residence of a center of Opus Dei in London by a lady-friend of hers. Then I asked her which year did she make the visit, it was sometime in 1977; while I pondered on this coincidence.

From that moment, it was quite clear to me that this woman, my fiancé, will most probably be my wife one day! However, the journey was not easy. I had to demonstrate my commitment and made substantial effort to win her heart; in order to convince her that my ultimate reason of marrying her is to love her, to make her happy and that our marriage will make us both good. I promised her that I shall strive to be a good husband and a responsible father, with daily effort; to this day I am still in this mode of striving hard daily; I suppose I have won her heart. Time really passes quickly — we have been married for almost 30 years now. Today I am as happy, if not more than, as our time of courtship, and I do hope that she feels the same. At times, I crack jokes to our fellow couple friends by asking the husbands whether they remember the outfit, the dress and hair style of their wives, fiancé then, in their love-of-first-sight encounter; they all laugh with a sense of embarrassment. I suppose some of my friends do not remember anymore after a few decades; but I still do!

Happiness in Marriage

Happiness in married life is directly proportionate to the mutual respect that husband and wife have for each other, especially in the intimate conjugal act of marriage. Self-donation of love in a marriage involves substantially the mutual respect between the married couple; precisely this unconditional love offers the necessary sensitivity in caring for the mutual self-esteem between the couple. One of the most radical self-giving love between human beings occurs between a husband and his wife in their spousal love and commitment; second to this is the love of a mother towards her children. Mutual respect and acceptance is central to happiness in marriage and in the common endeavor to deepen and perfect the "communion of persons" within marriage is the daily effort of re-entering in love between the spouses. The perpetuity of marital love does not merely lie in the sexual intimacy, "it lies in everyday things…in finding joy on coming home in the evening, in the affectionate relations with their children, in everyday work in which the whole family cooperates, in good humor in the face of difficulties that should be met with a sporting spirit." (said St. Josemaria Escriva)

It is usually helpful to remind married couples, after several years into their marriage, to reflect on the fundamentals of marital love and keep in mind that in conjugal life there are different levels in the gradual discovery of the personality of the spouse, and of his or her individual psychology, and the expectations; and finding common interests to understand genuinely each other's needs. At times, it is also helpful to reflect on the essentials of marital love that are based on mutual respect and trusted friendship. Love at first sight is the first attraction of love toward one another. What follows next is a discovery of the personality of the beloved, the character and moral qualities; such as: honesty, gentleness, generosity, patience, solidarity, justice, charity, sincerity, industriousness and responsibility, etc.

Happiness in marriage requires daily effort similar to those early days of courtship, when couple do not see each other for days, they would be missing each other's presence, the time they spend together, holding each other's hand; as if saying silently "How wonderful it is to be with you." Spouses should anticipate the continual daily effort of falling in love throughout their marriage. Genuine love refreshes and rejuvenates the marital relationship; starting from the affection of the first love that builds the passion, mutual love, trusting friendship and the fruits of their love — their beloved children; to the mature period of marriage without any trace of aging. To love is to will the good of another person. Genuine love requires sincerity between spouses; as love is not selfish, it demands total self-giving with a commitment of giving oneself unconditionally to your spouse.

A Sincere Love

If a person is not sincere with oneself, very likely he would not be honest with others. Love in marriage is founded on self-giving love — "I married you in order to love you; and I want you to be happy." This self-giving love is characterized by the willingness of outpouring oneself to the beloved: "I love you very much, I love you more than myself, and I will take care of you for the rest of our lives." A love that aims to benefit the spouse, the willingness to give up one's selfish inclination knowing that to love someone might involves some discomfort and inconvenience. In the mind of the wife: "I am happy that I am able to make you good and happy" and in the mind of the husband: "Be able to make her genuinely happy makes me proud and satisfied and as self-fulfilling husband."

Genuine love is in the details particularly when marriage enters into the first decade. Quite often we hear the husband says: "Yes, I love my wife very much, but I don't know why I always forget to celebrate her birthday!" To dedicate at least some minutes each day to think of tokens of affection and kindness toward one's spouse; to give her a phone call during the day to thank her for being a loving wife; an embrace on entering the house, a little pleasant surprise to spouse from time to time that could work wonders. Spousal communication should not be limited to get things done at home; a good husband should be a good listener and be patient with his spouse; he should find time to be alone together, having a heart-to-heart conversation in a restful environment is probably the best way to promote mutual attraction and confidence. A wife is inclined to seek affection through means of affirmation of love and fidelity of her husband; while the husband is inclined to look for affection through seeing how satisfied his wife is with him and how proud she is to have him as her beloved spouse.

A Moat of Defense

When marriage enters half-a-decade or beyond, spouses must be sensitive not to allow their love to age and to grow cold; with daily refreshment of their spousal love, sincere and genuine communication, the married couple would be able to navigate smoothly in the course of their marriage. However, there are possible external factors that would slip in between the marital relationship if the couple take their marriage for granted and think that "we have been married for ages and we still are, so what could anything happen?" At times, a married man or a married woman of good and happy family presents an attraction to a lonely-single individual beyond any logical explanation. The potential intertwining love–sex relationship could multiply if the married person is careless or innocent in this matter. We need to build a line of defense that I name it "Moat of defense."

A married person must be sensitive of how to keep a cautious distance from an unrelated opposite sex member in all possible circumstances where the first spark could be ignited; be it in working relationship, neighborhood, offsite training-program, on business travel, or any form of social gathering. Expressions of closeness that is only reserved with one's spouse should not be shared with others. Examples: being alone with a person of opposite sex in a enclosed environment such as office or conference room, in a car, intimate dining occasion, social drinks after work hours, or spending time side-by-side in a business or professional trip, etc. It is naïve to think that to confide an intimate personal problem, or to obtain advice on a problematic family situation, with a person of opposite sex who is not the spouse could ease or resolve the marital conflict. This perception is absolutely misleading that could cause serious consequences to a committed marriage beyond repair. Experience tells that in these cases improper intimacies will facilitate opportunities for unnecessary closeness that would build intimacy with a friend of opposite sex. In the beginning, the casual acquaintance would seem insignificant, and that is precisely what makes it more dangerous. Thus, any attempt to talk about personal problems usually suitable to one's spouse; or to listen to personal matter of another person is a clear sign of building up intimacy with a "stranger." This type of dialogue is likely to develop into unnecessary closeness between two individuals leading to disastrous consequences — a tiny spark leading to a fire that could consume the entire forest of a marriage.

Any attempt to seek understanding or attention of opposite sex who is not your spouse in order to fill the emotional void must be avoided. Any professional or working man or woman must also be emotionally smart and mature enough to see the potential danger of infidelity; and at times prudence in such matters is a clear indication of responsibility and truthfulness in marital commitment. "If I truly treasure the pearl at home, I shall love it, bury it in the ground and take good care of it so that no one else will take it away from me."

Expression of Love Between Spouses

The primary condition for a family is to provide a formative environment for the character development of the children that is founded on the genuine and secured love between the parents within their marriage. If the mother quarrels with the father in front of the child, even though later she may shower her child with many kisses, the child would have experienced a deep injury already. What the child wants is to participate in the family, in the love and a stable relationship of the parents. The responsibility and commitment of raising a child in good character is equivalent to, if not more than, committing ourselves in unconditional love for the spouse as to provide a safe home and happy family through a stable marital commitment.

Commitment

Expression of love between spouses is built on mutual respect and understanding. As we have seen, a man has a different way of expressing his feelings and emotions from the woman, at times a tiny issue could be exploded out of proportion due to the expressions of either one of the spouses.

Logically, there are moments of disagreement, or even disappointments in marital relationships, when the husband does not live up to the expectations of the wife, or vice versa. Mature couples who are happily married for ages would say that to aim at a genuinely fulfilling and happiness in marriage requires sacrifice, patience, understanding, creativity and the humility to say "I am sorry"; and it is only then the married couple will find his or her own happiness by giving oneself and making the spouse happy. It is recommended before the end of each day, before going to bed to think of two questions: "Have I been able to show my affection to my spouse?" and "Does she notice it?" Carelessness can be misconstrued as lack of love, disinterest or disrespect, especially for the man who tends to be more forgetful and careless in matters of intimacy in marital relationship. The wife might think: "If he does not remember to greet me, or to open the door for me as we were in courtship, or gives me a call from his work place or on business trip, he does not think of me anymore; probably he does not love me as much now!" An insensitive husband could cause unnecessary conflict with his wife simply due to carelessness and forgetfulness.

Marital love should be thoughtful and creative, such as a simple gesture of accompanying the wife to see a doctor, remembering anecdotes of the time during their courtship, going for a walk alone to be with her, or giving her a rub on the shoulders after a tiring day, and doing the simplest thing with care and delicacy. At times, it makes a huge difference when the husband expresses his love for his wife by being present with the family and children as much as possible during the weekdays and as well as during the weekends. Or the husband is sensitive enough to engage an active dialogue with her at the right moment, a call from work place, letting the wife enter first through the door, be a good listener when she wants to be heard, to press the button in the elevator. Husband should learn to strive harder! He needs to refresh his loving manifestation as youthful as a sportsman and as caring as a grandfather. Last but not least, the husband shall occasionally remind the wife of things that have special meaning to her, e.g. the color of her dress, or her hairdo in their first date...yes, many many years ago. Love is in the details, and must not be allowed to age, love should be a daily refreshed by both the spouses.

Managing Expectation

We quite often see many couples hiding their individual expectations over a period of time without simply commenting, or expressing it with each other. When spouses are not aware, or do not understand the emotional need of each other, it often becomes an obstacle in love and caring between the married couple. The cause of this could be that one of the spouses is too busy with his or her work, or busying with house chores that leave no time for each other simply to relax and talk. Or it could be when one of the spouses feels uneasy or uncomfortable to express the inner feelings toward the spouse due to the temperament of the other; or it could be the simple reason of negligence of one party, or both.

Any expectation could be hidden and gradually formed into a "justifiable perception" without much rational thinking of wife towards her husband, or vice versa. At times, these thoughts arise as a result of the anxiety derived from a hard day's work at home, or self-pity, or from the conversation with in-laws, or from comments of others, or lack of interests of the husband, negligence of the husband at anniversary or other special occasions, or due to temperament, or simply feeling lonely, etc. Quite often, the husband fails to understand the expectations of his wife and may not even know the underlying reason of an emotional outbreak from his wife. The hidden expectation unresolved over a period of time, whenever a window of emotion arises, the seemingly happily married couple would break into quarrels. Quarrel is fine as long as it is not frequent between the couple while they would learn to love each other more in the process of understanding each other's needs, and is a sign of affection. However, if quarrels are allowed to escalate into constant disputes between married couple that hurts one or both of the spouses, it will damage the harmonious spousal relationship and of the family. If such situations are allowed to persist, they could cause alienation between the spouses and further misunderstanding among the married couple.

Effective Communication

Communication is to convey a thought or feeling, to share a personal insight or to understand someone, to stay connected or provide access to another person. Men and women have different ways in expressing emotion and communicating. It is interesting to note that we have different expectations in our communications. Woman-wife tends to seek attention and affirmation from her husband as a good listener. In a normal conversation, the man-husband likes to go straight to the point and talk about the issue and finish it, and get on to the next one; whereas, the woman-wife enjoys the process of conversation when she already knew the solution even before she starts talking. Husband is happy when he sees his wife happy, content and satisfied, otherwise he would see it as his failure and would possibly start to blame someone else. At times, the wife paradoxically wants a dream husband of "as energetic as an athlete, as sweet as a loving fiancé, and the maturity of a grandfather."

Frequently, women use questions as a way of conducting a conversation and of showing their involvement in what is being discussed. On the contrary, men use questions simply to obtain information they wanted. At times, interesting situations develop in a normal conversation between husband and wife that could trigger our thoughts about communication skills of men and women. At times the husband, upon hearing questions from the wife, genuinely tries to resolve problems when in fact the wife was not looking for solutions because quite often she already has the solution. However, what she is looking for is understanding, acceptance, affirmation and awaits some affection, or a sign that husband is indeed showing interests in the wife, or what she is thinking at that particular moment. At times, she would repeat prior conversations in her current ones, making the conversation seems like overlap and "illogical" to the husband-man altogether, until she is totally satisfied; while the husband finds this confusing and at times intolerable. In the context of this seemingly mismatching conversation, the wife would find herself an unpleasant surprise of not having been properly listened to; while in the husbands' perspective, the issue has been thoroughly talked about and probably resolved, why bother the repetition like a broken record. The man-husband is more inclined to talking about events such as, politics, economics, sports, normally with a clear objective and ends while not enjoying the process of conversation such as listening to comments from his wife. We can draw similarities to such characteristics from the example of changing diaper for the baby: the wife enjoys or even sings songs while changing the diaper; while the husband changes the diaper quickly and gets the job done, that is it. He feels good by doing the job neat and fast, and he is proud of it. When the wife is not aware of theses proclivities, she might think that the husband's impatience stems out of listening to her comments, or taking no interests in her; tiny incorrect perception would often translate to lack of love of the husband.

The husband should be sensitive to and be aware of the differences and complementary aspects of women, understand that his wife is not a male, so she is logically different from men. The reality that his wife wants to share details of her thoughts and sentiments with the husband is what usually makes her happy. If the husband would realize this particular characteristic of his woman-wife, he would learn to become a good listener and naturally both would be able to conduct mutually informative and peaceful conversations as well enjoy the process of spousal communications. The mere fact is the wife wants to comment and share her experiences of certain situations; for example, of people in the party which she went with her husband simply because she wanted to share something of herself — her view and sentiments — with her beloved husband. The husband should be extremely happy and satisfied that his wife is opening up and is more intimate with him, as a husband and trusted friend.

At times, the man-husband is so numb to be able to observe this intimacy between spouses. On the contrary, the husband may misconstrue to think that this intimate sharing from his wife is a gesture of her consultation in order to resolve a problem, and he thinks that he is obligated to provide a solution. When the topic becomes recurrent and is repeated in the same conversation, along with added details from the wife, the husband may build up anxiety as viewing the conversation becomes more difficult and complicated. He might again misconstrue that the reason for his wife to repeat the same topics is because he is unable to resolve the problem for her. Then, the supposedly frank and mutual communication between the married couple becomes a battlefield of crossfire. What the wife essentially expects is understanding and support, serenity and strength from her husband. Perhaps, a little praise, or a pat-on-the-shoulder from the husband would make her happy and satisfy, giving an affirmation to the wife would make her feel secure.

Both husband and wife should keep in mind that their spousal love, genuine friendship and openness of hearts should be founded on mutual and robust communication, with patience and willingness to self-improve for the betterment of their marital journey. Effective communication between spouses involves exchange of intimacy of two bodily persons; Between "I am" and "you are." The following conversation between a loving couple perhaps would illustrate the genuine and intimate spousal communication founded on trust and friendship. A husband said to his wife one afternoon on a weekend when he was free from business travel: "Darling, I don't know what am I going to do if something happens to my job." His wife answered; "Don't worry too much, you will still have our family, your four lovely children and I. We will stand by you no matter what happens."

Managing Anger

Disagreements in marital relationships between husband and wife are indispensable, in fact, occasional minor quarrels between the couple can be quite healthy as long as they do not have any lasting effect; such petty squabbles are also a sign of affection and care between the couple. However, anger is a different story. Anger is a selfish act and a serious disorder of human passion. It is made up of a series of segments consisting of several stages ranging from the feeling of being offended and misunderstood or a sense of being victimized, then if self-pity is allowed to kick-in, the next logical thing to happen is rage, a retaliation or revenge. The first phase is when a person detects that he has been offended in one way or another, and gets upset. Afterwards, he feels the urge to device an attack at the offender, and to get even. Frequent explosion of anger between husband and wife could damage marital love and mutual conjugal relations between them, therefore, it is important to learn to control and to manage anger properly.

To overcome anger, primarily it would be good to know how it operates. The good news is that it is within the reach of everyone to exert some control over his or her anger. Above all, the person must be convinced that majority of offenses that he feels are not always valid, and the offense might not necessarily be real as well. It is often an impression formed by a superficial observation that becomes a perception in the mind, or from a previous experience in the memory, it is not necessarily factual. That is why we need to identify clearly the difference between perception and facts, whenever we hear the words "I"; "I think...", or "I believe what you mean...!" or "I feel bad because you don't love me..." all of the above "I" is based on the perception which is formed by her (his) own opinion. Mostly, misunderstanding that occurs between people is the by-product of misconstrued "led-believed" observation and when an incorrect perception is formed, either immediately or gradually over a period of time, in the mind of another person.

To understand the anger; we should ask ourselves why we are angry. What is the actual ground for my anger? What are the circumstances and conditions that could cause the pressure onto my uncontrollable emotional outburst? It is worthwhile to consider and reflect on the condition that causes the ill-passion of anger. It is essential for a person to face himself and his own defects as the human virtue of fortitude comes into play: a mature man-husband should not run away from any problem, but to face reality and the challenges of his own defects. And, it is also for justice sake that a man must be responsible for his own actions, otherwise someone will get hurt; in this case his spouse, the wife, is the victim. In a genuine self-reflection, a person might find that the cause of his or her anger originates from his own inferiority complex, for example: personal defects, work related stress, egoism, childhood experiences, pride, self-pity and/or touchiness, dissatisfaction with own performance, or his looks, or his financial position etc. A person with a mature personality must know how to master, self-control, himself or herself. People who permit emotional moods to dominate their minds and intelligence are considered weak in character. Marital relationships may improve after mutual forgiveness and a commitment to improve his/her defects and shortcomings.

Fidelity in Marriage

Marital fidelity is indispensable in order to maintain a mutually loving and respectful marriage. Fidelity requires strength of character of the couple involved and sources of energy and strength come from purity of heart and self-sacrifice. The ability to be faithful to one's spouse in marital love originates from the virtue of temperance — the ability of self-mastery or self-control. Temperance requires the power of self-denial and self-sacrifice to be effective and active, while fortitude gives strength to a person to persevere in the midst of difficulties and disappointments. Therefore, marital fidelity is a commitment of the spouses who have mutually consented to be faithful to each other for life as to the point of reference of exclusivity of marriage that was mentioned earlier.

Marriage starts with a vanity promise of any kind similar to a masquerade party for bachelors, in which every man and woman is nice, sweet and romantic, however, soon enough when the music stops and the masks are off; the reality of the real selves are revealed. A married couple who have no interest in commitment and fidelity in marriage cannot love each other with genuine spousal love. There is nothing as timeless as love, it is only in a marriage that a man and a woman achieve that complete belonging to each other which they long for as a result of spousal love and friendship, and develop a willingness to forgive and move on with their lives. Fidelity is one of the fundamental requirements of marriage, spousal love and fidelity have to be cultivated "inside" the person and integrated into his or her "inner self" that leads to self-giving and life long commitment.

Self-giving love is not only the soul of marriage; but also the soul of the marital act. In contraceptive sexual union, the spouses use one another for their individual selfish pleasure. In effect, they do not treat or respect one another's personhood; they treat each other as objects of pleasure that eventually constitutes sin as discussed in Chapter 2 "Knowing the Origin." Contraception thus violates the principle of personhood and is shown to be inherently disordered and irrational. Because it is opposed to "the truth about man" — the truth about who and what we are, about our bodies, about our masculinity and femininity, about our personhood.

Conclusion

As this chapter entails the deeper meaning of the marriage as "Communion of Persons", possession of *human nature* is *integral* and *substantial* between the married couple, precisely because of this — "you and I" — the married couple is capable of profound relationship of knowledge and love between themselves. Marriage is a journey of love between the spouses, while communion entails knowing the spouse better and better each day through the deeper meaning of self-giving love.

The union of two persons in one flesh is not just biological, as it is in the case of animals. The attraction among animals is purely physiological, whereas the attraction among human beings is physiological, psychological and spiritual. Only in this manner will the spouse be able to receive one another; the husband loves the wife and vice-versa, not only as one should love himself but also with the love for another self. Spouses become "a single union of life and for life." However, marital spouse is also a human being and as such, he or she may be imperfect in the eyes of the spouse. 'The person who we married was so charming and attractive' will inevitably change over time, from a purely human perspective that could cause some disappointment.

Love is a fundamental passion of human person, without love we can never be fully human and respond to the corresponding good which is the impetus for perfecting a purposeful life. What some people love is not a person but the experience of being in love. Sexuality of a person is unique and unrepeatable, as unique and distinctive as, if not more than, our finger-print or the pupil of our eyes. Sexuality within marriage naturally accounts for more than the sexual act itself, sexuality of the spouses, founded on fidelity and spousal friendship is enriched by every positive occurrence within marriage. In turn, a harmonious spousal relationship based on communion of persons enriches the life of the husband and wife in marriage in such a way that they both learn to improve and complement each other's personality, virtues and defects, toward perfecting one another in their mutual path of life.

A marriage founded on sexual passion lasts only as long as the lust or animal passion lasts. Love among animals is tied down to what can be tasted, touched, seen, and heard; but love among human beings is as universal as goodness, commitment, inner beauty, and truth. One effective way to find out the character of a person is to get him to answer the question: "What do I love most? What have I been craving for most in my heart?" "Where your treasure is, there your heart is too." There are two basic categories of love that human beings possess, self-love and the love for others. Love exists not in isolation, it craves the involvement with others because love is essentially a relationship.

When "self-love" outgrows itself to become "selfless love," would be the "love of benevolence" in its essence which explains almost everything good that happens to our world; charity, brotherly love, sobriety, trusting friendship, justice, understanding, magnanimity, fidelity, peace, commitment and solidarity, etc. When we apply this "love for others" concept in marriage, the loving relationship fuses the individuals together as "one flesh" through communion of persons. The marital spouse is committed to integrate one's life into a mutually shared undertaking; it likens the merging of an individual and personal path into an integrated marital path, physical and spiritual, together. If this unity does not happen in marriage, then it ends up becoming a self-complacent relationship, i.e., two egoistic individuals who live together. Though their bodies are together, their minds and souls are set apart.

The reality of life is a journey towards fulfillment of our human destiny and potentiality; it is inevitable that sometimes it necessitates joyful sacrifice through love and perseverance in order to navigate through this common life. Marital love will be perfected when due sacrifices of the married couple is exhausted. I would like to close this chapter by the following conversation between two loving spouses:

The wife asks her husband: "After so many years of marriage, do you still love me?" The husband replies: "Of course, I love you."

The husband says: "My dear, if I stumble on the way, will you pick me up?"

The wife says: "Of course I will, my love."

The husband says: "Never give up on me, ok, promise me?"

The wife says: "I will never…, give up, no matter what, my love!"

The wife continues: "You too, don't you ever give up on me!"

Chapter 5

Work to Serve

In the early days of my career in mid-1980s when I was working in a multi-national food and beverage company, I undertook an overseas business trip. My colleague, Bob, said to me: "I work hard; and I play hard, this is the way of life, you should know!" Bob was one of top company executives of the company. He was one the very few executives who had direct control of the "secret formula" of the cola concentrate. He was a big man probably weighing over 250 pounds, too heavy for his age as he easily lost his breath after climbing few steps on the stairs. He appeared most relaxed while sipping his fifth or sixth shot of whisky-on-the-rock and would happily sink into a leather couch of the hotel lounge as if he has totally forgotten the hustles and bustles of the busy schedule of our extended business trip. As a young executive in the company, I started to ponder on these words "work hard and play hard" of my colleague, on what it might seem to have any relevance to our professional work, but the subject dropped off from my head as soon as I arrived home from that particular business trip. I did not bother to think about it as I was working really hard to acquire the knowledge and skill of business. I had used most of my energy to understand the fast-moving consumer goods and its manufacturing expertise and process management. There were plenty of industry knowledge and business skills to swallow for a new fellow like me — quality control, purchasing and sourcing of raw material, engineering mechanics of plant operations, industrial engineering, design layout of factory, accounting, marketing and sales distribution, and last but not least financial modeling and scenario analysis for investments in manufacturing plants which the company had decided to make. It was such a tough training during those years, my role was a

113

combination of three departments altogether; plant and business operations, marketing and sales distribution, and business development in negotiating new joint ventures in several major cities in China. The investment initiative was considered very strategic to the company at the time, a key milestone in Asia, but I only knew it in my later days.

These words of Bob remained a myth to me until years later when I had assumed a bigger responsibility that I came to realize what these words really meant. "To work hard and to play hard" phenomenon is not the propriety of my colleague, Bob, it is actually quite a common language amongst the circle of senior executives of large corporations, as if there is mutual understanding that says; "since working so hard for the company, we deserve more than others to enjoy life." It sounds quite materialistic to me as if the purpose of working hard is merely for an exchange of maximum benefits and pleasure through spending money while playing hard. I make use of the conversation of over a-quarter-of-a-century ago for the sake of discussion in this chapter without pin pointing anyone, and I believe Bob would not mind as this is for a good purpose. It was my first encounter with this important relationship between responsibility and the associating authority. The power comes with my work responsibility at my disposal, and I can freely choose to exercise it for the common good, or for a selfish reason of my own.

The reason why I have included this chapter on work in "Mirror of Love" is because work by itself is an integral part of human activity. Work is also an inseparable entity of family and society. Work, in its essence, primarily aims at serving an objective, or several objectives. However, it is not an easy task to talk about work here in Asia as the concept of work is pretty well "defined and understood" in the sense that working hard is a common phenomenon, a well accepted social norm. In general, people work extremely hard in many parts of Asia, or at least they appear to be working very hard, and working for long hours. To work is to serve a purpose, but "to serve who, and to serve what?"

To Work as to Serve

While time slipped through my fingers like the running water in the past several decades, in an international conference in recent times, I came across an interesting conversation with a few young corporate executives in the cocktail lounge of a hotel. A young investment banker said proudly while looking at the far end of the conference room: "By this time next year, I'll probably have made enough that I can retire and do something I love" which seems to have impressed the other two business acquaintances. In the common language of today's business world, "If you are smart and work hard, you can retire at the age of 35" sounds quite common and appears relevant amongst young and successful individuals. I believe what it really means is that if you can afford the money then forget about whatever professional job you may have, simply retire and have fun in life. It seems to separate work from fun as if hard work can never derive fun that you have to be retired to do something else that you love. This sounds as if work itself is some sort of a curse or cancer of which people want to get rid of as soon as they can.

We all need to work, one way or another, to serve a purpose, or several purposes altogether. We work in order to survive, to earn our living, to bring bread on the table, to bring home the money for raising the family, for education of children, for paying the mortgage and expenses, etc. I suppose this is the most practical reason why we all work, whatever undertaking it may be, manual or intellectual. However, there is another perspective of why we should work besides the purpose of earning our livelihood and for the support of family. Man naturally craves to work for the purpose of manifestation of his given talents. "Man is born to work, as natural as, bird is born to fly." In a paradoxical analysis, if a bird is unable to fly, it would be seen as a handicapped bird; perhaps it will become the laughing stock by other birds; following the analogy, if man does not work, or does not know how to work, he would be seen as a handicap as well.

During my early-20s, I took a trip to a fishing village in a Southeast Asian country, an excursion with an intention to experience life in a remote fishing village. We had a fantastic opportunity to secure the temporary use of a local chalet that was built in a traditional structure of bamboo and timber looking over the impeccable blue ocean from a small hill. Though we were confronted with the absence of the modern facility of the city, we were extremely thrilled of the idea. We had no electricity, no television, no air-conditioner, no telephone nor electric fan, no wi-fi, mobile phone, or mobile devices such as tablet PC, and there were no lights after dark, except a few lanterns that burned on kerosene. Life was really simple, I learned to appreciate things that the nature provides for, everything else have to acquired through effort; for example, if we failed to catch fish that day, we could probably go hungry without meals in the day. The village people were so kind to teach us and helped us to cope with this "new life" of ours. What we saw as inconvenient was all very natural and normal to them — they intuitively understood the essence of their work through fishing, planting the crops and raising the cattle and slaughtering livestock's at a certain time of the week, and to share amongst different families, as they had no refrigerators to store the slaughtered animal stock. It was such a rare opportunity for "city-people" like us to experience the life of fishermen for a week or two during summer. One morning before dawn, we were awakened by a head fisherman who asked us to help out in preparation of the fishing net of the day. Though all the fishermen looked slim in their body build, they demonstrated tremendous physical strength similar to top athletes of cross-country marathon when throwing or spreading the fishing net for a catch, and these operations were repeated many times during the fishing hours. We, the young adults, supposedly full of energy and strength, were dwarfed by the physical strength and the determination of these fishermen. What a lesson learned!

Work, as part of the nature of human being, is a means to an end. It is an indisputable tool that helps realize the given talents of a person in order to fulfill his life purpose; without which a human being tends to lose his purpose in life. We all need to work, in different undertakings and professions, such as fishermen, manual labor, engineers, medical doctors, farmers, bankers, lawyers, teachers, bus-drivers, architects, businessmen, housewives, public servants and politicians according to one's talents and preference, and in the process of our work to serve the family and the common good. Any honest and upright undertaking, be it manual or intellectual, enables a person to earn a livelihood and to support his family and children, it also a means to realize his potential in contributing service to the common good of the society. Diligent work is important, and as crucial as the heartbeats of a person. "In the sweat of your face you shall eat bread..." (Genesis 3:17–19, Navarre Bible) reminds us of the necessity of human work and undertakings for the fulfillment and realization of the given potential in meeting our objective in life as a useful human being. On my return trip back home, I began to appreciate the work of these fishermen and their simple lives. My respect for them grew as without these fishermen, we probably will not be able to buy any fish in the supermarket for meals, neither vegetables nor fruits if they were not supplied by the plantation farmers, or meat by the cattle farmers. The work of these fishermen, plantation and cattle farmers have contributed indisputable service to the common good of the society that most of us are the beneficiaries of their hard work. Thus, if work can be regarded as being of service to each other in the community then it makes more sense that we should do our work the best we could, so that we in turn will receive the reciprocal benefit from other's service in this global village.

We can think of many other types of work in different sectors of our society in serving the common good of its people. The trip to the fishing village amidst nature has cast a lasting image of work in my mind as a young man, the intensity, decisiveness and the determination of these simple village people taught me a great lesson of what work really means in its most simplistic language. So far, we have been led to see that any diligent work as to serve at least three purposes; to earn a livelihood to serve the family, to manifest and develop our given talents for good use, and to serve the common good of the people through our work. Later on in my life, I realized that had I not worked, I would have fallen "sick", both physically and psychologically; my inner self had always urged me to work!

A Childhood Memoir

I suppose when a person reaches certain age of life, he is more inclined to reflect on his past, his achievements and failures, his career and his well being, his family and his destiny; however, some people begin their self-reflection as a habit from early years of their life; I am one of them. When I look back at different phases of my life, I consider myself to be extremely blessed to have trodden such a wonderful journey in life so far. I had a tough childhood with some sort of learning difficulties where I would struggle to overcome my study hurdles with tremendous efforts; I would spend days and weeks on a piece of school-work which otherwise would have taken only a day's work of average kid of my age. Despite the learning difficulty, somehow I was mysteriously able to overcome this deficiency during my early adult life, through great efforts.

One of the most effective ways to get to understand a person is by engaging to work with him, or her, for a relevant period of time. From a managerial perspective, some corporations would conduct a 360-degree perspective and profile analysis on a candidate of any key senior position, the circle of his work; of his relationship with superiors, subordinates and peers, of his social circle, and of his family circle, etc. In this case, it is most logical to trace back to the root of what have influenced me most as an individual that might have made me of who I am today. I recognize that there are two distinctive phases of development; one that is of the history of the family where I grew up from and events prior to that, and the other phase is the path I have chosen in search of a prosperous life and a professional career; that could be likened to swimming in the wide open ocean without shores.

I was born into a family of seven brothers and sisters; I am the forth-in line, right in the middle of my clan. My father was the second son of the eight children from my grandparents, and my father became the first in line after the death of his elder brother when he was very young. In the early 1900's, my grandfather, who originated from Taishan, a city of Guangdong province, had built a very successful business of manufacturing and distributing Chinese herbal packaged medicine in glass bottles. The product was distributed throughout Guangdong and some Southeast Asian countries. This "specially formulated" medicine was pre-cooked and manually bottled into tiny glass bottles and was famous for curing diarrhea and intestinal infections which at that time was a common and serious illness in Asia. My grandfather had managed to build a brand of the family owned medicine and the business was very prosperous. The company he owned had commissioned two ships for the transportation of the packaged medicine in bulk to Indonesia, Malaysia, Singapore and to the Chinese community in Thailand. I still vividly remember the photos of the two ships that my parents exhibited to us when I was a small child, but later on we lost track of the photos as we moved homes. The brand name of this medicine was "Zhu Zong-Xing" (in Mandarin) which literally translated into "Prosperity in the Chu-Family". It was so popular that it attracted copycats in several countries in Southeast Asia. On one occasion, upon receiving a report from the wholesaler in Southeast Asia, my grandfather became aware of the seriousness of the copycat situation as he had experienced loss of business orders and was receiving telegraphs of complaints from his business partners. Before the problems could be totally resolved, the war had broken. My grandfather died early, leaving my grandmother and eight children who were all boys plus one, the last in line, the youngest girl of nine who was found, wrapped in cloth, outside the main door of the mansion where my grandmother and her children lived. Out of mercy and compassion, my grandmother decided to adopt this baby girl as her own daughter, her only and youngest daughter who later on became my closest auntie in my father's generation. She was married to an overseas Chinese, a family man, now living in a Southeast Asian country with her five children, they are also close to me up to the present day.

My father graduated from a high school "Wah-Yan College" (in Cantonese dialect) which was run by the Jesuits, in Hong Kong Island. He was well educated of his time, he spoke fluent English and was active in the social circle of schools, social clubs such as The

Jockey Club, etc. Many of his friends were English nationals, foreigners and Chinese. While he enjoyed his teenage and pre-adult life, being the eldest son of the family, my father had developed a strong sense of responsibility in helping my grandmother in running the family business while assuming the role as the eldest son in fathering his younger siblings.

His role of fathering his younger brothers became obvious through consistent persuading and reprimanding one of my uncles to study hard at his primary school which my uncle had always tried his best to escape classes. After years of persistence and efforts, my father was confronted by his younger brother of his ultimatum, my uncle had decisively refused to continue his studies and he wanted to be let alone. Later on in his life, this uncle of mine admitted that my father had exhausted every means in forcing him to a proper education but failed, my uncle said to us that he had himself to be blamed. He worked as a car-driver for most part of his life. Another uncle of mine, a young brother of my father, developed some sort of skin disease during his teenage years, that consumed the tissues around his knee which almost paralyzed him and he could not walk for months. In order to get him to school and attend classes, my father decided to carry him on his back to and from the school during a period of several months. The act of my father had motivated the eagerness in studying of his younger brother; later on this uncle of mine led a relatively successful career and became a senior officer in the court of Hong Kong for most part of his life. He lived a good life and later he moved to the United States with his family and lived there for many years before he passed away.

From his late 20s, my father experienced major twists and turns. This was also the time when the war broke out in China and Asia. Hong Kong, a colony of the Great Britain back in those years, was occupied by the Japanese army. An incidence I recall from the memory of my father perhaps could give an idea of the monstrosity of the situation during those years when Hong Kong was under occupation of a foreign arm-force. The entire Hong Kong, Kowloon and New

Territory were under mandatory curfew by the Japanese soldiers after six o'clock each day and everyday, lights-out was mandatory in every household and street after dark. So the normal practice of the residents was to cover all the windows with layers and layers of curtain, or cloth in order to block the dim lights from inside of the house or apartments. One evening, my grandmother and her clan noticed that there were heavy poundings on the main door of the house where she and her children and servants and helpers lived. No one dared enough to answer to the door as it was obvious that trouble awaited right outside, and it was imminent. My father, being the eldest son, had no choice but to answer to the door. In a split of a second, he found himself in shock and almost collapsed when two Japanese soldiers appeared fiercely at the door and holding him at knife and gun-point, while shouting loudly with words that were not comprehensible to my father. Later on, my father described to us that he could clearly see the barrel and the knives which were mounted on the rifles. It was a lucky incidence that nothing more serious happened except that my father was slapped on his face coupled with pulling and shoveling in physical intimidation by these two fierce intruders. My father was speechless and probably too shocked to say anything except a 'yes' followed by another 'yes'. Finally, the two soldiers reduced their aggression and left. Later on, one the servants admitted that he had forgotten to close the curtain completely in one of the rooms and that lights from the inside was seen from outside, in the darkness of the street.

When the war was over, life in general was tough, there was scarcity of material and food, my father was still able to acquire substantial resources through his extensive networking of friends, such as milk powder, meat and chocolate, and the family was able to feed all the children and a sizeable community of helpers from China who were looking for jobs in Hong Kong. They all lived and worked for my father and the family while consuming plenty of the remaining resources and reserves of our family. This help of my father during the war had extended to many of his friends, amongst them some were foreigners, that included the godfather of my elder brother, Mr. and

Mrs. Dragon. My father had married my mother in the early 50s when they met in Hong Kong. My mother was originally born and raised in Shanghai, China; she was a beautiful young woman. I have vivid memories of her interesting stories about her experiences after marrying into this relatively large and traditional Chinese family of Guangdong origin. My mother at the time was seen as an outsider by her sisters-in-law, brothers-in-law and relatives because she was the only woman who originated from Shanghai, which was then considered a northerner, not a native of Guangdong, or Hong Kong.

My grandfather died relatively early leaving the family business to inexperienced hands. My father was in his late-20s, and my grandmother did not have much experience in the business in those years. The two ships of the family business were gone with the war, followed by unsuccessful business deals. In our estimate, those business deals and transactions were initiated and executed by some dishonest people and relatives in Taishan, China as well as people in Hong Kong. Therefore, within a few years, my father lost all his investments and properties, and the business went from bad to worse, leaving almost nothing left in the family company. The worse was still to come, my father and his company was in debt; our family house No. 20-something on Connaught Road West, Hong Kong Island which my grandmother once owned and lived with her nine children perished together with the mysterious debt. At present, our family house, that we once owned, has been converted into a multi-storey building standing proudly on the same piece of land, and of the same address overseeing the Hong Kong harbor. The only difference is its ownership.

My guess is these series of unfortunate events had happened around mid–late 50's when my parents decided to leave a nice house where my elder sisters and I were born, and moved in to a much smaller apartment in Kowloon, I was then about three years old. During those years, life was tough but we were happy to have each other as a family. The situation at the time gave me the opportunity to learn many skills and gain knowledge in repairs and maintenance at home. I was literally responsible for fixing everything at our home, from changing the bulbs of rooms to fixing door-hinges, from painting the iron gate to fixing the electrical power cord, or to repair pipes of the water leakage in the bathroom, as my mother thought it was a good idea to run her budget, while I enjoyed to help and be depended upon by my mother and my father. I continued this practice in my own family after I got married, especially in the early years when our children were still young, showing them work is to serve with an effort.

After these episodes and the war aftermath, life was back to normal but the living environment was far from safe and conducive especially in the scarcity of material resources in everyday living. My father worked in an office as an employee to support the basic necessities of his family. He endured drastic changes in his lifestyle and his identity, from a relatively wealthy employer of a sizeable company to the position of an employee in a small company, a huge adjustment indeed. I supposed my father swallowed his pride substantially and it took him many years to adjust to his life of a simple man of the time. My mother too had to work to provide extra support while taking care of her-more-than half-a-dozen children at home and of their studies. Life was not easy.

Essence of Work

Work is a universal need of society and its citizen, it is both a right and duty of a human being to exercise his or her inner talents in work to achieve the common good, and as well as, personal development; besides, work makes a family economically independent. Although work is a means of manifesting our given talents, the expression "personal fulfillment and development" should not be flaunted relentlessly as an excuse of, or a justification for, the disorder in family life as opposed to a mutual co-existence of a happy family and a successful professional life.

Economic conditions of a family could very well be the main reason when deciding whether both husband and wife should be working.

The reality is that many families cannot survive on a single salary due to high costs of living in both developed, as well as developing cities. It is pity to see some husbands, or both husband and wife, take on a second job in order to make the ends meet in their family. When this becomes necessary, parents will have to take extra measures to accommodate this imperfect and yet necessary childcare during their absence from home.

Is Workaholic any Good?

I remember a phrase that I heard from someone, "work is to serve people", not "people to serve work". Though to some people, workaholic may sound impressive, but actually it does not have a positive connotation. Today we can see many aspects of our professional work where many people are "over-worked" due to financial reasons to make their ends meet. In order to gain adequate income for their family and children, many people conduct either manual or intellectual work for long hours, or some are even "forced" to work several jobs in order to survive the ever-escalating cost of living. This kind of working on multiple jobs, if extended to a prolonged period, will drain the husband or the couple's energy and would certainly affect the marital harmony and well being of the family. Thus, the role and duty of the state is indispensable in ensuring appropriate administrative policy that guarantees adequate employments of its citizens, with fair wages and proper housing policy to support families and children.

In other situations, there are people who do not want to work hard simply due to laziness, or some desire early retirement upon accumulation of enough wealth; or there are people who work hard for long hours, or at least they appear to be working very hard, at their offices, during meal times, after work hours, even bringing home their work to the family, or they stay up late in the office.

As opposed to people being forced to "over-worked" for long hours due to economic reasons, we see another aspect of work life emerging as a result of this new phenomenon of professional "addiction" to long hours of work life. Quite often, we see office buildings still lit up beyond midnight as there are many people working in the offices. Restaurants, café and bars near these office zones are still wide-open after midnight simply because there is demand from customers of surrounding office buildings who need to continue their work after late night while drinking and dining. This long-haul working habit has become a life style among different professionals across various industries, it seems to be a socially acceptable lifestyle of "life goes on after dark". In many cases, the workaholic lifestyle would indisputably exert great pressure to family members and children, if it is continued over a long period of time. Frequent travel for work is another problem that exerts tremendous pressure onto the husband-father, working hard to keep his employment while being away from his wife and family. Not only does the father face work pressure in business travels, both physical and mental, at times, pressure arises from loneliness in an extensive trip for weeks, or even months. Though these situations are quite common in our society today, yet some honest and upright professionals see the need to reverse the work place to a more family-friendly environment.

Professional Work of Women

In the distant past of our human history, women did not have the need to work, their main focus was attending to household chores. However, the picture has changed substantially today, women are actively participating as professionals in the fields of education, research laboratories, space ships, military barracks, finance, theaters, banking, film-studios and so on. Many women have demonstrated their natural ability to work in relevant and important positions in our society. Having said that, there are places in the world where men–women equality in dignity has not been well developed as opposed to the rest of world, where women rights are not as equal as their male counterparts. In these countries, women are seen as secondary citizens to their male counterparts; often women are treated worse than animals, while sexual abuse and gang rapes of women are seen as acceptable social culture. Thus, causes for lack of opportunities in fulfilling a woman's full potential deserve a closer look by the man-husband, and by a responsible government as a whole.

In the last decades, in the larger circle of the international arena, we have seen woman demonstrating and achieving professional capabilities and positions which were exclusively reserved for men in the past. Through this development, woman has corrected the bias that women are only capable of work in the family and household chores because of her physical and psychological structures, in the male-dominant society of the past. "There is an urgent need to achieve *real equality* in every area: equal pay for equal work, protection for working mothers, fairness in career advancements, equality of spouses with regard to family rights and the recognition of everything that is part of the rights and duties of citizens in a democratic state." (*Letter to Women*, number 4, JP-II, 1995). To be able to cope with such a rapid and arduous change successfully indicates that a woman's intuition and unique professional competence brings with it such a potential to be ready for job. The woman who is capable of running a house, able to care for others, minute after minute, through necessary training and timely exposure in a stable and continues manner, is capable of undertaking any professional challenge.

The woman-mother, having overcome obstacles in professional development in the tasks that were traditionally reserved only to men, has enabled her to develop more substantially into her womanhood. Given the above finding as it is, professional work and domestic chores of the family, would enable the woman to realize her inner potential for any challenge; in this respect, a working mother has to cope with more challenges than before in balancing between different functions of her role. Today, there are important positions occupied by competent women; as women executives and professionals and as leader of States, and they have all proven that they can do certain jobs better than their male counterparts.

A conscientious mother would carefully evaluate if her professional job would turn her into a stranger in her own home, transforming her from a simple provider to her children and a cohabitate partner to her husband. Moreover, the married couple should look at this with an open mind and with common sense and compassion that women do have the right to participate in the public functions of the society and also the necessity of self-fulfillment of their natural given talents. However, it would be unhelpful if this issue enters into an argument with people who have pre-determined idea of women liberation in the society. On the other hand, men will also have to revitalize their true role in the family. They should not see themselves as purely financial providers and physical protectors entrusting the thousand-and-one daily problems of family life to their wives. The role of husband and wife within the family in educating and upbringing of the children should be mutual and complementary.

Domestic Chores are Professional Work too

Today many wives and mothers, in the West as well as in the East, are practically compelled to work outside the home because of economic conditions, and this could be a terrible injustice. In some cases, women are hired for well-paid professional jobs, while men assume the duty of domestic chores. Men with predominant mentality as the head of the family would feel ashamed of not able to perform a natural task as husband-father to support the family. At times, this sense of defeat is viewed to be outdated in the third millennium; given that the situation of each family is different. So long as the situation of husband's unemployment was not caused by the irresponsible attitude of husband to escape from his duty to work to serve, then as soon as a positive situation arises, he should get back to work.

On the contrary, domestic chores are of good educational value, highly dignified and important to all members of the family. These duties are creative, are an effective tool in the formation of our children and also help in sustaining the matrimonial relationship as everyone in the family gives some part of himself or herself to the common good within the family. Domestic chores contribute to family unity in a simple but mysterious way. The fact that domestic task is not remunerated, if it is done by wife and husband, has no reason to undermine its value. Besides, the possibility for self-fulfillment is infinite for the woman who gives herself completely all her life for the welfare of home, husband and children. This situates wife-mother perfectly in the context of service, which "expresses her talent in the service of others in ordinary life." (*Letter to Women*, number 12, John Paul II, 1995)

JP-II said "Motherhood, because of all the hard work it entails, should be recognized as giving the right to financial benefits at least equal to those of other kinds of work undertaken in order to support the family during such a delicate phase of its life." In his Letter to Families, insisting that the work women do within the family unit must be appreciated and recognized, he rightly declares that "the 'toil' of a woman who, having given birth to a child, nourishes and cares for that child and devotes herself to their upbringing, particularly in the early years, is so great as to be comparable to any professional work."

Indeed, it is a reality that today in many Asian countries, it has become quite common that some of the domestic chores can be delegated to domestic helper, particularly in families where both spouses have the need to engage in full time work. This, of course, depends on the family income and whether grandparents would be available to help or not. In other cases, the tasks will need to be shared among the family members, especially the children at different ages would need to be educated that they are not always on the receiving end, they should be aware of the need to contribute as members of the family. In a family, everyone needs to work and contribute to the overall welfare of the common good of the family.

However, parents who are both employed professionally should not misconstrue that their domestic helpers could take their place in baby-sitting their children most of hours of the day in their absence, just because their work demands late working hours. Though, it affirms that a mother has the right to seek active employment in a professional environment so long as this does not jeopardize her indispensable mother-wife role within the home and the family, just as the work of the husband-father outside the home does not jeopardize his indispensable role as father-husband within home and family.

After their wedding, quite a few women discover they are suddenly expected to do things for which they are quite unprepared. Many young married women find that these were not in the "marriage curriculum" nor were these ever been explained to them. Even though some women may have received some instructions or attended related courses, they find themselves unable to cook, iron, or run daily household chores at home. As wives, they are examined in a subject — housewifery — that most women are not aware of. Or simply, some women of the modern society, with their incorrect mindsets, think that house chores reflect relatively low qualification of women's ability. As a result, many women are not willing to carry out this important task at home which is a source of family unity and education of children.

I could not even begin to imagine a home without feminine touch. It is obvious that a welcoming home can never be manifested to its fullness without the involvement of a wife. The femininity stands out in a marital relationship through the expression of her capacity as a woman in receiving others, her husband and her children. This capacity, deeply crafted into her womanhood, irradiates through her feminine attractive personality. Family home is a reflection of the personality of its inhabitants, a place of love and life, for an intense and happy family life where members learn to love and make sacrifices through love, to develop and be developed as well. When these feminine characteristics of the wife are applied in a family home, it is obvious to see that the decoration and style would reflect the personality and the likes of the wife; through the details of the dinning table cloth, the color of the curtain, the texture of the sofa, and setting of the living room and the kitchen, etc. in order to facilitate a comfortable and conducive happy family living for her beloved. Love is in the details. Managing a family home and house chores are actually complex work, they are as important as, if not more than, any professional work outside the home. It deserves more attention and respect from everyone within the family, especially from the husband which may be slow in appreciating because of the weakness in his nature. The husband should understand this and get to know it before he could possibly appreciate what is behind the brilliance of their family home. However, quite often house chores in its essence and significance are reduced to something that is too basic and even seen to be boring that even women of our modern society are not motivated to get themselves involved, much less than to embrace this important task of managing a beautiful and yet efficient family home. I can think of a few key capabilities of home management from a business perspective.

1. *Multi-tasking*

When my boys were young, I used to motivate them by explaining why multi-tasking was important and thus trained them in handling different tasks within a short spectrum of time. On an average, men have a natural weakness in handling several tasks at one time when compared with their women counterparts. A woman is naturally more integral than a man as discussed in an earlier chapter. Simple operations of the house chores as we men perceive are actually quite complex; let us take a look at the everyday life of a typical young pregnant mother with her first born — 18 months old toddler. "When the toddler cries persistently while the mother is preparing food, she needs to investigate what is the cause of the toddler cries, the toddler could be hungry, or wet, he might have hit his head somewhere in the room, or some other reasons. Suddenly, she remembers that she is in the middle of making the soup for the dinner, that she needs to wash and prepare the ingredients and mix them in the cooking pot on time to be cooked before her husband reaches home in two hours with his parents for dinner. Then, the telephone rings, she catches the crying toddler and runs to pick up the phone. She finds her own mother is on the other end of the line asking how things are, without knowing her daughter is right on top of several tasks at the same time while the grandson is crying loud. The young pregnant mother ponders if she should tell her mother that she is cooking a dinner feast for her in-laws tonight..!" Organizing skills in household chores is so essential and important as well, managing a household also demands the use of the intellectual faculty in creating, ordering, planning and executing which are all necessary to make family life enjoyable and interesting to everyone in the family members. While the wife carries out the household chores, her mind is constantly active attending to almost infinite number of other things; from the planning of dinner and its ingredients, cleaning of the house and setting, from washing of clothes to arranging pick up of her children from the school, and shopping for groceries at super market and arranging delivery, etc. A million and one things happen in our households that need the attention from someone, and the most capable person for such tasks is the wife; the husband must be smart enough to realize and appreciate it.

2. *Flexibility*

When a child cries or hurts himself that needs immediate attention and solution, frequently the original task of the parents/mother will be interrupted and a new solution would be developed to cope with the change of environment, for example, bathing a baby while simultaneously attending to the toddler boy that has fallen from the chair, managing the burnt chicken in the oven, etc. This means the wife needs to find an alternative to a chaotic situation and an unfinished task, be it dinner or other matters of the house.

3. *Resourcefulness and Creativity*

Managing and balancing resources of time and money in various forms is never an easy task. If we could take a moment to look at how the heads of state in numerous leading economies in the North America and Europe could fail their financial budgets that created a financial tsunami sweeping across the world resulting in such a tantamount of problems everywhere, we would better appreciate the difficulties in managing resources in our families though at a different scale. Time is never enough in household chores, handling a thousand-and-one things at the same time, according to schedule while managing variety of tasks and within a tight constraint of money.

The husband must learn to value the work at home, keeping profound awareness of its values, its practicality and the dignity of household chores while appreciating his wife dearly. In numerous situations, we see few husbands that are ready "to get their hands dirty" regardless of their professional achievements and are actively and willingly involved in the household chores that could even include cooking the meals and cleaning of the bathrooms, side by side, with their wives and children on regular basis.

Through such co-operation between husband and wife where actions speak louder than words, the dignity of housework is reinstated. And if we pour out our genuine self-giving love for the service of man (woman) and for the common good of family, it elevates this simple work of ours to a supernatural plane which is capable of tying us to the higher objective of our destiny in heaven through sanctifying our ordinary work — be it simple or sophisticated, labor or intellectual. Society has an obligation to recognize the invaluable work that women do within their homes. "While it must be recognized that women have the same right as men to perform various public functions, society must be structured in such a way that wives and mothers are not in practice compelled to work outside the home, and that their families can live and prosper in a dignified way even when they themselves devote their full time to their own family."

I believe most readers would agree with me that only nature and special skills of most wives would help in facilitating this important task of household chores. A wife-homemaker possesses a great human heart of love, deeply crafted into her womanhood, the willingness of serving the common good of family and creating an enjoyable home that enhances happy family life. Thus, it is logical to overcome and rectify the narrow mentality of the society that advocates honoring women more for their work outside the home than for their work within the family. This primarily requires that the husband should truly esteem and love his wife with total respect for her personal dignity and her work as the "Minister of Home" in managing one-thousand-and-one things in the domestic house chores. Society too should chip in and develop conditions favoring work at home.

A Man in the Making

The episodes of my father and my grandfather had not only changed the course of our family history, they also helped shape the course of my life. The events that happened in the course of the past two generations remained invaluable lessons to me, I learned that each person has his own destiny in life, my grandpa and my father had theirs, and I have mine. I began to be aware during my early teenage years that things have to be acquired with effort, and there are no free lunches, and my destiny is in my own hands, and in God's hands. I knew that I must be able to grasp the essence of all the necessary professional knowledge and skills in order to navigate safely through the path of my career and my family life. Looking back to my career in the past 33 years, each and every step, every critical decision that I have made and the corresponding achievements so far; I have so much to be thankful for. I simply cannot let a day pass without giving thanks for the blessings in my life, for who I really am and my family, wife and children; and for everything I have done; and my professional work, the social projects that I am involved with and people and friends whom I got acquainted with.

My Early Days

When I was at my pre-teenage period, probably between eight to nine years old, I had a leukemia-related illness that I had to cease my schooling for several semesters. According to the doctor's advice, I could not conduct physical activities of a normal boy of my age; simple sports like football or basketball or any kind of active physical exercise was a luxury to me. I recall that I was to watch from a distance while others had fun in riding the rollercoaster, running around in the football field; their excitement in the fields, screaming and shouting, were simply out of my league. During this period, I ended up following my mother everywhere she went as we had only a temporary domestic helper; quite often our daily journey ended up in a nearby church. I vividly recall what my mother had said to me at times when things seemed to turn unpleasant; "You are a good boy, be good!" By observing what my parents did and how they lived their life, I gradually learned the "essentials", when my father went to work as an employee, he demonstrated virtues of fortitude, industriousness, humility and honesty to accept his fate in working hard to support us in the family.

Competent Work

From the experience of my father and my grandfather, I came to realize that to carry out professional work requires knowledge, skill and experience. Such competencies helped them make a huge difference in the face of challenges which they had encountered during their time. In the early years of my career, I developed a strong sense of curiosity in knowing everything that came across my path, and I would not easily let go until I had a good grasp of understanding the meaning behind the superficiality. There were many valuable lessons I drew from the historical lives of my grandfather and my father, in the experience of their work and their family life. The difficult times they underwent in different environments and their personal experiences provided a basic framework of who I am today.

My Early Career

As time passed, my career prospered well, I grew from an engineering consultant to an industry of fast-moving consumer goods of beverages, from electronics to telecommunication, from lighting industry to regional management and later on to a conglomerate of listed companies. In the mid-80s, when I was working with a beverage and food company, we used computers that were mono-screen in green color, they were more or less text-based workstations in contrast with the mobile data/audio/video communication devices of today. The use of financial modeling, in critical and progressive analysis, in the business world was not as common as it is today. The general perception at the time was that these financial modeling concepts were mainly for the bean-counter, the financial people and the accountants, it was rarely for people in business management. The idea of "management accounting and scenario analysis" for business managers was not as common as it is today.

However, as a newcomer, I was absolutely mesmerized by this management tool that was only used by the senior finance and accounting people. One day, I decided to visit the Chief financial officer (CFO) to chat about the financial models and I remember he was a bit surprised of my move. Since then, financial models, scenario and progressive analysis became the fundamental management tool for me, and for some of my managerial colleagues in the company. It was a great tool to the extent that I could visualize the overall financial results, such as; return of investment (ROI), return of assets (ROA) and profit-generation capability of the entire joint venture during the business trip in the hotel room, by inputting and manipulating the variables on sales and, cost-of-goods-sold, seasonality curves, financing cost and amortization criteria; at the time, 5 years for manufacturing equipment and 10–15 years for factory building, etc. Within two years, I was instrumental in soliciting two joint venture contracts which the food and beverage company was very determined to establish in the two major cities of Beijing and Shanghai from the beginning. The Chairman of the Board then, Donald Kendall was so excited that he decided to fly himself personally to China to witness the signing ceremony of these contracts.

Mr. Donald Kendall was a man of stature with silver white hair that concentrated on the sides and back of his head and was a good looking mature man in his late 60s. He was the key figure in the financial committee that supported the Republican Party then. That trip was the first time I met him. After the contracts signing ceremonies with Chinese dignitaries, the dragon dances and firecrackers and the feast, work was initiated to build plants within the strategic timeframe and locations together with a concentrate plant in Guangzhou, a city in the Southern China. In the summer of 1985, I was summoned by the company headquarters in New York to set on a trip to accompany D. Kendall and his family on a private trip in these two cities of China where two beverages plants were to be built. It was obviously an important task as it was widely understood in senior management circle of the company, "either you make it, or you fail it", which meant that anyone might possibly get sacked in this kind of close-encounter with the Chairman of the Board. Anything could have happened.

I must say it was quite an experience to me; I remember the head of the regional management was kind enough to forewarn me of this, while a few senior fellows jokingly gave me their blessings and said: "do whatever you can, but don't call me." That was it! since to organize an event of this kind requires some specialty, especially in China. In those years, China had just "opened" its door to selected foreign companies (from 1979), and those that focused on advanced technologies were the most welcomed; while fast moving consumer goods from the West were considered luxury items, as the senior officials said to us many times that Chinese people do not need the cola drinks, and they do not miss it. Unlike the China of today, in those years the clothing that people wore had only a few colors, blue, grey and green. There was only limited brand-taxi running in the streets, traveling visitors had to hire their own taxi-cars in order to get around between ministries, meeting places, factory and hotel. Therefore, I decided to hire a US-based PR company in Shanghai which helped organize the entire program of Don Kendall. At the recommendation of the PR Company, we hired one of the only two Lincoln limousines in Shanghai during the five days visit.

When Don Kendall and family arrived from the airport to Sheraton hotel, the latest international hotel in town at the time, the US Consulate general in Shanghai and the Head of Sheraton in Asia and staffs were amongst the lines of welcoming guests at the entrance. As soon as the crowd of people accompanied the family to their room and I tried to bit farewell with "see you later at dinner"; Don Kendall stopped me and insisted that I have a drink with him and his family and he himself poured me a drink, a whisky on the rock as a gesture of thanking me. It was quite a scene to me, at my 30s, when this relatively interesting event took place. On one morning, I was invited to join the breakfast together with Don and his family in the presidential suite. While we were chatting about the business, Don Kendall received a long-distant phone call that he stepped away from the table for a few minutes, and I had a chance to talk to his two teenage sons, one was ready to go to college after the summer, and younger was in the line of next years. Don came back and told me that it was George Bush, Sr. on the phone informing him that a senior cabinet member had met an accident by falling off from house back.

Not only did I survive the trip; I was highly regarded by the senior management in the headquarters. Later on, I had the opportunity to meet up with Roger Enrico, who was then the President of the Company, during a trip to Beijing for an international Marketing Conference. We had a celebration after the conference at the hotel, where he bought us one of his favorite Mexican drinks, "Tequila with one or two coffee beans." Roger Enrico was also the writer of his controversial book "The other guy blinks." I had a rewarding career with this food and beverage company for years before I was solicited by a European electronics conglomerate through a close friend of mine who was the Chancellor of the Embassy of the same country of origin of my new employer for many years to come.

Horizontal Verses Vertical

The years I worked in the multinational food and beverages company taught me many things; amongst all that I have mentioned already, knowledge-based management is a key from which I have derived "horizontal knowledge" and "vertical, or the depth of knowledge".

Horizontal knowledge entails a broad information and knowledge base across various disciplines and/or industries, whereas, vertical knowledge entails a less than broad information and knowledge base that focuses on one or two particular disciplines or industries. Vertical knowledge tends to stretch from top to bottom, it entails more substantial depth of knowledge, skills and experience, industry peculiarities and particular behaviorial patterns. Whereas, horizontal knowledge tends to be stretching across a lateral horizon, its emphasis is on broad base of information, knowledge, skill and experience across several disciplines; such as general management of a team, or an organization that involves work processes across various teams of different disciplines.

As the lead-manager of the negotiation team in the food and beverages company responsible for establishing investments for two joint ventures, I soon came to realize that I have to gain vertical knowledge; the knowledge and experience that is specific to this particular industry of fast-moving consumer goods; its overall industry behavior, how a cola drink is produced, quality control, from raw material to finished products, its inventory turns, its specific packaging distribution system and the key factors that impact on the total cost structure, etc. In order to establish the two successful joint ventures and get the business going, I needed "horizontal knowledge and skills" in process management, finance and accounting, cash-flow management, to effectively communicate company's objective with the authorities, partners and stakeholders, device strategies to achieve the planned objectives while the technique and knowhow in motivating different groups of colleagues and team members to work as per the going-forward plan, in order to achieve the anticipated results of the company.

An Afternoon with an Investment Banker

Some years ago, I had an interesting conversation with an experienced investment banker. Sam was the head of investment banking division focusing on chemicals and pharmaceutical industries. While having lunch with him, I asked Sam: "It must be a quite tough to quit the chemical industry and become banker, how did you handle it so well?" He looked at me and replied: "Changed industry? I have never studied nor worked in the chemical industry, nor the energy sectors. My first degree was global business and I have always been a financial guy, a financial analyst until they promoted me several years ago."

Then my curiosity grew even more and asked: "Then how did you make investment recommendation to your clients? Have you ever visited these companies and see how they operate and how the products are made?" Sam in his certainty replied: "No, never. Not even my boss, my colleagues, nor my guys." He continued: "Well, you know, there are tons of analytic reports and financial papers about them and we read a lot everyday, it is too many, we don't have time to go around seeing actual thing ourselves!" I have nothing against the work of Sam, or anyone in the investment banking sector, I simply use this as an example as it is seasoned topic, and it is relevant to our discussion.

Both vertical and horizontal knowledge are necessary, one is not more important than the other, the gist is to maintain a good balance of each type of knowledge and skills according to a particular industry or discipline, and continue excel in each of the arena as one's career progresses. This awareness and experience helped me in the subsequent career in electronics industry.

My Years in Electronics Industries

"Greater the power, comes greater the responsibility" is the righteous perspective of people who possess power. As my career prospered over the years, I have realized when a person in a position of authority, almost every single decision that he makes from senior position, or is instrumental in making a collective decision, would affect the life of many people; stakeholders, employees and their families. Thus, it is important for people who are in a position of authority to realize, how to dispose the power he or she possesses with great care and responsibility for the mutual benefit of the company, employees and stakeholders. However, to acknowledge this concept is relatively easy to say than done, as power by its nature is so attractive that it could blind the conscience of man.

From fast moving consumer beverages of a US-based corporate to a European electronics corporate culture was definitely not a straight jacket so to speak. This electronics corporation was reputed for its fundamental research in science; and also very strong in research and development (R & D) of applied science, but it needed improvements in product development and in the process of commercializing its products and services. It was one of the most challenging time of my career where I had to make special adjustments to a different industry, electronics industry. As soon as I began my new career with this electronics corporation, I was sent to the headquarters in Europe for two months to meet up with the people and to see the various operations, the laboratories, R&D and manufacturing plants in different sub-industries. This electronics company operated eight different independent vertical companies; from semiconductor to medical equipment, from lighting to consumer electronics, from telecommunication equipment to business electronics, etc.

My first assignment was as the Liaison Officer of three-giant technology transfer contracts between China and this European country. Every two-three months I found myself in offices in Europe and different cities in China, especially in the telecommunication arena. Soon after our second son was born, I was asked to join the lighting company, which was the most profitable and a significant business within this electronics corporation. I had a larger responsibility with a mandate to grow the business through acquisition or establishment of and joint ventures with manufactory facilities in the lighting industry in China and Asia. During those years the company had become a champion in almost every aspect in the industry. Two keen competitors, from Germany and USA, had been trying to lure our managers in Asia over to their companies. After several technology exchange seminars for the experts that we had organized, the Chinese national office for the electronics industry made it a point to adopt our lighting technology as the design criteria for the country. Our electronics company thus gained a strong position and recognition in the industry in China and Asia.

Moving up to the Region

In the following years, I became the head of Asia Pacific region of another business; my responsibilities increased as the head of Asia Pacific Middle East and Africa (MEA); geographically it included China, Korea, Japan, India, Pakistan, Australia and New Zealand and everything in between; and the MEA region that included the African continent and more-than-a-dozen Middle East countries where the businesses were managed from UAE and Johannesburg Europe, Africa and Middle East had become one of the frequently visited continents. I soon become a Corporate Director of this European conglomerate that had approximately 280,000 employees worldwide. In this corporation, to be a Corporate Director meant that you belonged to the inner circle of the senior executives of the company, the upper tiers of the top management, very similar to the membership of a prestigious club, a vested senior employee. As a corporate director, your job assignment could be in various roles, you could be the head of a regional business or several businesses, or the head of global business worldwide, or a senior scientist in research and development. In one of the corporate meetings in the European HQ, I had the privilege of sitting next to the principal scientist of the group R&D in fundamental science, an English national, a colleague of mine and a corporate director, who was pursued as the target guest-of-honor by some large Japanese companies.

In the business world, it is an indisputable honor to become a corporate director; I am convinced that it is very attractive to everyone of the 280,000 people workforce within the company. Throughout my corporate life, I had the opportunity to become an expatriate for half-a-dozen times, but my wife and I deterred any possibility of becoming an expatriate family with great effort. We know very well from professional perspective, expatriate assignment entails a prosperous career development; yet it also means constant moving job locations and homes, and it also means changing schools of our children and their friends. I would not deny that it is a good career path to many aspiring executives, but we have a personal view on the subject.

A Business Trip with My Son

In one of the business trips to India during a summer month, I took my elder son along with me, primarily to spend more time with him. With the help of my colleagues and customers, between offices and meetings, we were able to make use of a weekend when we all took a train trip within India and the places we visited and things we saw became an educational trip for my son, and also for me. In a separate trip to India where I attended a business conference of over 120 local business executives and owners from various parts of India, I had the opportunity to share something about family values. The conversation was predominantly focused on business strategies, business issues, supply chain management, and other interesting subjects.

During a coffee break, I decided to shift the conversation to a different topic, so I asked an open question to all of these important business people of their country: "How is the television here in India, how does it affect your family and children?" Before I could even elaborate with more examples, responses were overwhelming so much so that we "over-spent" 30 minutes in the conversation discussing the negative effects of television on our children and families. These business people were quite unhappy with the content of some the programs imported into the country, they were all struggling, together with their wives, trying hard to rectify the problems.

I knew from the early days when I assumed a bigger responsibility, I would be torn between my work responsibility and my family obligations, a typical problem of many contemporary corporate managers. However, I also knew many of these successful executives of multinationals ended up with broken families. The decision was simple; between family and work, I had chosen the former, to say good-bye to the attractive and promising career of being a corporate director in the electronics corporation after more than a dozen years of service; it was a tough call. After an elaborated farewell party and farewell notes from all over the world, my e-mail box was almost burst. I returned home a simple man, a father and a husband, happy and relaxed without any corporate burdens on my shoulders until I got in touch with one of the wealthiest men in Asia, who owned several publicly listed companies in Hong Kong and other businesses spread across different continents. I then began a new chapter in my career which continues until this day, however, I am obliged to withhold details of business activities.

Work Attitude

When I hear people talk about work attitude and related issues, I seem to have a good idea of what exactly it means. Under the influence of materialism, work has become a mere money-drilling machine, or a means to get rich. In different parts of the world, people who get rich in a quick way are considered smarter and more attractive: as money makes the world go around. If money were the ultimate objective for work, then it would seem logical to me when people with money aim for early retirement. However, this has defeated the original purpose of work itself. Work is not a curse but a means to an end for every human person, who genuinely needs to work not only for exchange of financial benefits, but in order to lead a fulfilling and meaningful life, and in the service of others. In my opinion, a person should work irrespective of his or her financial position, whether he or she is wealthy or not, whether he needs to work for money or not. Even when a person achieves substantial financial position, he or she should continue his or her professional work as to manifest one's talents and to serve the common good.

If we look up the word "attitude" in any English dictionary, it says: attitude is "the manner, disposition with regard to a person's tendency, especially of the mind." It further says: "It is an expression of an action or emotion; for example, a threatening attitude or a relaxed attitude." Attitude and its two little cousins "behavior and manner" of a person tells something about the personality and character of the person. "Attitude" is an interesting word that deserves a closer look.

On a weekend Friday, I took the underground Mass Transit Railway (MTR) that was packed with people. I saw a young man in his early-20s stand up and gave his seat to an old lady standing next to me. She was delighted and thanked this young man for his kindness. I then overheard a conversation of a couple nearby whispering to each other: "This young man has good manners, he has a kind heart." The question is: how does the manner of this young man on the train come from, what drives his attitude in response to situation of the old lady in the MTR?

Attitude is believed to originate from the inner disposition of a person that is founded on a group of values that give guidance to, and govern the moral behavior of a human person. These values find their origins in human virtues, or we simply call it character for which I would like to give a corresponding image-sense as of the "skeleton" of our body organism without which we can not make simple movements and actions. If "character" were the "skeleton and muscles" of my body, then "attitude" would be the "skin and body features" that give my external appearance; in which both are integrally fused together that form a perfect harmony of my body-system which enables me to perform actions and reactions.

Following the analogy, the attitude of a person is the manifestation of the character "domicile" within the person. But, the question is "can anyone make up his attitudes?" or "can attitude be falsified? I think the answer is "yes", and also "no". A person can falsify an action, through the manner or a response to a situation, or a question from someone; however, it is not easy to falsify one's insights over a long period of time, nor is it easy to falsify a perspective on an important issue, such as his views on a moral issue without being noticed. In other words, the attitude of a person is a kind of portrait of the inner personality of the person. Under normal circumstances, a person can falsify some aspects of his personality, but he probably cannot falsify every aspect of his attitude. For example, in normal circumstances, the wife who lives together with her husband will clearly notice the smallest details of the personality of her spouse.

To aim at forming positive attitude, one must start to instill virtues and form good character in a person preferably from early age. However, merely having good attitude is not enough, to achieve the best possible objective of "work to serve", a person needs to have a righteous intention, or rectitude of intention. For example, if a person whose genuine intention of joining a renowned charity is for fame, in order to rub shoulders with rich and famous, instead of serving the original aim of the charity; then he does not have the necessary rectitude of intention to its fullness. We shall further discuss "Rectitude of intention" in section "Purity of heart" in chapter 7.

Liz's Summer Job

On a hot summer day, my friend, Norman, telephoned me to ask for a favor to get his graduate daughter, Liz, the position of a management trainee in a large corporation. My friend believes his daughter could have a good career start while learning the basics of a potential managerial job. I agreed with him and made it my personal business to secure a position for Liz whom I watched grow up from her young childhood, but I had not seen her since her pre-teenage year. After a relevant interview by the human resources department and successive department heads, Liz was hired. Norman, the father was a happy man and so were we, everything seemed to be fine. However, after several weeks, I received a call from the department head of this large corporation who said with embarrassment that Liz could not cope with her colleagues and peers, she challenged everyone in the team and refused to follow normal working procedures and the duty of her job. When her superior tried to mediate the situation, she said to him "My job is not to take phone calls, as simple as that. By the way, they are asking me to do this and that, they all tease me, making my job difficult…!" Liz ended up leaving the position and the company in less than three months, she disappeared completely from our scene. My friend, Norman, was devastated and apologetic when I saw him last time; when I gave him a call, he did not give any reply.

A Selfish Act of Work

If we look closer at our materialistic world and how we really live our work life, we would have a better idea what the reality it is. The example that I am giving below is the real work life of an individual who had made work merely an instrument to achieving his selfish desire for money and comfort. In many of the work places today, offices and factories, boardrooms and clinics, the reality is that many of these work places have become battle fields for human struggle for power, fame and profit. There are several groups of people who hold different perspectives about work; one group that believes that it is alright to be ignorant or could not care less of what the truth is; and the other group has the ill-intention of making work place a tool for selfish wants, and the third group possibly belongs to those who have least responsibility, in other words, a pool of professional people who have little or no ethics at all. This echoes the terminology we have used in the early chapters "technically capable barbarians", they tend to do the job with minimum responsibility, it does not matter if anyone gets hurt in the process, as long as they get by and get their maximum benefits. Their professional work life likens the mummies who have no heartbeats and no conscience in dealing with issues and people. The forth group belong to those who want genuinely to do a job as good as he/she possible can, for the purpose of serving three objectives plus one: family, personal development and fulfillment, and for the common good. Last but not least, people in the forth group would strive to link the diligence of their hard work with heaven, giving thanks to the Creator for the opportunity and benefits that may bring in the service of others.

Work Ethics of Henry

The following is a real life story that had happened many years ago in the mid-90s. A previous managerial staff of mine, Henry, whom I knew for years, had relevant academic and professional qualification but left the company to pursue his career elsewhere. After a few years, I learned that he was laid-off due to redundancy in the company which he had joined. He was looking for a job and asked me if we could re-hire him. I was then running other businesses within the same company, and I had sympathy for him. After talking to the senior managers of different divisions and the human resources and after "twisting a few arms", I brought Henry back to one of my divisions of the professional lighting business. Soon I realized from my colleagues that Henry had changed a lot since his last departure, he was found lazy and always late in offices and meetings, he was careless, made empty promises and committed serious mistakes with professional customers, the architects and engineers and government offices, creating problems and potential loss for the company. Besides, his lax attitude in work had created a huge disparity in the working culture that we had instilled in the company and amongst all the managerial colleagues. We gave him several chances to correct his behavior in the hope that he would improve. Most of the senior managers disapproved of his conduct, especially the head of Finance and Accounting.

After exhausting all possibilities, I decided to let him go, as I felt that I was responsible for his employment in the first place. After he left, we heard that he set up his company and led a luxurious lifestyle, driving expensive cars and shopping at the luxury stores with his wife, etc. His lifestyle was short lived and soon he founded himself in huge debt while his business had failed, then he filed for bankruptcy and disappeared for good. His debtors were all over the place in search of what and who may have any connection to Henry in order to get a part of the debt Henry owed them. Henry's debtors were so keen in finding him that they hired a debt-collecting company to search all the previous colleagues and friends of Henry who had worked with him side by side; the incidence had created nuisance and unpleasant experience to some of my divisional managers. I felt bad for them and finally we sought police involvement to resolve this nuisance. After the incidence, no one wanted to deal with Henry, who had little ethics, both in work and human relationships, he had utilized his colleagues, abused the trust of friendship and also his business partners as he cheated their trust, while he had benefitted from the ugly ordeal.

I wonder if Henry's conscience or the state of mind would allow him to sleep at nights thinking how deeply he is indebted with much of other people's money. In my opinion, even though Henry had escaped the legal responsibility by filing for bankruptcy, he was morally responsible for the debt and the damage that he had caused upon others, his debtors and their families. Let us say from a paradoxical assumption that one of the debtors of Henry had his wife divorced him due to his financial burden which was, directly or indirectly, caused by Henry's selfish or careless act. To cause a broken family could be a serious moral liability. Yet, Henry's liability would likely be adding up as negative consequence of the children of this divorced family; the possibility of these young children being abused in the absence of their natural parents. A seemingly simple ordeal of greed and selfishness may tantamount to absence of moral responsibility; Henry might have a long payback time!

Rules of the Jungle

Relentless corporate culture likens a killing field; "either I am doomed or you are dead". I have witnessed instances of relentless desire in people climbing up the corporate ladder by stepping on others' backs, their fellow colleagues through making false accusations with "arrows" shooting from different directions. At times, a corporate boardroom appears similar to an arena of beast-fight for survival, or a theatre where ruthless human acts are displayed against each other. It is quite common to see boardroom and professional work place turn a blind eye to justice but accepting the rule of the jungle as the game-plan; "the strong survives, while the weak dies", reducing human and work dignity to mere tools and instruments in achieving selfish objectives.

I recall an incidence that reminds of this ruthlessness in senior corporate culture. A newly appointed regional head, Ron, of a small business unit who was desperate to climb up in his career, arrived at the management office of Asia Pacific region one day. He knew a person of his own nationality who became the head of global business and a member of the board of a large European conglomerate, let us call him Jim. I personally knew Jim, long before Ron did, at his home country before Jim was promoted to the Board. My regional superior at the time, Kix, was a hard working and efficient man, who could build his own swimming pool by himself at the back yard of his home. We were friends. But Ron was a very smart fellow and somehow he became a friend of Jim. I recall one time at a corporate dinner with live music and gourmet food, Ron had poked his head out from the far end of the long table, with a glass in his hand ready to make a toss. Jim, the board member, was sitting next to me while Ron made his toss, Ron said: "I like to make a toss to our new chief Jim, Sir, I want you to know that if you say "jump" anytime, I will jump." There was a two seconds delay before each of the 15 senior corporate executives realized what the toss really meant.

In the following months, we continued witnessing the ugly corporate drama. Ron, who was a newcomer, was after the job of my superior. He managed to achieve his goal, through false allegations, with a board member of this European conglomerate. When I heard the announcement which was made during a dinner party to remove Kix in such a humiliated manner, my heart sank, but I knew I was not alone. For the benefit of doubt, I did give Ron a chance to show his, once ugly face, the true side of his humanity. I worked with Ron for years afterward as he needed my expertise in running businesses in Asia and China, while I kept my eyes and ears wide-opened. Even the smallest sign of change for betterment would have been an incentive for me to forge ahead to stay on with Ron, but unfortunately his ruthlessness in making other people suffer, owing to his pride, for his selfish gains had deterred my enthusiasm. I have enjoyed my professional work and have strived to do it well as much as I could all these years. However, when work was motivated by human incentives, such as getting a promotion or compliments from people whom I worked with, I was easily discouraged whenever things did not turn out the way they were supposed to, or ventures that I was in charge did not result in tangible success. But, when the motivation for my work turned to the supernatural objective, to give glory to my Creator, then the focus was no longer on me. The end results were the realization that I am only an instrument in the process of getting things done well through work, an instrument to meet the purpose of "work as to serve". After a short period, I was offered a regional responsibility as the head of a new business for Asia Pacific, Middle East and Africa regions, by the headquarters of the same European conglomerate; and I moved my regional offices to include Taiwan and Singapore.

A Bus Driver

While giving final touches to this book, I came across a piece of local news. A 26 year old man had decided to quit his managerial job at a financial institution which earned him good salary, to become a public bus driver. Because driving bus was his childhood dream, with the encouragement of his parents, he was daring enough to abandon his big pay job to chase the dream of his life. With his academic excellence where he had scored 9A's in his public examination, his career life would have been financial rewarding; however, he chose otherwise. He said in an interview that after months of training and qualifying, on the first day of his life as a driver, he felt that his life was never this happier. He was happy because he could realize his wish to serve the needs of the aged people, making sure they would have a safe and comfortable ride. What a noble dream of this young man, a lesson to many others.

A Barber and A Doctor

I have always been very easy with my haircut throughout my life, in other words, I am not prepared to spend a lot of money on my hair, unlike my peers; simply because I think all haircuts, whether they are done by the hair-dresser or hair stylist, or designer, or barber, more or less are the same to me. That means I will look for a qualified barber at a minimum charge. Since 12 months, after the previous young barber had left for his migration, my wife and I came across another young barber, Raymond, a nice fellow in early-30s. Over the last months, during haircut sessions, when Raymond was busy with his scissors, we developed a good rapport; we talked almost anything: his future plan, his fiancé, his dream and career, his dog and its life, his concern and ideals, etc. One day, when he was cutting my hair we talked about how fortunate people like us are while many people are homeless and live below the poverty line. He asked me what my view was. Then I told him how my wife and I brought up our children on the concept that to love is to give, not merely to receive, how my son and his friends helped out in the charitable homes for the homeless at the center of "Missionaries of Charity", a branch of Mother Teresa's foundation located in Sham-shui-po district, Hong Kong in his free time. Raymond is young man with a good heart and I encouraged him to do some charitable work to help the poor and needy with his skills. Weeks after, when we met again, he told me it was such a good idea but his good will to help was not warranted by several charities. Then, my wife suggested that we should introduce Raymond to the sister-in-charge at the center. He was able to give haircut service to over 20 aged men and women, who cannot afford to have their hair cut at barber shops. Raymond was hilarious when he described the scene to me last week during my regular monthly haircut session. Here is the conversation between some of aged people and Raymond that I find interesting to share with anyone. An aged man said to Raymond: "How nice of you to have you willingly cut my hair, we used to have a nice old lady who could not see too well, she struggled to give us haircut, look at me, this is how she cut my hair and I was a bit worried that she might have my ear cut off one time." According to Raymond, the man's hair looked a bit chaotic. Another woman said to Raymond: "Young man, thank you for helping us here, you are so patient and you cut so well." And Raymond answered them in a long line up, "Grandma, it's fine. If I don't, then I might as well don't come at all." Such a good reminder to us that, any form of diligent work, even a barber's job, is directed as a service to others, and for free!

In a similar way, one of my friends, Pablo, who is a medical doctor upon hearing the story of the barber Raymond's charitable act in giving free haircut to the aged and homeless people, wanted to do his share. He has decided to give medical consultation to groups of aged people at the center of the "Missionaries of Charity" and he has also, on his own initiative, given the necessary medicines for free to the less-privilege people on the monthly basis. I think charitable work could be "contagious", that attracts each other, especially for people with kind hearts.

Balancing Work and Family

A military general once complained to a close friend the: "You know, I don't get it. In the barracks where I am a commander general, when I give a command, everyone says 'yes, sir'; when I say to my fellow lieutenants, or my commanding officers, 'do this', they will do it without a fuss. However, when I get home, I am nobody, I am totally lost. As soon as my wife hears me entering the house, she asks me to do things; at times, even worse, she will ask me to pick up something at the nearby laundry shop. And my kids, they have no respect for me, my five years old wanted me to act as a horse and let him ride on my shoulders, it's ridiculous!" "You know? I am a general and I have no say at my own home, what a mess!"

When discussing the problems of husband-father in reconciling professional obligations with marital and family responsibilities, we find that these were the same problems in the past. However, today it is a problem that must be faced by wives and working mothers as well. Due to collapse of the global financial market in the recent years, that induced social and economic imbalance worldwide, cost of living has escalated, there is higher unemployment rate and scarcity of jobs which exert unnecessary burden onto many people among the younger generations and countless families which in turn create social unrests, directly and indirectly across the continents. In many cases due to job requirements, frequent traveling takes the main bread-earner, the father-husband or in some cases, even both spouses, away from their family thus depriving children's rights of having their parents present in their upbringing. Nine out of 10 people who I asked "what is your priority in your life?" replied "family comes first and work comes second; but in reality, in their daily lives, the actual priority is: work, work and then work! The disordered priorities of life are well accepted by many people of our modern society as if the importance of family and children are subordinated to the demands of work and social life.

A clear manifestation of "balanced life between work and family" is that man is the subject, not the object of work. Work must first and foremost support the dignity of man in order that he can perform truly, earning necessary income to support his family and children and also be able to fulfill his potential as a person. A husband should never use his professional obligation as an excuse for his failures in carrying out marital and family responsibilities. A man is married to his wife and not to his job, and if his job begins to take the place of his wife and family, he initially will find himself motivated and energized in his doing his task, but quite soon he will find himself disoriented, a lonely person and unhappy and he will soon wither.

The professional work of husband and wife, of father and mother, should be compatible with the essential vocation of spouses on the one hand, and with fatherhood and motherhood on the other. Parents who use their professional jobs as an excuse to minimize giving themselves to their children according to their needs, or not finding the necessary time for mutual sharing as a couple, are undermining the very foundation of their marital commitment and the welfare of the family.

Husband and wife should feel equally responsible, each one assuming the complementary role in the cultural development of their children. Both partners will have to weigh up their material and affective needs in every case. They should analyze the most dominant features of their characters and capabilities, so that whatever the situation they would always provide maximum service to their family as their top priority. Thus, each spouse would have the opportunity to achieve their personal fulfillment in life through different stages of their own vocation in marriage, to which they should orientate their conjugal commitment for the benefit of the mutual and selfless love in marriage.

Marital love needs time and patience. It is quite easy to deceive oneself and look for material substitutes that will never match the need for the sharing that true love calls for. Quality of time spent in family life is only possible when there is enough time to spend with the family. Without giving in to make-believe and to illusions, one has to begin with the actual amount of time he or she has available for each other. From there, he would have to cultivate, as much as possible, an intense family life.

Intense family life does not mean the husband-father acts as an observer by watching others, his wife and children or helper, to be the buzzing bees; he himself has to participate in the household chores, be actively involved in serving the needs of his family members, for example, making the family dinner an enjoyable occasion for everyone on the table, creative enough to prepare a funny story to tell his children, sharing the day's incidence that has moral education values with the spouse and children etc. Somehow, it must be the mystery of human nature that only when the husband-father starts to discover through active involvement in creating an intense and happy family life together with spouse and children, will he be able find true joy and true satisfaction of his inner desire for love and beloved.

A happy and satisfied husband-father would be very unlikely to look for other forms of happiness and satisfaction outside the family, thus intense and happy family life; and strong spousal commitment is the natural "firewall" in defense of the integrity of the marital spouses from temptation of all kinds.

The use of an integrated work–family–personal diary could be an effective tool for balancing work-family life. The habit of entering the schedule of professional appointments, family schedule and personal appointments in one diary would greatly help in managing our time, for example, reminding us the simple but very important appointment of watching your son in action at the school sports. Thus, the family schedule may be noted on the same page signifying that this schedule is as important as professional or personal meetings and will easily be kept in mind. Unless it is done this way, the appointed time with the family will always certainly be buried underneath the thousands of urgent matters of each day.

If a client of the company would like to make an ad-hoc dinner appointment at 8.30 in the evening followed by another program, especially when it is foreseeable that the husband-father needs to be home at that time with his wife and children, then the husband should try his best to defend his "family-turf" from his superiors and clients, and ingeniously device to re-schedule the meeting to another time slot so that the client would not feel neglected. This little tactic is necessary because such incidences happen all the time in any organization. If one does not take extraordinary measure to defend the "family turf", eventually everyone will suffer. In reality, it is also good for the client to be reminded gently every now and then that he should also return to his own family at that hour. At times, scheduling business entertainment with clients or business partners during lunch hours would leave ample options for family time and has proven an effective way in managing balanced work-family life.

When at home, it would be good to turn off the cell phone or computer from certain time onward of the evening while letting people know about it, so as to minimize disruption of family life on a regular basis. It is recommended that husband and wife should mutually discuss before deciding on the family schedule, or on occasions when work and family schedule clashes. The recommendation of the wife should be heard and respected, as these matters of scheduling do not concern only one but the welfare of everyone in the family. Both husband and wife would have to consider special changes in the schedule like work overtime as it is time taken away from the family.

Home is not a Board Room

The following is a true story of a couple who are successful in business. The husband is the chairman of the board, while the wife is the vice chairman in the same company. Their dining table at home had soon become the boardroom where corporate and business issues were discussed on the dining table while having dinner with their children. After some years, their children were nowhere to be found at dinner time, just the two of them who remained arguing business issues at home, soon enough their marital lives were tense, unity was jeopardized. My advice is: "when you leave office everyday, lock the door and also the work behind the company door. Minimize, if possible, to bring your work home, as much as you can". Then "before arriving home, you should be psychologically prepared for another activity — family — and no work please. The focus at home should be to bestow attention to your wife and the kids, crack a few jokes to make them happy and let them see and feel that you have been thinking of them; and you enjoy being with them. It is very important." The time between the closed office door and the door of our home should allow the husband-father to psychologically prepare for a different type of activity for his family.

Fulfilling one's responsibility and commitment in marriage is also a source of joy and peace. Married couples have natural needs of each other, children have needs from their parents, they need to wake up from the illusion that marriage will take care by itself without much effort from each member of the family. It is absolutely essential for married couple with good professional careers to realize the underlining danger and opportunity to lead a well balanced family, professional and social life. And be able to reconcile professional obligations with marital and family responsibilities by maintaining and balancing professional, family and social life — these are keys to happy and successful life. There should be a clear distinction between the three important sectors in our life: family, work and social life. Proper allocation of time to each sector with little effort is required to maintain a healthy segregation between them and yet a smart integration of all three will definitely help foster a well balanced life. The reason is simple, because the source of strength, happiness and contentment in one's life primarily comes from a healthy, happy and fulfilling family life; the natural sequence can never be vice versa. In other words, to achieve balance in professional and social life, one must have the foundation of a happy and fulfilling family life, with the spouse and children.

My Days in NGOs

In 1988, my wife and I came across a family enrichment program through a Spanish friend of ours who was with an international organization (IFFD) that promotes family enrichment activities. We were so fascinated that we decided to get involved and from then onward we started our journey of professional counseling in parenting and matrimonial love matters that brought knowledge, skills and experience to hundreds and hundreds of married couples and families.

People learn the essentials and values of work primarily at home. Without proper formation from parents through intense family life, our world would likely be operated by capable but irresponsible people, "technically capable barbarians". Family is the most ideal environment that fosters proper upbringing of children. Children brought up in a family where they have seen and learned the dignity and value of work would become responsible individuals not only to raise a family, or possess a good profession, but also capable of contributing to the common good of the society. St. Josemaria once said: "...you must understand that God is calling you to serve Him in and from the ordinary, material and secular activities of human life. He waits for us everyday, in the laboratory, in the operating theatre, in the army barracks, in the university chair, in the factory, in the workshop, in the fields, in the home and in all the immense panorama of work. Understand this well: there is something holy, something divine, hidden in the most ordinary situations, and it is up to each one of you to discover it,..."

To be involved in non-profit charities is also work, in fact the essence of work as to serve becomes much more visible as you do not get paid, yet you will most probably end up subsidizing the charitable endeavor while dedicating your free time. At times, you might invite unnecessary trouble when faced with people who suspect the efforts and enthusiasm that you willfully plowed into the NGO.

My Spanish friend, Rafael, once said to me when we were on trip together many years ago: "It normally takes three preceding generations to make one generation good and righteous". It did sound special to me especially as the comment came from a European, as it has a stunning resemblance with our Asian values, a famous Chinese proverb resonates: "It takes ten years to bring up a tree, yet it takes a century (approximately three generations) to raise a righteous person."

This proverb further explains the significance of raising a good generation; let's say if I want my children to be good and upright, first of all, I have to be good and upright. The reason that I am able to be good and upright is because I have been raised and fostered in such a way by my parents who believed to be good and upright was important to their lives and to their children's lives. But who had such an influence on my father and mother in making them who they were? It must have been started from someone who raised my father and mother, their respective parents, and from whom they witnessed and learned how it took to be good and upright. It is obvious that these values of being good and righteousness are cascaded down from one generation to the next from their respective parents, from my grandparents all the way to my generation and beyond.

Conclusion

From the beginning of the chapter, we have discussed "work is to serve". Everyone should work irrespective of his or her financial position, whether he or she is wealthy or not, whether he needs to work for money or not; in order that a person can manifest his talents through work and be useful at the service of others.

Work must not be an instrument of division between people and family, but as an instrument of unity. Work in our modern society plays an important role of bringing unity amongst the family members and spouses as in the case of 'work is to serve' family; but it also has a power to divide the unit of spouses and family, if family and work are not properly balanced and well managed. We are living in world which has a socially accepted culture that promulgates excessive self-indulgence and self-gratification in one's professional work. To lead a balanced work and family life is of utmost importance for the capable husband and the efficient wife to ensure their family gets the best of the both worlds, especially in a modern society like ours.

To do diligent work, a person should have relevant and good attitude to work with people and issues. He thus devices a conscientious solution; like the empathetic young man in the MTR. We know by now that good characters and values drive his attitude. However, merely having good attitude is not enough, to achieve the best possible objective of "work to serve", a person needs to have a decent and righteous intention, or rectitude of intention.

When the purpose of work is merely to serve one's own glory and self-gratification, it reflects "self-love". However, when the ultimate purpose of work is at the service of others, family and society, with the righteous attitude and rectitude intention; it reflects "love for others", which supplements the organic structure of this book, "Mirror of Love", and its values that we all try to instill.

Chapter 6

Father as Primary Educator

In a recent lunch gathering, when a friend of mine learned about the title of this chapter "Father as the primary educator", besides being curious, he kept asking me questions for the reasons I chose father, and not mother as the title? Is mother not the primary educator of her children as well? This was followed by plenty of relevant arguments justifying his point of view. I think my friend has a point there. Should I have chosen to use "parents as primary educators of their children" then it would probably appear to be more appropriate; probably no one would ask any question.

My reason for choosing the title is quite simple; the role of father in a family has been neglected significantly, and widely misunderstood, especially by fathers themselves, and even by some mothers and grandparents, whereas the role and importance of motherhood is much easier for people to identify and understand. Motherhood is naturally built within womanhood; it is then further fostered from the moment of her baby's conception through physiological and psychological experiences throughout the pregnancy and beyond; whereas, fatherhood is not.

Until recent years, when we walked through the section in a bookstore which exhibits parenting formation and child-care practice, we would probably notice that majority of the books are devoted in mother–child relationship in the upbringing of children, it is less common to find books that emphasize the importance of the role of a father. Thus, it is not the intention of this chapter to neglect the importance of motherhood, but to emphasize few aspects of true fatherhood that are fundamentally important for the child's development, in becoming a mature, well-groomed and confident individual. Obviously, fatherhood is a very essential and important role, it has an enormous influence on children's lifelong strength of character and overall developmental needs of the children. Unfortunately, the father's role has been substantially neglected and overlooked in many families.

Half-a-Dad

A young father is normally excited by his first born child and he probably will exert most of his energy on his first child, he takes special efforts to adapt to his new role as father. With the help of his wife, the new father would probably try to get involved with child-care, making effort to work and learn according to the tempo of his wife, he learns to enjoy taking care, feeding and playing with the baby at home.

Quite often, this co-operative child-minding situation of the wife and husband continues for a few years when the next child comes along, the husband-father finds himself quite satisfied with the second child, then he will probably look forward to their third child and the next ones to come. In many cases, when the elder child reaches two years old, the couple would spend substantial time in searching for the "best" kindergarten for this little creature. At times, this supposedly simple operation of finding school gives many sleepless nights to the wife, and perhaps to the husband as well due to the stress from his wife and her peer group. From the moment the child begins his/her life at a "renowned and quality" school, the excitement of the young father would seem to drop quite a bit. He would seem to be more relaxed and satisfied that the child is now in good hands, and is well taken care by the school and teachers; while his wife would take care of the rest, including overall parental education of the child. His attention towards the children will be swayed by his focus on his professional and social obligations; and gradually he would spend less time at home and so would have lesser opportunities to play with his children as before.

Time passes quickly before he realizes, his first born would start becoming a nuisance and disobedient to parents in years after the age of reasoning. It is highly probable that this father could not obtain any satisfaction from upbringing and educating his children, he would tend to re-focus his energy back at his work as his career prospers; while his wife would accept this reality in silence. The next event that would awake this father is probably a shock from a serious incidence of his teenage child; such as, drug or sex-related problem of the adolescence, which we see and hear from the daily news. This phenomenon of "half-a-dad situation" is becoming quite common in our society which grows beyond the boundaries of cultures and geographical differences.

In general, unlike the wife, the husband has a natural tendency of alienating himself from the daily physical encounters with his children, especially with adolescent children; he does not feel easy to show his affection, or being playful with his growing children. It may be either due to his nature, or character defects, or temperament, and therefore, a responsible father should strive hard to learn his fatherhood and device tactics to overcome his inclination to not becoming an affectionate father. In many cases that my wife and I have witnessed, the upsurge of "excused-fatherhood," situation in many good and intact families, quite often this "half-a-dad" situation is considered as normal and accepted by the couple-parents in our today's society, until one day when they would receive a wakeup call.

Dad, I Want Your Time

I recall a very good and interesting movie which my family and I watched quite some years ago, the characters and its story echo "Dad, I want your time." The movie is about two Asian families, one is well-to-do four-household family, an executive father and his wife and two teenage sons. The other is single-parent family, a handicapped father and a teenage son who lived in the edge of the society. This well-to-do family of four and a grandmother live relatively well and comfortably in a house, the father is a successful executive, very busy and immersed into his career, while the mother is kind hearted full-time housewife. The older teenager, probably about 15 years old has gotten himself into trouble with peer groups, peddling in drugs and shoplifting for money, gang bully and fights. The younger son craves for his father's time and attention but it seems his father never realized it.

Then there is upcoming school-play enacted by various students before the end of the school year where the younger son has an act in the play. He wants his father and mother to see him at the play. However, the pre-teenage boy could not get any affirmative answer from his dad if he would go with his wife to see the school play. The father of this child replied with strong conviction, "You know how busy I am and my time is so expensive, my son, but I will try." While the teacher asks each student to confirm the parents attendance, this young son out of desperation, decides to steal money from the tuck-shop of the school, but gets caught in the act, and the incident gets reported to the office of the school headmaster. The parents are summoned by the school of the theft and a meeting is setup at the school. Back at home after the incident, his mother is sad while the furious father waits for the pre-teenage boy holding a stick readily to beat the boy up. The father asks 'How could you do such a thing to yourself and to you family by stealing?' The son confessed with tears and says "I don't have money because I have given all my saving to my elder brother for he needs it urgently. I steal money from the shop to because "I want to "buy" some of your time, dad, so that you and mom would go to my school-play." The father and mother burst into tears with remorse.

In my opinion, the center-piece of the movie is "Do we, parents, really understand our children and their genuine needs, at different stages in their life? Do we know and understand them well enough to be able to offer our support? Do we have time for our children? Are we there when they need us?" The story in the movie helps us to see from the teenager's perspective common teenage issues that they face, the peer pressure, isolation and concerns they may have, instead of the usual parents' perspective of how we "interpret" what we like to see, based on parents' opinion and perception.

In the upbringing of a healthy teenager from childhood, a boy or girl needs to experience many aspects of her father. To experience who he really is, his voice, his embrace, how he does things or cooks meal for the family, she needs to have close encounters with her father, in person, in order to establish a realistic and genuine relationship with him. Furthermore, the child needs to experience the true personality of her father, his likes and dislikes, the time to play and joke with her, and the chance to ask him questions and to hear his voice, and his views about anything under the sun that may help her in developing her personality.

A father must learn to overcome the natural tendency of alienating himself with his growing children, he must realize that his role as a father has much more substance than to just having a fatherhood-by-title and bring home the money, while leaving conveniently everything else of children's upbringing to his wife. What a child craves for is more than her biological needs — food and sleep, academic education from the school. What she needs is her father's presence and his attention, showing his strong interests in her life and things that happen around her life, as a guardian, as a protector and provider, as a coach, as a truthful and trustful friend, a supporter, and a genuine father whose life would become the co-ordinates of children's life.

I Am Lonely, I Steal

A 11 year old boy, Tom, was from a well-to-do family, his parents owned several factories in China and they lived together in a three-story house. But the couple was always on business trips away from home and seldom spent time with the child so much so that Tom had his dinner by himself almost everyday. The parents had hired four domestic helpers thinking that they could take care of their pre-teenage boy whenever they were away; they give Tom a thousand dollars a day to spend after school hours, everything seems to be fine until one day when they received an urgent phone call. Due to the constant absence of his parents, Tom had asked his friends to come home and they played jackpot-game by throwing tennis balls at the line of vase in the living room, the winner was whoever could break the vase with minimum shots. Often against the advice of the domestic helpers, Tom continued his games in breaking many valuable vases at home, undoubtedly his act substantially irritated his dad and mom. But they were too busy attending to their business and conferences and after a few words of reprimanding, life continued the way it was.

On a particular afternoon during a weekend, Tom's parents received an urgent call from the police station saying that their son was caught shoplifting and was taken into police custody. The parents went to meet Tom at the police station, they were very upset and angry with their son and did not understand why he would steal things from the supermarket as he got lots of pocket money and things more than he needed. At the police station, the angry father almost shouted to the young teenage son: "Why did you steal at the supermarket? Didn't I give you enough money to spend?" "If you need more money, let me know, I will give you more. Why did you steal?" Even the policemen who were attending to the case shook their heads while looking at each other.

The parents took Tom to a reputed psychologist whose advice to the parents after the consultation was: "You son is extremely bored and frustrated because you, the parents, are nowhere to be found. Remember he is only 11, he needs to be with good companions and should feel needed. I believe that he got nothing else to do but to destroy things to arouse your attention. Obviously, breaking vase did not work out, so he thought by escalating the problem to shoplifting, he might be able to catch your attention...!" Tom's mother looked at her husband in puzzle and remorse.

A growing child wants to know his father, play with him, to see how his father does things at home and at work, how he loves and respects his wife, the mother. Through family life and activities at home, children are able to visualize and feel the love of their father toward them and their mother. The children believe that they would gain the necessary knowledge and values from their parents. It is important for the father to realize that the sustained interest and attention that he has toward his child is of paramount importance in educating and forming the personality of the child during the formative years. Unfortunately, it is only a vague image of fatherhood that is one of the most common missing-links in the modern society, whereas search of a proper and real fatherhood is seemingly a luxurious item in our modern world.

A Day in the Park

William is a father in his mid-30s, he once told me how much he missed his father's touch and embrace as his father was always travelling on work since William was a child. One afternoon during a weekend, William took his son to play in the park and his memory flashed back to his childhood days in the park when he remembered many kids would play with their fathers while he would play alone supervised by his helper. At times, he did not know what was bothering him, he could only remember that he felt unhappy and less confident than other kids of his age. He continued telling me that how he had missed his father playing with him in the park. The strong arms of his father throwing him up in the air, or having him ride on the father's shoulders as a young boy, the chance to listen to his father's ideas meant so much to him as a child. As a grown up man, whenever he listens to any father–son dialogue, in real life or in a movie, he would sigh afterward. Every now and then, my friend would find himself still missing something significant deep down in his emotion crevices; he thought it may be the wisdom and affirmation of his father, and the chance to ask him things about life and his presence when he needed him. Unfortunately, his father died years ago without William opening up to him.

Where is My Self-Esteem?

An adolescent desperately wants to be accepted by his peers as the social norms of our modern society emphasize the importance of gaining respect of their peers in their social circle. Quite often, a teenager could easily be misled to believe that in order to gain respect and acceptance by his peers, he has to adopt certain behavior to please others in the peer group. One of the important aspects for teenage children is to understand the difference between popularity and self-respect. Children should know that friendship without respect is mere familiarity; people may be liked for the good laugh they provide. However, is it worth losing his or her self-respect, or in more serious situations, the virginity, in order to gain acceptance and popularity in a peer group? There could be many reasons for an adolescent to seek acceptance from his or her peers, however, one substantial reason that stands out from the rest, is the loneliness and relatively low self-esteem of the adolescent who has little confidence of her or his being. The ten-million dollars question is what drives the self-esteem and confidence of a child?

In a casual conversation with a child psychologist friend of mine, we discussed this issue. An adolescent's low self-esteem is a direct attribute to, or the cause of, substantial lack of parental attention and care during his or her upbringing. In other cases, the reason is due to the absence of a clear father figure during the upbringing from early childhood to adolescence. In our modern society, there are thousands and thousands children that grow up without the intimate interactive life with their father or mother, or simply with very little presence of the father from the early years of their life. The absence of fatherhood in the life of a child is quite common even in an intact family, needless to mention in a broken family; and the situation is not getting better.

I Am Not Pretty

Beth is an 18 year old good-looking young woman who finds herself in and out of rehab center for drug addiction and abuse, she has been a drug addict for years. She ran away from her bailing officer thus was chased after by the law enforcement agency. When she was caught, she was found living with a man more than twice her age in a dirty container-turned home, in a pile of junk and dirt. The woman officer who caught Beth asked with sympathy: "You seem to be a nice girl, you are pretty. Why do you do this to yourself?" Beth did not like to talk at first, but after the woman officer told Beth that she is also a mother and that she has great sympathy for her, Beth started to sob and said: "I am not pretty, I am never pretty and I am useless, please don't let me come out again, because I deserve to stay there. I am helpless and I don't know what to do." Then the woman officer continued with curiosity: "Who told you that? Your eyes are pretty, your hands are pretty and you feet are pretty." Beth then said while rocking her body to-and-fro in tears: "My dad, he always shouted at me when I was young that I am nothing, I am ugly and good for nothing. Nobody wants a little dirt like you." The woman officer and her colleagues had their eyes wide open in awe. The above is a true story.

The absence of a clear father figure has substantial effect on a person throughout, the subsequent character defects would likely be revealed from the teenage years and beyond, in different aspects of her entire life. This often happens in families when parents are too busy in making a living, or due to the fact that the parent-father has little idea of the importance of the role of father on child's upbringing, or he sees his father's role could be substituted by his wife in his "absence." At times, in some tragic situations the father may be permanently absent such as, in a divorced-single-parent family; or the father may use abusive words onto the growing child either due to his anger in life or simple selfishness. When young children have direct contacts with their father who gives them his presence and affirmation by being there, while taking a personal interest in their upbringing, the efforts of such a parent-father will build self-esteem and confidence among his children, boys and girls alike.

The necessary affirmation from a father to the child is likened to consistent words of assurance to the growing child "don't worry, my son (my daughter). I am your father, and you are my son. I will take care of you no matter what happens." These seemingly simple gestures of assurance from a father have "miraculous" effect that plays a vital role in affirming the masculinity and femininity of the children. It is quite sad to see that this simple manifestation of love and care between a natural father and children of an intact family is overwhelmingly missing. For the daughter, she needs to have a trust-worthy man in her upbringing, her father, to affirm her femininity and identity and to demonstrate that she is being treasured as female person in the family for who the person she is, not merely for her physical attributes, through his fidelity to his wife, their mother. Then the teenage daughter would be fully aware that she is not an object, of man, merely for admiration or pleasure. This assurance of the father would facilitate the teenage girl to be groomed to her natural maturity.

A teenage girl from such an intact family would thus be well groomed in both psychological and physiological maturity that would help her to identify whether a pursuing male is a "predator" who aims at exploiting her innocence and beauty, for the selfish purpose of his physical and sexual satisfaction. When the relationship between a father and his daughter is cultivated from young age, mutual trust is established and is constantly enhanced through mutual dialogue and family life and activities, it serves as intuitive affirmation from father that strengthens the well-being of the daughter, her femininity. It further enhances the confidence of the young girl and brings about greater clarity of her goals in life. A teenage girl, from her infancy, learns the truth of her feminine being from her mother. Through close contacts and natural affinity and a heart-to-heart dialogue with her mother, the girl will gradually learn her lifetime project, as a wife and as a confident mother.

Father's Affirmation

Who needs affirmation? Every child needs affirmation from his or her parents, especially from the father. What does affirmation do to a child? We could anticipate an overwhelming response. In giving life to his child, a father says to his new born baby: "My baby child, you are the fruit of our love"; or "I am your dad, don't cry, I will take care of you." When talking to his son at the age of reason in order to give direction in life, "Son, what do you want to become?" To foster generosity, "Let's prepare and bring some food to the poor and needy on Christmas eve." To foster a hobby, "My dear, let's play the piano in the chapel first to see if you really like it, then we shall talk about whether to buy a piano or not."

In the past decades, our society has witnessed more and more young people emerging from childhood with serious problems deriving from weakness of character; immaturity and irresponsibility, drugs abuse, loss of virginity, gang fights, sexual abuses, moral indifference toward other fellow human beings, multiple sexual partners, marital instability and divorces etc. Research reveals that there is a common trait among these troubled youth: they all have weak relationships and little respect for their fathers. Without the powerful but subtle and natural ways by which the father evokes his presence and takes personal interest in his children's welfare — an effective tool in forming the children in family life — many children end up with weaknesses and uncertainties in their adulthood, a near certainty of creating time-bombs ready to explode anytime.

Such children, in their adulthood, would retain the weaknesses of childhood such as uncorrected tantrums and self-centeredness and other bad habits; and they would continue to remain self-centered, immature, irresponsible, self-indulgent, incapable of making any relevant commitment in many aspects in life. Due to their lacking the necessary strength of character, they are easily influenced by peer groups, or by indiscrete media and could easily be confused in their sexual orientation whenever temptation arises.

Men have different perception of sense and sensitivity from women, the mind of a man is normally more sensitive in the "image sense" than the mind of a woman, thus, the man in general, has a stronger inclination of response to the senses and sensuous matter, whereas the woman, in general, likes attention especially from opposite sex. Though women's inclination to draw attention from her loved ones is natural; attracting attention from a stranger merely by displaying or exposing the female physical features may not be the smartest thing to do. A woman who is confident with herself, her inner being and her external beauty, tends to have lesser inclination to attract attention from men.

A Movie Star

Below is a story of an infamous Hollywood movie star, Jenny, in her mature years. Jenny had a very successful career in entertainment, but she had also gone through a number of failures in marriage that ended up in several divorces. The story of Jenny strongly indicates that her father was the missing-link during her formative years. This was revealed in her insecure attitude in her relationships with different men; she said once: "I was always a courageous woman, capable of confronting governments, but not men." Whether her father was the reason for her volatile sex-relationships with men, we do not really know; but it definitely tells something about the significance of a proper fatherhood in a girl's upbringing. In all her relationships with men, Jenny became the woman who would pander to the wishes of her men turning into a chameleon adjusting to the different environment.

Jenny's father was a man who did not show his emotions, and unable to communicate with his daughter, worse still; when Jenny was a child, her father used a lot of abusive language to put her down, consistently telling her "no one will love you because you are ugly and imperfect." These words coming from a father, who is supposedly the most loving and reliable protector in the family, could definitely damage, to a certain extent, the personality and carve lasting scars in the life of the daughter throughout her entire life. The huge emotional and psychological void caused by Jenny's father was filled up by various men in her adult life, "the men in my life have made me who I am today." It is sad to see that this missing-link of fatherhood could cause so much pain and suffering to many individuals and families.

If only we, fathers, could wake up from the illusion that sways us man-father from the role of responsible fatherhood, we would see more and happier children and families.

In the eyes of the children, their father is a hero no matter how successful or unsuccessful he may be in his career. Thus, a father must uphold this leadership profile as a hero in the minds and the hearts of his children. A hero protects his family from intruders, he provides a roof for shelter, a hero loves and is concerned about the wellness of his wife and children, a hero does not cheat, he works diligently and does not tyrannize the weak, a hero is responsible and lives up to his promises, etc. A father should aim at becoming a "hero" of his family. He is his children's greatest friend, and unconsciously a model and source of confidence, humor, wisdom, security, leadership and happiness. To a certain extent, a father facilitates in his children a sense of purpose and direction in life; the fatherhood serves as the co-ordinates in his children's lives. The common trait of successful fatherhood is that his wife and children respect him and deeply feel his presence, his love, his caring, his commitment and strength of character through out his entire life.

Affirmation from a father does many extraordinary things which seems to be invisible but it definitely sounds magical to a 10 year old daughter, "You are not only a beautiful girl, but also very smart and intelligent too, because you are my daughter, I love you. Let's go to hiking this weekend."

A Sex-Addict Son

Arthur is a teenage boy whose father is a successful entrepreneur owning many businesses including a publishing company. His father and mother are happily married and live a comfortable life together with their three children. Arthur is the only son, the middle of the three. Arthur's father is not only a busy man, he is also involved in many social activities and clubs that take him away from home almost everyday, he rarely has dinner at home with his children and wife. The relationship between Arthur and his parents is average, but he seldom sees his father, and rarely talks to him on personal basis. Arthur's father shows little interests in the welfare of his son, he pays little attention on what he says and what he does. Because of their comfortable lifestyle, Arthur has help from his private tutor in his studies. While he has plenty of idle time on his own, quite often his mother will have to check on him whenever he locks himself in the room for hours wondering what is going on and what is going through her son's mind.

Arthur's mother is a loving, diligent and capable woman who knows something is not right with Arthur while growing up to his teenage. In summer when Arthur reached 16, his mother found that he was having cyber-sexual relationships with several young women with the evidence of the expenses on the credit of his mother. In fact Arthur had started his pornographic habit since he was 12, sunken for four years in the muddy world of sexual fantasies. Since the discovery, Arthur's mother has been seeking help from psychologists, therapists, and educators to cure Arthur's addiction in sex and sexual fantasies. This is an on-going battle as we speak.

Man as Father

We live in a world where innumerable human persons have not been engendered by a father and a mother united by a bond of love that constitutes a community of love and life within a functional family. The dissociation of parents–children interrelationship is, more or less, equivalent to the dissociation between conjugality in fatherhood and motherhood, and this has fundamental negative consequences to a child in acquiring his or her identity and personality development during the upbringing.

In the absence of proper marital union, or when the conjugal union is ruptured between husband and wife, it could negatively affect the personality and cause serious consequences in the life of the growing child. In a broken marriage, the disassociated fatherhood, in direct conflict with the motherhood, and vice-versa, could introduce a missing-link of parental love and intimacy into the life of the child. The child will have difficulty in understanding why the two most important persons in his life who had promised to love each other would choose to stop loving each other, and stop loving me? It is hard to qualify and quantify the magnitude of damage that fall on this young child, but it is definitely a drastic blow to the young causing perennial and possible deformation of character.

The child misses the true image of a father or a mother, the fundamental truth about male and female, what it takes to be a man or woman, and the truth of genuine human love. The confusion in this little creature could lead to a puzzle of "who she really is", her true identity and how much she is worth, in the eyes of others, her peers. If this symptom remains unnoticed in the early stages, this hidden problem is highly likely to escalate during the teenage period. Needless to say, any physical abuse of the child, at early age, by a family kin or a stranger, would make the situation even more devastating.

Fundamentals of Fatherhood

How does a man get to experience his fatherhood? First, and foremost, he has to become a biological father, through the help of his wife in giving birth to their first child. This man would begin to experience his fatherhood from the time he hears the news of pregnancy of his wife, he then psychologically prepares for the existence of the child, through seeing and touching, the womb of the mother. With today's medical technology, young parents can "see" the images of their unborn baby with the help ultrasonic equipment.

How does a man discover this natural ability of his fatherhood? From whom does he acquire the knowledge? A young father can possibly learn his fatherhood from several sources: firstly, from his own biological father and mother, or from the grandparents. In a large family, a young fellow grows up seeing and observing how to take care of his baby sister, or baby brother, as part of his daily life routine.

The young boy sees how his own father helps in the child-care, as well as, the intellectual, psychological, physical and spiritual needs of his siblings, younger and older. Secondly, if the primary source is not possible as in the above, a young father could also learn fatherhood from his own wife; thirdly through external sources, such as from studies or seminar or courses, and through close observation of the nature.

It is quite common to see that the primary source of transmitting the knowledge and knowhow of fatherhood from father to son is missing in our society today. The reason due to "excused fatherhood" has been mentioned earlier in this chapter; it is also due to the sad reality of increasing number of divorces among couples in our modern society. Therefore, it naturally makes the secondly source even more essential, where the husband learns his fatherhood from his own wife. When a man becomes a father through the genuine conjugal love with his wife that brings forth the new baby being the fruit of their love, he realizes that no one else knows and love this little unborn creature better and more than he and his wife. They have started their journey of fatherhood and motherhood from the day of conception.

From marital love, a woman becomes a mother from the moment of conception. As one contemporary writer puts it, "it is simply stated that an adult female will be naturally transformed into a social mother when she bears a child, however, there is no corresponding natural transformation for a male." JP-II said: "A father has to learn his own fatherhood from the mother." Whereas, the wife should facilitate her husband's fatherhood by allowing him to be involved with his own children; knowing that the well-being of children requires the loving presence of their father. To give emphasis on the importance, men who learn their fatherhood from their own fathers are more readily to become mature fathers than otherwise. A father must 'insert' himself into the bond between mother and child by an initiative similar to adoption; where this initiative is essential and autonomously fostered by the mother in order that children of both sexes are properly oriented to outside world.

Nevertheless, maternal values are not thereby repudiated, fathers too may embody a fatherly tender attribute without ceasing to be a man-father. However, the good news is that the exclusivity of the mother–child bonding is enriched by the personality and authority of his father and allows proper growth of the child and prepares him for the future extra-familial society. Men tend to be more differentiated than women in their responses to people and situation, men are more goal-oriented; their male identity depends to a much greater extent on what they could achieve more than a woman does. While a woman's nature tends to be more integral and wholesome, she could naturally initiate and execute multiple tasks in a simple and orderly way. Both husband and wife are complementary and provide a home for shelter and protection, they have a natural tendency embedded by the nature to educate and form their children's physiological, intellectual, moral, social and spiritual aspects of life and; but they need to discover and develop this embedded talents within them.

Like his counterpart-mother, father has an indispensable role to play in the education of his children, a role complementary to hers. Precisely because of the characteristics that define a mother as a woman, interiority, depth of being, tranquility or the peace of deepest ocean, she has a predominant role to play in educating her children and when their personal needs are of paramount importance. The father, too, has great responsibility here in caring for them and treating them with tenderness and affection, providing guidance in life and particularly a sense of purpose of their existence; and a sense of direction and responsibility in their life. Where the woman "allows" a child to grow, the father "causes" the child to grow.

Give your Child a Sense of Direction

The role of the father in his children's education becomes more and more crucial as the children enter their teenage years. He must help introducing the external world to the child; he must watch over his child's friends, to help him to think intelligently and foster maturity to avoid corruption by seductive hedonists and materialistic ideology. As his son matures and grows in strength, and probably would grow physically stronger than his mother and his sisters, and perhaps his father as well. The energetic young man may be tempted to abuse his strength by dominating over the will of his mother and sisters. Therefore, the young man must be taught self-mastery by his father, and that a strong and upright man who is also honest and responsible will not abuse his masculinity to tyrannize women, or lord it over them because of his superior physical strength. The male competiveness must be properly channelized through persistent help and example of the father, that being upright, gentle, generous, responsible and loving are positive traits of matured masculinity.

Can I Meet your Dad?

During a management training session, several young men in their late-20s talked to each other during coffee break: "I wish I could have a dad like yours who like to share his insights, ideas and his wisdom and experience in work and in life. Going through a cause and effect analysis of the social, political and economic perspectives of various issues facilitates you to see a clear horizon of the panorama of your life objective. Now I understand why you are so good and well-informed, full of confidence and wise amongst us, and always willing to give anyone a helping hand." One of the young fellows continued: "Can we meet your dad one of these days.., for his advice? For a sense of direction?"

A Protector and Provider

At times, a male teenager may need to be disciplined for the purpose of correcting a moral behavior, and the father is solely responsible for this, while a daughter would need the protection of her father to affirm her in her femininity and show, by his faithful love of their mother, that she must treasure her female attributes, so that she will not become an object of man merely for admiration or pleasure. Through the natural affirmation, the father will assure his daughter that he loves her dearly as his daughter, that he treasures her for who she is, not merely for how she looks; the young female will grow in her self-esteem, she will not allow anyone to exploit her femininity and sexual attraction. In this fatherly love, the father has provided his daughter the necessary affirmation of femininity and maturity to her womanhood.

The responsibility of husband and father, begins as the provider of the family, but does not merely end as the protector of the members of the family; as there many other aspects of fatherhood as mentioned earlier. Referring to the truth of the recognition of whole woman-hood as mother, a sister, a wife and a daughter, it all begins with love, which is charity, and in justice as well. Besides different aspects of fatherhood, one of the fundamental roles of the male-father and husband in a family is to protect; to protect the family from intruders and thief, from contamination and corruption of the mind of the children caused by media and strangers behind the computer screen. Other aspects include protecting the women in the family from masculine domination, or intimidation toward women in the family, the possible suspects are the males; the father-husband and the son as well. Children, especially boys, should be taught to understand being the "head of family" is not equivalent to superiority. True masculinity will never put women under his suppression. True masculinity of the husband and father means protection, equality, mutual consensus with his wife-mother, love and care for women-daughter, and genuine friendship that is built on trusting relationship of the spouses.

Domestic violence is one possible outcome against women in the family. Other serious and more dramatic examples of incitement of prostituting wife or daughters, incest, rape and the sexual harassment of children, by the father or male friends of the mother. Society perceives these as brutal forms of injustice of the husband-father perpetrated on his own female family members. These unfortunate incidences do happen from time to time in our society, in different parts of the world. In fact, recent findings from new reports indicate that these crimes have not diminished, and show an upward trend of getting more serious. That is why fathers must be reminded of their role in fatherhood that any inclination toward tyrannizing women must be stopped and "killed" in its first sparks, during the formative years of a male child.

The most effective way to stop this horrific trend of some male inhumane dominance is to provide a proper chastity education to young children. Teach them that respect for the opposite sex should start as early as the child knows the difference between boy and girl. One of the greatest challenges of a man, by far, is to raise his children well. Character is simply the integration of good habits — virtues into a person that reflect his fundamental values of what constitute a good human person. These are internalized, habitual, permanent habits and attitudes, at times, they are called virtues, by which man deals with life, in all its circumstances. Whether we call them virtues or strength of character, they comprise the essence of what we admire most in people: "so and so is such a good and kind-hearted person with such a good character and with well-defined manner!"

Faith, Hope and Charity, Prudence, Justice, Fortitude and Temperance are the main virtues, or strength of characters which are absolutely necessary for a person to navigate his or her life in our society. A philosopher wittingly said: "Character is whatever left-behind or remained in you after you have gone broke or bankrupt." When we visualize a bare person minus his money, assets, reputation, fame and all his materials possession, then whatever is left behind, or that remains in the person is his character. Without any exaggeration, we can say that the criteria of success or failure of a father-husband in his life is primarily focused on "how good the formation he gives to his children," this genuinely constitutes the success or failure in life of a married man. To be fair from the parents' perspective, though we can qualify the input of formation and education that of a father gives to his children, we simply can not qualify or "guarantee" the outcome of the child in questioned. However, quite unfortunately, many fathers, due to some good reasons such as being too busy at his professional work, are unaware that his absence presents a problem to his children's upbringing. Without any malice or intention at all, many fathers fail to exercise the moral leadership and the rare opportunity to instill the necessary strength of character in his children from the very early stage of their life.

The question is how would our children acquire the strength of character, as they certainly are not naturally born with them. Youngsters learn the strength of character, most essentially and deeply, from their mothers and also from their fathers. If children do not learn these strengths from their parents from early childhood, especially from the fathers, for whatever reason, they usually grow up without them. In the absence of the physical presence of the workaholic father during the upbringing of these lovely toddlers, they have little or no idea of what a true father should be and what it takes to be a man-father themselves when they decide to get married one day. When turning into their pre-adolescence, they would have already gotten use to the life without father, thus the image of true fatherhood is naturally blurred and unclear to them. This lack of the true image of fatherhood would unfortunately be carried on to next generations due to the fact that they have never experienced the strong fatherly love and the necessary affirmation, formation, protection from their own fathers.

Woman as Mother

During the months of pregnancy, the bonding between the unborn baby and the mother is established and is gradually nurtured; this close bonding is so intense that it will extend to the rest of their lives between the mother and the baby child. The young woman is transformed physiologically, psychologically and emotionally from a girl to a mother throughout the course of her pregnancy.

As we know, when new human life comes to be in and through the marital act, it all happens within the young wife and mother. A mother accepts and loves the child as a person whom she is carrying in her womb. This unique contact with the new human being developing within her gives rise to an attitude of human being who profoundly marks the woman's personality. In general, women are more capable and natural than men of paying attention to another person and that motherhood develops this predisposition even further. In the process of development of parenthood, husband and wife reach a new level of communion of persons by outpouring their mutual love beyond themselves, that self-giving love between the spouses finds its way onto a new focus — a new human life — their own offspring who is entrusted to their care, love and education.

Through this special matrimonial love between husband and wife that opens to new life, the married couple assume the state of being a father and a mother. The pregnant woman begins to realize her state of motherhood through the physiological, emotional and psychological changes, while the man should make necessary efforts to realize his state of fatherhood by closely observing and learning from his wife. The state of being a mother, and that of being father, is proper to the nature of man and woman who are destined to marry and establish a family.

In other words, by fulfilling the duties and obligations of his natural fatherhood, and that of her natural motherhood, it will facilitate husband and wife to achieve the proper state of their parenthood. Though, it is the husband-father's responsibility to lead the family, his authority is not, however, to be confused with, much less identified with, the exercise of power and domination. Authority is a principle of co-operation, thus a role of service to a community — in this case — a family. Marriage and family life involve intimate and continual co-operative thoughts and action, and to cultivate unified decision is the proper task of authority within marriage and family. Furthermore, authority in family is not domination, but responsibility, a mutual sharing of the power and the consequence of the couple's mutual decisions that are aimed at the wellness of children and family, at all times.

Motherhood also implies from the beginning a special openness to the new person. In this openness, in conceiving and giving birth to a child, the woman "discovers herself through a sincere gift of self." The gift of inner readiness to accept the child and bring him/her into the world is linked to the marital union, should constitute a special moment in the mutual self-donation both by the woman and the man. The woman's motherhood in the period between the baby's conception and birth is a bio-physiological and psychological process which is better understood in our days than in the past, and is subject of many detailed studies. Scientific findings fully confirms that the psycho-physical structure of women is naturally disposed to motherhood — conception, pregnancy and giving birth — that is a consequence of the marital union with the husband man.

Home is Where the Mother is

Once Mother Teresa picked up a child from the streets and took him to a Children's Home, gave him a bath, cleaned his clothes, everything, but after a day the child ran away. He was found again by somebody else but again he ran away. Then she said to the sisters: "Please follow that child. One of you stay with him and see where he goes when he runs away." And the child ran away the third time. There under a tree was the mother, she was cooking something that she had picked up from the dustbins. The Sister asked the child: "Why did you run away from the home?" And the child said: "But this is my home because this is where my mother is." (*Ref. Mother Teresa*)

"Home is where the mother is" so much truth in it. In the little mind of this boy, that the food pieces were taken from the dustbin was all right because mother will take care of everything, she will have it cleaned and cook before she let me eat. It was the mother who hugged the child, who wants and love the child; the child has his mother around, that was all he wanted. In a spousal relationship, husband and wife share a similar foundation of self-giving love, as discussed in Chapter 4.

Shared Parenthood

Parenthood is shared by both the father and the mother. Although both of them together are parents of the child, the woman's motherhood constitutes a special "part" in this shared parenthood, it is realized much more fully in the woman. It is the woman who 'pays' directly for this shared generation, which literally absorbs the energies of her body and soul. It is therefore important and necessary that the man be fully aware that in their shared parenthood he owes a special debt to the woman. Even though the man shares his parenthood with the woman, he always remains "outside" the process of pregnancy and the baby's birth; in many ways he has to learn his own "fatherhood" from the mother-wife. The child's upbringing, taken as a whole, should include the contribution of both parents: maternal and paternal contribution. However, in any event, the mother's contribution is decisive in laying the foundation for a new human personality.

Leader at Home, Leader at Work

Over several decades, fathers have lost much of the moral leadership at home, it is quite unfortunate to see that there are many fathers who remain unaware of this erosion of the true fatherhood in family and its serious implications for their children's future happiness. In our contacts with many families particularly with fathers, many think that they are adequately fulfilling their fatherly role simply by providing a home for their family's comfort and living, and then from time to time be able to participate in family activities, mostly on weekends. Or they thought that by planning good quality family holiday excursions in resort hotels; or with a "well-defined" excuse of giving freedom to the children by letting them to do whatever they wanted, could help fulfill their role as a father and husband.

Unfortunately, they are wrong; fathers and mothers often will not find out how wrong they are until their children reach early teenage and beyond. As we have discussed earlier, when children grow up without esteem for their father's strengths of character, they would show weaknesses in their overall character development. When children reach adulthood, they would be somehow out of balance and relatively "feeble" — immature, irresolute, self-centered, preoccupied with comforts and pleasure, uncertain of themselves — that they would be often seen as creating trouble for others in order to justify their existence and contribution, or merely having fun of a destructive nature.

Children from upper-middle class families almost never see their fathers work; while most of the time they see their fathers at leisure around the house or having a glass of wine while watching the news of the day, or while joining an enjoyable holiday trip living in a five-stars hotel, playing golf during the weekends or leading a vibrant social life in the evenings. Whether it is for recovering from the pressure of his hard work or not, is not so relevant, because children would never be able to understand this leading to a cold relationship between father and his children due to the fact that their physical contact through family activities such as dinner at home, in sharing the days experience, in discussing a view of the news, sharing his insights as a professional, working on the house chores, fixing the broken door-hinge or washing the car; are bare minimum, or none.

1. Today, home has become a place merely of play and enjoyment rather than work and shared responsibility: There are affordable electronic gadgets, implements and domestic helpers in all households today to help with fixing things, cooking meals etc, while the playthings are all over the place: TV, video games, computers, i-pods, table-games. Air-conditioned car with hired-driver has also made the life much too easier than in the past.

2. Conversations with the father in present times is minimal: natural and serious dialogues between father and his children by which the children learn about dad's life and his character, his work attitude, his likes and dislikes and his views about things in life, about right from wrong, about what it takes to be a man, sharing stories or photos of his childhood, is extremely rare.

3. Children and adolescents today function as consumers, not producers: the meal that needs to be cooked, and house chores, washing and cleaning are done by domestic helpers. Children of well-off middle-class households, have very little idea of laboring to get things done, much less the need to contribute to overall welfare of the family and to the society at large. They have been totally deprived from the rare opportunity of experiencing how to get things done at home, and later on in the society.

4. Television and other entertainment media have become the principle means by which children observe the concept of adult life. If a family has no or very little presence of the father, then some other adult male serves in his position instead... the notion of "dad" does not display strength of his character, dad is perceived to be a relatively weak individual, likeable, leisure-oriented due to the absence of the true dad and his rightful father-hood image. Then, celebrities or pop music singers would conveniently become the icon or heroes of the children through their seemingly attractive and successful lifestyle.

A Drug Addict

A psychologist friend related to me a rather sad situation of a middle-class family in which the only son, Ben, was in drugs as early as 14 years. After several sessions of consultations with the psychologist, Ben revealed that he was an unhappy young man because his father never uttered a word to him in person, the father always related his words and ideas through his wife, i.e. Ben's mother. In a certain sense, Ben was puzzled and disliked his father as he interpreted that his father may not have had any interests in him. He used drugs to pacify his emotions and thought that drugs would make him independent and make him a man too! How pathetic this situation is?

A Drunken Female

Wendy is 19 years and has been raised in a single-parent family in London, she is the only child. Her parents had divorced due to character incompatibility. Wendy's mother is a hard-working woman who raised the children by herself with financial support from her husband. Wendy's mother has a bitter relationship with her husband after the divorce, somehow this resentment finds its way into the minds and ears of the four children, including Wendy. After midnight on a weekend, Wendy was found heavily drunk and lying unconscious and her parents were nowhere to be found at the time. Police and paramedics were involved and Wendy ended up in a hospital for days before she was released. She was intoxicated to alcohol at her prime years of life!

Conclusion

I would like to close this chapter on fatherhood with the story of a ship captain that I find very relevant to fathers of our modern society who are torn by their work which may have caused time constraints in spending time with their families. Many fathers who complain of their work have very demanding schedules, with frequent travels and being away from home making them almost impossible to live a consistent and fruitful family life. Though some of the fathers want to revitalize their natural tendency of becoming good and responsible fathers, they are physically and mentally exhausted. True enough, perhaps these fathers are genuinely too busy, and simply cannot find opportunities to spend time with their families, wives and children. Whenever there is an opportunity, I share the following story with fathers who intuitively love their families but need necessary encouragement.

A Ship Captain

A ship captain, due to his life-long profession as a seaman, had developed relevant skills and knowledge in sailing large ship across oceans and was considered an expert. However, his profession took him physically away from his wife and his six children whom he treasures and loves so much each and single day of his life. Depending the seasons, at times, he will have to stay away from his family up to six-months, however, there are occasions when the time away from his family was shorter. Although this was a profession he chose, he hated the fact that this profession kept him away from his family, his wife and his children, for long duration of times. As steering ship was the only skill he possessed, he couldn't pursue other professions due to financial reasons and the need to support his family well. He struggled to bear the pain of not being able to spend time with his children, talking and playing with each one of them, and to be with his wife. He deeply missed his family during his journeys and on each journey he prayed to finish the long-haul trip as soon as possible and return home to his beloved. He was keen to sustain his relationship with his family and devised a unique way of achieving this...

What this ship captain did was, after his work each evening and dinner, while his colleagues enjoyed drinks, socializing and merry making, he retired to his own cabin. He would write a letter to each of his six children individually everyday from Monday to Sunday, the cycle renewed itself every week, non-stop. He would be telling each of his children what his dad had been doing on the ship that day, and how much he wanted to be with him or her, and how much he thinks of them. Individually, he referred incidences to each child; for example, "Mary, you told me last week your friend has won a race, she gets good result, how is she in....?" Or to his son, "Peter, you told me about the captain of the football team wanting to recruit you in the school team, I think it is a good idea, do you need to buy a pair of football shoes..?"

The letter he wrote each day, seven letters a week, he sent them off by mail whenever possible, as often as every week. Each of his children received one letter a week from his father telling them stories, and conversing with them individually of personal matters and encouraging them on a regular basis, as if they had their father living with them. This ship-captain continued doing this through out the many years of his career whenever he was sea sailing from port to port, month after month, year after year. The story has a very good and encouraging ending; with all the children of this captain-father grown up well. All his children have grown up healthy, physically and morally sound, good and responsible young men and women. Almost all of the children have completed their university education and landed in good professions, are married with wonderful children. This captain and his wife have been living happily together after his retirement from his captainship.

In the difficult situation of the ship captain who was also father, he demonstrated his creativity, his fidelity and self-giving love for his wife and children, and the effort and sacrifice that he made have eventually become the good of his children and family. We can clearly observe that strength of character is manifested through the life of the ship-captain, he is a leader in his work, and a leader in his family, a leader by examples.

Chapter 7

Is Chastity Possible?

During the coffee break in a conference, the following conversation was heard: "It is so difficult for teenagers to live a chaste life today" said a well-dressed lady-mother. A young mother replied: "Yes, especially to teach our children to be chaste." The well-dressed lady continued: "Look at the popular TV programs, they all display either violent or sex, and these are so easy accessible by mobile devices, it's terrible." Then she continued: "Most of my friends are really doubtful if ever our children could live a chaste life!" A voice joined the conversation: "I think to be chaste is difficult, but not impossible" and the two women turned their heads and looked at this "intruder", a mature woman who was a mutual friend of both ladies.

"Is chastity possible to average people at all?" is probably a question that not many people would be ready to give a straight answer. In fact, we normally do not hear people talk about chastity, as if this word is only reserved to a rare few, perhaps for the monks and priests, or people out of the ordinary. Once a concerned mother commented: "Oh, I really don't know what is happening to my son. He just turned 12 and has suddenly become immersed in pornography, locks himself in the room for hours, claims that he is playing games, but as a mother, I know!" Another parent murmured: "I am not sure if I still know my teenage girl anymore as I used to, her behavior seems absurd and at times mysterious!" These questions and comments are quite common for parents of typical teenagers in the junior high school.

Chastity is positive affirmation of what true love is toward another person through self-mastery in thoughts, words and actions of human passion and sexuality. Chastity founded on purity of the heart enables a person to see and to understand with clarity that a person needs to be chaste before he or she can truly love another person with self-giving love. Otherwise, quite often, people equate love to sex.

Lust finds its root in inordinate self-love, infatuation in another person for satisfaction of a desire or sexual pleasure, thus destroys true love and mutual self-donation between two persons, male and female, within marriage. A lustful person is usually addicted to sexual pleasures, his mind and his heart are infatuated with the desires of wanting sexual satisfaction, any time and anywhere. To some contemporaries of our today's society, chastity sounds like an alien from the Mars "for me to refrain from sexual pleasure? So weird, no way!" Though chastity seems to be out of fashion to most people, there is evident that some upright, healthy and decent people, young and old, do not only believe chastity is possible, but also actively leading a chaste life in their respective situations, for good reasons.

A Sensuous Touch

During a recent holiday trip in Europe, my wife and I were having a coffee in one of the open café that is set on a beautiful square, piazza something. There was a family, a husband and a wife with three children, who were sitting in another café some 20 feet away from us. The youngest boy must have been about five year old and sat on the lap of his dad, while leaning his arms onto the café table with his back against the chest of his father. I tried to signal my wife to take a look of the loving scene of the father and son. Suddenly we saw something strange — the young boy started to move back and forth, and then we noticed something quite "beyond-the-ordinary". The father put his right hand under the tiny shirt of boy and started caressing the back of the boy, from his groin to the neck, up and down, back and forth. The five year old boy seemed to be enjoying this extraordinary action, while his wife and other children were sitting with them. Later on, worse happened as the hand of this man turned to the chest of the boy caressing the entire front part and the neck and ear lobes of the little body of his own son!

My wife and I were so disgusted that I almost stood up to question him about what he was trying to do to this young boy. My wife reminded me to be cautious in the tourist area and we ended up keeping our eyes closed for minutes and started to pray for this little boy and his family. How could such absurdity happen in a family? I simply could not comprehend, how ignorant is this father? At one time, we doubted whether this man, in his 40s, was the genuine father of these children; we thought so because their faces resemble each other.

Whether this man knows the seriousness of what he had done to his own son, I really do not have an idea. With the benefit of doubt that this middle-aged father does not know, what he did was caressing the most sensuous parts of this little creature that would create a strong sensation to the body and mind of this boy. This will leave a lasting mark in the boy that caressing and sensuous touches transpiring to "love and sensational feeling" are inseparable. "My dad loves me, what he did is to make me feel good; that must be ultimate essence of love!" Of course it is so logical for the boy of five to think and feel this way because he simply has not seen or been exposed to true human love. The little mind would think that "love is mainly in the sense" thus as he grows he would be inclined to believe that love equates to sensuous feeling of touches and that without sensation there is no love. This is the cause of the fundamental confusion of what true human love is; love is not merely an emotion; as love is to *will* the good of another person; as opposed to self-satisfaction and self-gratification.

We can imagine that the life of this young boy would get complicated as he grows up. Not only would he not understand what chastity is, but he also would remain ignorant of what it takes to be clean in the heart, in the mind and in the body. Whenever an opportunity arises that favors the inclination of sensuality, whether from the touches of a male or a female, the already-weakened will-power of this boy in his teenage, will simply submit to any sensuous temptation, like melting chocolate under heat. Parents, please wake up! Do not destroy your own child (children) by your own hands.

Why is Chastity Essential?

We have discussed what lust is, what damage it could possibly bring to an individual and to a family. Lust is a disorder of man who merely uses sex as an instrument of satisfaction of his or her own desire for pleasure. It is an obsessive desire to use another person's body, or image, for satisfaction of his sexual fantasies and desires, thus it violates human dignity of the persons involved. We have seen the horrendous negative effect of lust that produces multiple types of related crimes, directly and indirectly, to human passion and sexuality as described in early chapters. By now, we know how lust operates and where it originates from — the disorder of human passion due to the original sin, while man (woman) has a strong inclination to sensuous pleasure of all kinds. This inclination includes over indulgence in delicious food habitually, falling in love with the comfortable feeling of the senses; enjoying laziness, idleness in the mind and in the body; over indulgence in material possessions, such as luxurious items and branded goods for the body. Not excluding the sensational feeling of being privileged, meditating the sensuous joy in the mind which finds its root primarily from pride and vanity, "My joy comes from the fact that I am privileged few who can afford many more things than average people, such as these glamorous luxurious items."

The opposing force of lust is purity of heart and chastity that primarily focuses on "love for others". If chastity is absent in the life of a single person, young or old, male or female, it likens a pilot who is flying an airplane without his navigation system in place; or a man with eye-impairment who is driving a car without wearing his lens; or a surgeon who conducts a heart operation without thoroughly cleaning his hands and without proper medical qualification. In a marriage, something substantial and important would be missing if chastity is not found between the married couple. In the absence of chastity, the conjugal love and union will be imperfect, as the sexual union of the spouses will become a means to an end, merely for satisfaction of a sexual desire, either or both of the spouses are then reduced to object(s) of pleasure. Thus, the married couple will not be able to love each other with self-donation of love of their personhood, physical and spiritual, of their substantial beings. Like all human actions, marital spouses that are truly in love with each other, would be motivated to exercise their free-will to decide whether the conjugal union is a "self-giving act of love" for the beloved, or should it be an act of "self-love" merely focusing on sexual pleasures, consequently reducing the spouse to an object of pleasure. Thus, it is essential for anyone to foster chastity within marriage, and outside of marriage.

In normal circumstances, chastity cannot be won without a fight, a fight against oneself, of one's inclination of self-complacency, and self-love that could further promulgate into sensuous pleasure of various kinds; such as, gluttony, covetousness of material things and comforts, and of course relentless desire of sexual pleasure. In my entire adult life, I have not met anyone who does not need to struggle to achieve chastity either in marriage or single. In reality, some people may need to struggle more than others, just like in terms of temperament, some people might be more emotional than others.

Purity of Heart

One of the most effective ways to cure lust is "purity of heart". But it is easy to say than done, as it takes tremendous efforts to overcome a bad habit, a vice, especially a sensuous moral issue such as lust. The most ideal scenario is to start young; when a child has a clear idea of what chastity means and how it operates through the role model of his/her parents at young age; the job of achieving chastity is almost half-way done. We shall discuss the "HOWs" to conduct chastity education in the following pages of this chapter.

We should be aware that precautionary measure is always better than remedial measure in forming and educating children of good character from an early age, particularly in chastity. Someone may ask: "how early should we begin chastity education?" Well, experience has taught us that it should begin as young as the little toddler boy or girl is aware of the differences of opposite sex. Starting from mutual respect for the particular features of the opposite sex; for example, when a toddler boy enjoys to rock the toy-house in rapid motion and all the little furniture within it; he should be taught to respect his little sister who likes to play with dolls and toy-kitchenette. The toddler boy must not be allowed to trample, or ruin the doll or the toy- kitchenette setup whenever he feels excited or bored in playing with his own toys. When he does the "damage", which will very likely to happen sooner than later, the boy must be taught to apologize for his bad behavior, parents must educate the little boy that he should respect girls and the "girly things". He should not be allowed to despise in his little mind that "those silly-girly things!" In the process of child upbringing, a young boy or girl should properly learn the differences between them, and their respective particulars and inclination, and they must learn to respect each other. For example, boy and girls are not advisable to take bath together after reaching eighteen months old, for a basic reason of modesty.

Chastity, in its essence, does not entail merely the external purity in human sexuality and conjugal relationships; it also means purity of the mind and purity of the heart of the persons involved. A chaste body finds its root in the purity of heart. "Anyone who looks at a woman lustfully has already committed adultery with her in his heart."

Rectitude of Intention

Purity of heart is not only limited to chastity, it also entails the purity of intention, or rectitude of an intention of a person to achieve good. An intention is what a person has in mind and plan to do, after deploying the faculties of intelligence and will. The intention becomes an action after the person wills it to happen. Rectitude of intention determines the righteousness of an intention, it further qualifies whether a person has the righteous intention to do good to himself, or to others. For example, a husband says to his wife in their wedding promise: "I marry you in order to love you and make you happy; and I love you from the very depth of my heart!" When everything this husband does, or is going to do, has a pristine aim to achieve what he promises to his wife, then he has the necessary "rectitude of intention".

An intention can be good or it can be vicious depending what is on the mind of a person, and what he sets out to do, or to achieve. A young mother whose intention is to ensure that everything she does is to give the best in nursing her baby. Even though she may have made small mistakes as in overfeeding her baby in the first week due to her inexperience, her intention was as pure as its original form in the nature of her motherhood.

An Educator

An educator was hired to evaluate and improve the overall curriculum of a school. However, besides carrying out his work, this educator had something else on his mind: to gain control of the management committee through manipulation of people and system in order to advance his career and for monetary return. This educator ended up creating messy situations in the school; he did not have a righteous intention as he claimed to be, thus he did not have the purity of intention in his work.

A Broken Vase

A teenage boy, Sam, who accidentally broke a valuable glass vase while kicking a ball in the living room which was forbidden at his home. He was scared for his fault. While his parents were on their way home, different thoughts went through Sam's mind "what should I do? I can't seal these pieces of glass back together!" "Should I tell the truth?" "Oh, no. I should say: 'I don't know, someone must have done it.'" "OK, that's what I will say to my parents.'" In the face of a temperamental dad and a kind-looking mother, the heart of Sam pounded quickly and loudly, he silently muttered to himself "I can't lie to my parents, I have never lied, and I've promised I'll never lie." Finally, Sam decided to tell the truth that he has broken the vase, himself alone, no one else. Aside from being brave and honest, this teenage boy has rectified his intention of being honest with his parents, "I want to be honest, I tell the truth!" Rectitude of intention can also be rectified through effort and self-struggle to be righteous.

Two Tales of Donation

Let us say a male donor wanted to make a sizeable donation to a charity to gain access to a prestigious club of the rich and famous for vanity reason, whereas a donation made by wealthy woman who has an ultimate objective to help and support the poor and needy in the slum area, wanted to remain anonymous. Even though both made their respective donation in the name of charity, their intention is wide apart. In this case, the wealthy woman has right and pure intention in her donation than the male-donor did.

A Writ of Bankruptcy

When an honest and hard-working man in his late-50s somehow is "forced" by his debtors to declare bankruptcy due to the declining industry and unfavorable market environment that causes the failure of his life-long family business, he sees bankruptcy as the last resort, he feels shameful of his own failure, whereas, a relatively young business executive turned businessman, willfully chooses to declare bankruptcy to evade debts from his debtors in his seemingly failing business. Prior to declaring bankruptcy he transfers assets under his name to his wife and relatives in order to protect his wealth and to minimize his "losses". Though both men declare bankruptcy, their respective reasons and intentions are fundamentally different. In the case of the older hard-working man, bankruptcy is the most unwanted and shameful in his life, in his mind, he has decided that one day he will make up for the loss of his debtors, whereas in the case of the young businessman, besides dishonesty to the court and to his debtors, he has built his "success" on the pain of others. He has a twisted mind and unclear conscience; and his intention is far from righteous and pure.

A Different Kind of Love

A divorced man, Gan, in his 30s married a good-looking lady, daughter of a wealthy owner of a media company. Members of the both families and friends were happy for this lovely and romantic marriage. Gan had a different objective: he was not only attracted to the beauty of his wife, but also the wealth that her family possessed. Gan obviously "loved" his wife dearly, he did every possible thing to please his wife and the father-in-law; however, after years into their marriage they did not children. After a few years, Gan was found to have an affair with another woman that became the direct cause of his wealthy wife to divorce him. Gan had a golden goodbye from this broken marriage.

Gan not only achieved his lustful objective of maximizing his sexual pleasures with a beautiful wife, but fulfilled another objective of a comfortable and luxurious life and substantial monetary benefit. Gan used the marital relationship as a tool to achieve his selfish objective, he obviously treated his wife as an object of pleasure and instrument of fulfilling his desires of enjoyment and money. I think there was no trace of chastity, mutual self-giving love, exchange of personhood, openness to life and purity of heart in this unfortunate marriage. Observing from the external behavior of Gan, it is highly possible that he has a twisted mind and malicious intention from the beginning of this marriage; however, we cannot be sure as intention belongs to the interiority of a person. No one knows for sure, except the man himself and his Creator.

Chastity in Fashion

Modesty is considered the little sister of chastity. Modesty in dress, in the church, or on the beach, the way a man looks at a woman, or the way a woman looks at a man, the way a person sits or is lying down, in visiting places whether it is appropriate for a married person, etc. In a recent trip to Europe with my wife, we witnessed an interesting incidence in a Catholic church that we went in for a liturgical celebration that reminded me of modesty. While most people in the church were in silence awaiting the mass to begin, a group of young men and women, probably tourists as we were, came in and settled down in the pew in front of ours.

The young ladies were wearing skirts to its maximum shortness, exposing their bare legs in the light. Besides my wife and I, other people in the church, especially parents and families, felt offended and showed their disapproval pointing to this group of young female tourists. Soon enough, we heard some steps coming from behind the church, two nuns walking hastily and stopped in front of the row where my wife and I sat. They murmured some words to the two young women sitting in front of us, and handed two pieces of colorful scarf-like material and signaled the young women to wrap around their waists in order to cover their bare legs. The female youngsters then followed the "instruction" of the nuns in an apologetic manner; everyone in the church including my wife were happy and relaxed from that moment.

My wife and I appreciate fashion and fashionable and contemporary design, artifacts and interior designs of houses and condominiums. Fashionable clothing is good as long as it reveals the natural beauty and dignity of women. But some designers equate fashion to nudity, or semi-nudity. Some women are addicted to this fashionable lifestyle by adopting whatever the designers "dictate" them to wear. This is where modesty comes into consideration, at times we see that fashionable women clothing overwhelmingly displays their bodies unnecessarily that could be counterproductive; a unwarranted image of indecency and distasteful look.

A Bridge We Must Cross

Teenager's curiosity in opposite sex is inevitable; whether we like it or not, our children would probably go through a period of turbulence and confusion while growing up, especially during the teenage period. It is the duty of the parents to provide proper formation and education to their children long before they enter into pre-teenage stage of life to enable the youth to ride through the storms smoothly during the years of their volatile teenage period. It is essential for parents to know and understand the significance of instilling some key moral values in upbringing of their children, especially in the area of temperance and fortitude. Thus, they would be more readily prepare their children to overcome any possible temptations that their children may face of sensuous and sexual nature during their teenage and beyond.

Teenage is a stage of human development, similar to any stage in human life that has its particular need of parental support. Similar to infancy, the little creature demands parents' constant attention of care and nurture to the baby with food, sleep and playtime. During infancy, she needs her parent's attention and with necessary stimulations while playing, she learns well through different movement and senses: touching, crawling, walking, throwing things and playing. Teenage is no exception, the youth has her natural needs but she is substantially different from the other stages in her life development. Under normal circumstances, a teenage girl would have nearly achieved a full-grown physical body as her mother; however, the anticipated corresponding maturity is absent. A view merely based on external features of the teenage girl could be a deception. A teenager possesses a tremendous power similar to that of an adult and yet most of the teenagers usually are not aware of this procreative power — the power to generate another new human life. Under the influence of hormones which are normal for growth and are a catalyst of vitality, and with unlimited curiosity, teenagers are highly susceptible to committing mistakes under heightened human passions and sexuality.

Many parents think that it is too early, or too difficult to begin a proper education about human sexuality to the child at his or her early age; when the child reaches pre-teenage, i.e. between 9 and 11, parents feel they are unprepared and too embarrassed to talk about it. When the child reaches teenage, parents tends to ignore it with the psychological thinking "my boy girl will know somehow as he or she grows up." Or the parents would find a logical excuse that "the school will teach them the relevant sex-education". At the end, most children enter into their teenage with the least idea about human sexuality and its corresponding responsibility. The price at times can be quite high.

How Close are you With Your Children?

From time to time, interesting questions come up in social gatherings among parents of teenage children, such as: "Who should influence your teenage children's sexual decisions?" Some parents would ask "Who actually influences the teens' sexual decision most?" Many parents are quite uncertain of the two questions, while some parents believe that they themselves should influence their child's sexual decisions. It is indeed, a ten million dollars question. Here we have results of a geographical survey conducted across several cities on "Who actually influences your child?"

Who influences the sexual decision of our children?

Parents	= 18%
Media and environment	= 32%
Peers and friends	= 38%
School teachers	= 8%
Religious leaders	= 4%

A rather crude survey on these simple questions was conducted, and the result from the respondents indicates an interesting percentage distribution among various parties: 18% from parents, 38% from friends and peers, 32% from media and environment, 8% from school teacher and 4% religious leaders. If we look at the distribution of influence among various groups, the picture seems reasonable and practical, but if we look closer of the aggregated percentage of influence outside the scope of the parents and put them together, the picture has suddenly become quite alarming. Percentage of influence from peers and media and environment scores 70% as compare to 18% from parents which is quite an overwhelming difference. The respondents of the survey are collected from intact families where their parents are married and actively pursuing ways and means to improve the education quality of the children. This even makes the situation more critical. Moreover, it is even more critical that quite a substantial number of parents are not aware of the seriousness of this reality at all.

Nine out ten teenage boys and girls feel if they are emotionally connected with parents and their genuine needs are understood by the parents, then they will likely to delay sexual experience than those teens who are not closely connected with their parents. The following are list of questions intended to give pointers to parents in education of their children:

Parents' reflection

- Do you share the hopes and inspiration of your teenage children of their future with warmth and encouragement? This question does not refer only to the academic achievement.
- Do you know about their friends (by their names) and their mutual activities together?
- Do you help to facilitate healthy recreation together with their friends from earlier years?
- Do you make family meals and quality time so enjoyable that your teenage children stay home for dinner on regular basis?
- Do you encourage and instill strong family values and establish a trusting relationship with your teenage children?
- Do you discuss important topics and share your opinions with them?
- Do you listen to their voices and see their body language that tells you something about them…everyday?
- Do you set guidelines and maintain high expectations (again, not only academic)?
- Do your children know and understand what you really want them "to be" and "to do"?

- Do they know the purpose of their life?
- Do your children know you at all (what kind of a person you are)?
- Do they feel that you love them, that they are important to you as your beloved children?

Primary Source of Education in Sexuality

Proper education of human sexuality is an essential part of children's character formation in each and every stage of their development, it is particularly visible when children enter into teenage. Parents need to know the subject matter well and with proper anticipation to be an effective coach and role model. Quite often parents would only take action when children encounter problems in matters related to human passion and sexuality, at times it may be a bit late. It is important for adolescents to realize that teen years are for friendships of all kinds, but not for extensive romance. Discussion of sexual morality should be conducted with care and discretion that aims primarily at preparation for a life-long loving relationship, that is, marriage. Dating is not just a social activity; it is a long-term preparation of for a stable and happy married life.

Chastity Education

My humble involvement in parenting education at primary and secondary schools had taught me many good lesions in last decades where my wife and I had the opportunity to contact hundreds of parents and families. Some parents find the dramatic behavioral change of their teenage children from the first year in high school very puzzling; while some parents do not notice any behavioral change of their children. Noticeable behavioral problems of the teens often seem to begin from age of 11 or 12. Their concern varies from average teenager behavioral problems to some serious moral situations, such as addiction to electronic games, or strange hairstyles and weird clothing, spending long hours inside the room, spending long hours chatting with groups on social network, talking to strangers, premature curiosity in opposite sex and pornography, etc. In parallel to these behavior problems, it is noticeable that the school education of teenagers deteriorates and he often looks tired due to insufficient sleep, while he loses interests almost in everything. The boy (or girl) seems to be keeping some secrets from his or her parents, going out late without telling parents where he or she goes, and with whom; does not join the family meals, she is not interested to give the usual greeting to the parents and refuses to have dialogues; and often arriving home late at night, etc.

Some parents often wake up shockingly to see sudden changes in behavior of their teenagers that seems to act like a stranger thus causing great bewilderment to the parents. In reality, the-so-called "teenage syndrome" is highly probable to have begun from a much younger age through accumulation of bad habits and lax attitude in life. The reason is also partially due to the physiological, psychological and emotional changes within the teenager, with most parents believing that their child is still the little angel as he or she used to be as a toddler and continue to treat him or her as such, while neglecting to see that their pre-teenager has outgrown his early childhood. Most teenagers build up muscle tone of an adult, yet their minds are still in development mode.

A teenager desires to exercise freedom to make choices in life, he desires the power to consume unlimited alcohol, of spending large sums of money, of spending abundant leisure time in unsupervised activities. He craves for using his freedom, to wear fashionable dress and hairdo; to have tattoo imprinted on his body; and to go anywhere anytime, etc. This has become the dominant factor of "teenage syndrome" in claiming freedom. One of the reasons for the seemingly irrational behavior of teenagers is the hormones that are produced abundantly and is directly proportionate to the physical development of the teenager. These hormones — biochemical substance — produced in the teenager body have psychoactive side-effects that could cause erratic moods in the youth. That is why people sometimes say that living with a teenager is like sharing your home with someone suffering from temporary insanity. The common trait of the underlying problem is teenager's possession of the power similar to that of an adult, but he often lacks the relevant commitment and responsibility of a grown-up person. When such energetic and curious young people are exposed to matters of sensual and sexual nature under the influence of media, peer pressure, while under the influence of the psychoactive hormones; this could further amplify the already existing tensions between parents and their teenage children.

Parents who are aware of and understand the developmental needs of children in different stages of life would realize the significance of proper upbringing of children with them as role models in these critical years. This is the utmost important task of their life as parents. Parents are able to ride through this stormy teenage period safely with their children, not because they hold the magic formula, but they realize that responsible parenthood and proper parenting education require certain knowledge, skills and some sacrifice on their part. Because of their determination and willingness to learn, to be flexible and be good listeners, etc. both husband and wife could improve their relationships with their children and be good role models in parenting and upbringing of their teenage children to a pleasant and solid adulthood.

Sexual Morality is not a Myth

Some parents think that proper education in sexual morality of their children would come from the school, and some expect that there are programs that specifically cater to resolve problems of their children; or some parents even hope for a "quick-fix". They equate getting a "tablet" to cure problems of improper sexual inclination of their troubled teenage child as antibiotic to cure the flu. Unfortunately, there is no-quick fix in problems related to human passion and sexuality. Parents should expect the re-education process to be long and winding as they are dealing with moral behavior that has been developed during the years of upbringing of the young individual. In normal situations, teenage children's addiction to sexual fantasy and pornography do not pop out from nowhere, very likely this moral misbehavior has been developing quietly in the pre-teenage period for years without being visualized until the teenage cannot cover it up anymore. Consequently, to correct and make good of this vice requires substantial effort, time and self-determination to undo the unhealthy inclination, which was built over the years. It is good to start early.

One of the most effective means to educate young people in sexual morality is not from a certain special program on a specific symptom; but a wholesome developmental education in forming virtues through practicing good habits from young childhood by the parents within the family. It is essential to tackle the issue in the early years of the child's life, some experts prefer as early as the child could walk and run. Much later, the good habits that the child has been exposed at young age will be reflected in the personality of the teenage individual who has the necessary point of reference in moral behavior, and based on his own freedom, knows how to make the right decision, to lead a healthy, decent and almost untainted young adulthood life.

In understanding and educating chastity, two important human virtues jump out of the list, *Fortitude* and *Temperance*, besides, other principal virtues of Charity and Justice. Temperance is the ability to moderate and regulate one's passion through mastery of oneself, while fortitude is the ability to be daring in the face of difficulty. As in the case of Dick (in the example of "Is a heart-of-gold enough?" in the later part of this Chapter), even though a person is kind hearted, he could easily yield to his own yearning of passion whenever an unfavorable environment pops out in his face. When a person lacks the ability to master his own passion even though his conscience tells him what the right thing to do, he simply would not execute what he sees is right. He lacks the strength of the will.

More Tips in Chastity Education

Proper formation of human sexuality is no mystery, nor has it any shortcuts. It all begins with the fundamental knowledge and determination of the parents to see this as an important task which is as important, if not more, as the academic results of their child. At an early age, the formation could begin as simply as practicing generosity at home, sharing the favorite candies, or cake amongst family members, accompanying young children to bring food to the poor and needy, sharing toys with siblings or neighboring kids, reserving food for domestic helpers before the family members start their meals, instead of leaving the leftover to the helpers which may convey lack of respect and inhumane behavior.

Modesty

Another habit that has an important bearing on the proper education of human sexuality is modesty. The practice of modesty at home should be visible: from an early age, to segregate bathing sessions between boys and girls, wearing appropriate clothing for different occasions, pajamas for sleeping, bathing suits for the beach and not the-other-way-round, proper shirts for the boys and dresses for the girls when attending a dinner party, or going to church on Sundays. Movie entertainment at home is a good idea but it has to be carefully selected, preferably it should be educational, the scenes must reflect the spirit of decency and modesty. Help to foster self-respect in young children and respect for others, particularly respect for the opposite sex. Explain to young children the purpose of entertainment as a form of family gathering for relaxation and a change of activity, to refresh and relax so we could regain our energy to work again. At about the age of reasoning, parents should explain the pros and cons of video entertainment, the evils of pornographic film that corrupts adolescents and older generations equally. So daddies or mummies, no matter how "mature" you think you are in both mind and heart, there is no exemption, or excuse of "adult channels for adults only, dad and mom" as far as practicing decency and chastity are concerned.

At certain points in their teenage years, children need to learn about the importance of modesty and self-constraint and personal honor. Girls, unless being informed and educated well when young of what modesty really means, normally would grow up with less awareness of how her immodesty in revealing clothes and intimate contacts could inflame the passion of a boy of her age. At times, girls, either due to insensitivity or simply ignorance, are not aware that seeking attention and/or tender romantic experience in physical contacts with boys, could create serious moral problems for boys of her age. Boys, on the other hand, are usually attracted to girls for their looks, young men who merely seek physical beauty and attraction (in their spouses) could be committing a big mistake that they will only find out later in life. Boys normally assume girls are also attracted to good looking handsome young men, but boys need to know that morally mature girls from good families and sound education tend to be more impressed by boys who are dependable, have good character, are both considerate and tough-minded, kind and responsible.

Mature young women from good families are attracted to men who would be able to take care of his future family and be strong enough to provide for it, and that he would be capable of fulfilling his promises and duties as a husband and father — such as to instill certain disciplines at home such as timetable and simple house rules, to introduce simple job assignments at home, such as cleaning the table, washing the dishes after dinner to enhance the sense of justice and responsibility from early childhood. It is also essential to foster justice and charity in and outside of the family: from daddy obeying the traffic lights to donating to support the less fortunate families with toys and food at Christmas and festive time to instill a sense of solidarity in the little mind of the children. It is essential to show the child what generosity and solidarity really means through examples and practice in and outside the family; merely talking with lots of flowery words and not doing the act could induce confusion to the child that could produce counter-productive effect.

A Dish of Temperance

Like teaching any human virtue, unless parents are prepared to be the role model to their children, it is difficult for children to learn the most fundamental cardinal virtues of fortitude and temperance — to begin, a renewed customs of the family periodically related to the fortitude of all its members, including the father and mother. Parents should avoid going out at nights frequently, when occasion arises that is unavoidable, then parents shall try returning home as early as possible, otherwise the children may start to wonder going out late is normal. Remember the children are like the "mirror" of our life, how we live our life would be almost a replica of how they will lead their life. Occasional going out for a drink after dinner is not the same thing as going out late with friends several times a week on a regular basis. It is better to have gatherings with friends and families at home and to offer them food and drinks as children see everything.

I recall an experience from an international conference that I had attended several years back to illustrate the effectiveness of forming the virtue of temperance in young children. A marshmallow test was devised to study virtue of temperance in young children and its corresponding effect when grown up. A group of 4-year-old children were offered a deal in a study conducted by a university where a marshmallow candy was placed in front of each kid; if any child could control, and delay eating the marshmallow by 10 minutes when the professor (program conductor) was to return, the children who would endure their want for 10 minutes would be rewarded with two additional marshmallows. Before the test started, it was clearly explained to all the participating children that no reward would be given to anyone who will devour the marshmallow candy before the professor returned. A camera was installed to record what was going on with these young children in the room after the professor had left the room. Different 4-year-olds did different things. Some children devoured the marshmallows in a matter of seconds and minutes. But a few other young children managed to wait for the full 10 minutes and earned the two extra marshmallows. The hidden camera captured their various self-control strategies: some covered their eyes, some tried to go to sleep, others played games with their little hands, and some talked or sang to themselves. Those little creatures who were able to delay and control their self-gratification at the age of four are likely to live a cleaner and healthier teenage life and beyond. These young persons participated in the study after reaching teens and they demonstrated their ability to tamper their desires of different kinds, and master their sexual inclination for sensuous pleasure much better than their peers.

Practice plan-menu for family meals at home, which should include occasionally food which they like more, and food which they do not like, in order to educate them in virtue of temperance. Gradually, children will get the message of choosing something that is not their favorite willfully and freely is a way to learn and experience self-mastery as an objective. Children should learn to serve themselves as well as to serve others at the table without expecting others, or the domestic helpers to provide service to them. Parents need to device a norm in the family to teach their children to intake a little more of what they like less, and a little less of what they like most. I recall in the family of a friend and his wife who taught their eight children a song that they all sing several times everyday at meal times: "In our family we like everything, a little bit more, and a little bit less...!"

A Day in a Supermarket

Grocery shopping for the family can be an occasion of disseminating virtues to children. Parents may like to show the children that the purpose of shopping for groceries at the supermarket is to acquire food items that are strictly necessary even though the family can afford more than they buy for the sake of educating children to learn the value of sobriety at their freewill. Place in the pantry and the refrigerator what is essential and let them know that their parents look for most economical substitutes for food, drinks and other items for the family for a good and sobriety reason that they could save the excess for helping other people who are less fortunate. Children should learn to accept cheerfully unfavorable situations, in which something is lacking, of discomfort, such as no air-conditioning at certain times of the day, or to take the public transportation occasionally on weekends, etc. Parents should creatively provoke these situations from time to time to help children to see and experience little discomforts, cheerfully.

Parents should always explain the reason that practicing self-mastery, in acquiring things that he likes, is fundamentally good for the person himself as he is more in charge of his own wants and passion, and he has less burden of his own inclination and yet the little self-sacrifice becomes the good to another person which is the essence of charity. When a father stimulates his children to help in house chores or washing car on weekends, or to prepare family meal together — from shopping grocery, washing and seasoning, cooking, decorating the dishes, setting the table etc. — his children will learn a nice meal does not come automatically from the kitchen, delicious meal need to be prepared and things are done with effort. One more thing they could learn is "their father can cook as well".

A Taste of Sobriety

Parents should discourage their children from becoming slaves of fashion and branded goods. Sometimes, when the children are little and incapable of choosing for themselves, it is the parents who "project" themselves as most knowledgeable and choose the latest fashion as a sign of showing their affection to children which is unnecessary and at times could be damaging in creating a sense of materialism in children's minds. When there are several brothers and sisters, it is advisable for the children to get used to the concept of "inheriting" the used clothing without feeling of any shame. It is also good to receive clothes from other families who are friends or relatives, and make use of the occasion to explain to them the reason is not merely because of money. It is also a good habit to make the best use of things around us for the good reason of not being wasteful and for the reason of environment protection.

Children should learn to take good care of their own things and clothes so that they last longer; to fold their clothes properly, put them away for cleaning, prepare them for the next day, etc. Children should be made aware that clothes bought for them are just for covering and protecting the body. There is no need for any superfluous acquisitions of fashionable clothing; parents should help their children develop a sense of pride of being smart and be able to buy good quality clothing at reasonable prices. This simplicity will help them to be simple, contend and happy.

A Permanent Strength

Every human being needs to possess solid and good character to guide him in his sexual life during teenage years and beyond; thus in proper sex education, the core objective is to form the young person of healthy and good character from early childhood, amongst all other virtues, the virtues of temperance, fortitude, justice and charity are fundamental. Parents need to show the children how to use active self-control for better managing their own passions and temperaments in order to enrich other people's lives. Occasionally, it is good to have daddy, from time to time, demonstrate the virtue of temperance by depriving a beer and a glass of wine for himself as a sign of practicing temperance, while a cola drinks or juice for the kids in a family meal.

At an appropriate time in their young lives, it is good for parents to instill a habit in family meals to have less dishes or prepare some food which is less favorable to the taste buds, and parents should explain to the child the reason for giving less favorable things to oneself that would eventually achieve more freedom and make him a better and stronger person. Try to articulate to children in a positive manner that when one can say "no" to himself or herself freely, it is a sign of strength that makes him a better and stronger person. To aim at having fewer electronic gadgets or toys also enhances the practice of temperance. The virtue of temperance is the most essential and effective gate-keeper that enables human beings to know and to live a life of proper human passion and sexuality because it strengthens the ability to temper one's unwarranted desires in many aspects related to human passion, that also includes the inclination of sensuous pleasure of all kinds.

When experiencing pain or little sickness, parents should help children to learn not to become obsessed with getting rid of the discomfort feeling immediately. Try to encourage them not to be afraid of physical pain and discomfort from childhood, taking advantage of the opportunities that arise naturally such as walking extra miles before taking a rest in a family outing on the weekend. Teach them to accept any contradictions cheerfully and give importance to the struggle to overcome defects of character such as tantrums when young and bad temper when it extends into maturity. One very effective way is that the parents should try best to control their own passions and temperaments, otherwise it would be difficult for children to learn and master this struggle.

Parents should demand constancy in their children's study, their work, readings and to fight idleness, having nothing to do would promulgate other defects in life. Encourage them to engage in cultural and sporting activities that demand constancy and small sacrifices. Parents need to be smart to keep up the demand of the above practice at home without winding in repetition in murmuring to children (which they dislike), as children especially teens tend to have "short memories" in making effort and constancy as necessary. The virtue of fortitude would give the young fellow the ability to forge ahead in time of difficulty, when facing tough situation or uncertainty, he or she would not be back down. It is the ability of choosing to do the right thing during tough times. As if the words from the loving father whispers in the ears of the youngster in time of trouble: "Be not afraid, my son!"

The practice of fortitude, the ability of daring to face difficulty, not to give in without a fight or run away from tough situations in life, is another very important virtue required for living a life with proper human passion and sexuality, a very close sister to the virtue of temperance. One example is for parents to encourage their young children to pursue an extra mile during a family excursion in a hot summer day, or delay a glass of delicious cold drink after exercising, these would be some of the effective ways to instill the sense of fortitude and temperance in the mind and body of the young man or young woman.

Is a Heart-of-Gold Enough?

A mature man once recalled his younger days "I used to have a very good and kind heart, people would say to my father 'your son has a heart of gold.'" However, to have a heart of gold is not enough. This man, Dick, was married for over 40 years, with a lovely wife and two daughters, had left his family for another woman for a personal reason in the last 13 years, but he was torn between this mistress and his wife who was ready to forgive him if he decided to return home. Dick was brought up in a relatively upper-middle income class, his parents were good and honest people, he was always good to people, his friends and classmates, but he did not indulge in sports, particularly in activities that required great physical effort, such as climbing the hill or playing football in the summer days, etc. Dick had a habit of keeping himself "comfortable" in the body and in the mind, and tried to avoid hardships of any kind. Something similar to what we hear quite often in our contemporary society, "I like to take it easy with my life, and so on...!" and he was a gentle and not an aggressive person.

With the kind heart of his parents who thought that their son was kind and good and they respected his personal preference, thus let Dick alone in his comfortable way of living for the entire adult life. Dick was blessed with a little fortune that he had inherited from his parents, his professional talents had not been given a proper chance, while he lived on the fortune and a small business from his preceding generation. Everything seemed to be alright until Dick hit his 45th birthday.

In his mid-life, he did meet a crisis, a crisis of finding new love in a new life with a woman who was half his age. Everything that his parents had taught him, educated him in his upbringing indicated that this new love-affair was not right, in fact Dick knew it was wrong because he betrayed his wife, her love and fidelity toward him, and he had also betrayed his children, who he had held close to him in their younger days. But Dick was too weak, he could not make a decisive action to terminate the "butterfly" relationship with this young woman until much later in his life. Dick had only come to realize his grievous fault in life after many years in his remorse, and wanted to return to his wife and family in his advance age, but he experienced great difficulty. Eventually his quest to return home was accepted by his wife and family, after re-settling at home for a few months, he died with a hear attack at home where their children were born and brought up. This story of Dick remains a valuable lesson to many of us when this story traces its route to the ears of my friends that resonates in echo "Having a heart of gold is simply not enough."

To parents who specifically seek help to impart sexuality education to their teenage sons and daughters, well-formed character is fundamental and important for any person to lead a good, meaningful and healthy life. I summarize, as below, the key elements of forming children's character according to age groups as a general guideline of specific human virtues specially relevant to certain age group. It does not mean, for example, that at the age group of 8–12, virtues of love, sincerity, order and obedience of early years are no longer important, what it says in Table 7.1 is that it would be critical if the child does not know and practice those virtues under the specific categories of any age group.

In other words, virtues given within the years of any specific age group necessitate and include the developmental needs of a child, in short, a must have proposition. However, unless the child learns and practices these virtues in his daily life, in the family as well as at school, with the help of the parents as role model, Table 7.1 that contains valuable insights would be rendered useless in the upbringing of children of good and solid character.

Table 7.1. Critical path of human virtues.

Age: 0–3	4–6,7	8–12	13–15	16–19
Cardinal virtues				
Predominant virtues/age group • Justice	• Fortitude	• Temperance	• Prudence	
• Sincerity	• Obedience	• Generosity	• Modesty	• Prudence
• Obedience	• Charity	• Fortitude	• Simplicity	• Understanding
• Orderliness	• Order	• Perseverance	• Sociability	• Flexibility
• Love	• Honesty	• Patience	• Friendship	• Humility
	• Responsibility	• Industriousness	• Moderation	• Loyalty
		• Justice	• Respect for others	• Audacity
		• Responsibility	• Patriotism	• Optimism

** The chart is for general guidance of specific virtues applicable to different age group. Unless children learn to **practice these virtues** (character formation) from the **parents** in normal family life, this chart renders a little contribution in good children's upbringing.*

Foster Good Habits in Family Life: Good habits can be achieved through repeated practice of good human virtues, and family is the best environment to educate children of good habits, in fact, almost all virtues should be learned and practiced at home, from and initiated by parents. This strength of character that children acquire during their upbringing will have positive and lasting effect throughout their entire life.

It is the parents' task to form — much more than to inform — the children's personalities in all aspects of life including sexuality; fathers have to do so with their sons and mothers with their daughters. This formation does not simply consist in simple lessons of anatomy or physiology, but the lessons must have the tone of spirituality which corresponds to these truths: it is a divine gift, ordained to life, to love, to fruitfulness. It is necessary to speak to the children with clarity and naturalness, without going into details which are inappropriate for their age. Before setting upon this task, parents must be well prepared about what they are to do and how they must do it, reading from adequate bibliography or consulting others who have good experience in such matters. In a matter of such great importance as to provide proper education of human sexuality to their children, parents cannot afford to improvise during their conversations with children, or do a job half-heartedly. It is not enough for parents to have just one conversation and presume that their job in educating the child is done. As a matter of fact, it is necessary for parents to continue to conduct this formation with prudence especially during the pre-teenage period, clearing any possible doubts that may arise in the mind of the child. And to give child a clear criteria and adequate information about the changes which occurs in puberty, anticipating the possibility of deviations and the difficulties that they may face from external influence; teach them prudence for any intimate relationship with the opposite sex, while focusing on the concept of dignity of the body. The success of this education and formation is directly proportionate to the time of parents' active presence in the life of their child, the level of mutual trust and closeness between the children and parents.

Managing Free Time and Leisure

True leisure is not idleness, but a change of activity. Rest means recuperation: to gain strength, form ideals and make plans. In other words it means a change of occupation, so that you can come back later with renewed energy to do a better job. An idle person does not only work against the grain, but he also gets bored in his free time; he is sad, and easily discouraged and very often he is self-centered and inward looking. Whereas when a person works with love and diligence, the person is better positioned to work hard driven by the power of curiosity and self-fulfillment, to make good use of time to bring out the best possible effect of his or her work. Rest is a different form of occupation that is different from idleness at leisure. Consequently, leisure has a positive connotation; it may include activities of cultural, philosophical, artistic, musical or spiritual nature. On the contrary, if a person is only capable of focusing exclusively to produce things and results and singled-mindedly engage other people to do the same, he does not only limit his personal growth in other aspects of life, but also develops a single-polar personality and that of others as well. This makes it difficult for him to reach maturity as a person.

Only those parents who know how to use their leisure time well will be able to teach their children to do the same. They need to make choices between pure leisure through materialistic entertainment or activities that develop and enhance values, knowledge or skill. That means, for example, not depositing the children in front of TV set or computer game set, instead take them to the outdoor world where children gain the experience with nature, such as playing on grass, on the beach where children could feel the different texture of the surface that they landed their little feet on. Or help them to acquire a hobby that requires patience and effort. Thus, children will engage to acquire the knowledge and skill and be able to develop their talents at the same time. Upon growing up, they will be able to live and enjoy their respective leisure according to this criteria.

Artistic Values: Music, painting, sculpture could be exposed to children at early age, let them listen to good music from childhood and to the beauty of music and painting, without enforcing their passion and selection of any particular type of art. Children will respond and develop the sensitivity for melody and harmony in music, or would incline toward the art of painting and sculpture, etc. Some children could have multiple hobbies that may lead them into discovery of the world of science, such as interests in insects, creatures in the ocean and in the sky. All these hobbies would help to enhance their maturity levels and thus help in developing a balanced personality. Show children how to enjoy the 'contemplation' of works of art, by visits to museums, making available some art-books or architectural books, or good documentary of nature and of the animal kingdom etc. Try to expose them to things of the nature and beauty and if parents notice that their children have interests and talent, let them learn how to play some musical instrument from earliest childhood, or photography where they learn to see and appreciate the beauty of creation through the lens. However good these hobbies seem, parents should never force the children to learn and acquire these artistic hobbies merely from a scholastic achievement point of view.

Manual Work: It is essential for children to know that things are acquired with effort and skill, i.e. lunch and dinner do not just come out from nowhere, it is because someone has made an effort to buy ingredients, prepare them and finally cook them together such that the cooked food becomes an aromatic gastronomic delight! The best way is to expose young children to simple house chores. Thus, in households where domestic helpers are hired, parents have to walk-an-extra-mile to facilitate children's involvement in helping out in order to learn through seeing and doing simple jobs at home, and soon children will learn to be responsible for looking after the material aspects of the home. It will the best opportunity for a father to demonstrate to his children by carrying out small repairs, watering flowers, putting grease to door hinges, or cook for the family, or washing the dishes after dinner; these are great lessons to children, "if the head of the family and man of the house would do these things, it must be important." These will help educate children to live in a realistic environment as opposed to the concept of virtual reality rooted from internet world; and help develop their inner potential of industriousness, commitment and responsibility.

Reading books: Help children to develop a habit of reading, with attractive and pleasing reading material. Children's books are well produced these days, and there is a lot of material available. Get young children to express their impressions about what they read, and pay a lot of attention to what they have to say. And, if parents read the same books as their children, they will be able to talk about the subject-matter, content and characters with them. In conclusion, give importance to children's work at home, this idea can also be applied in other areas of education. There are interesting science fiction books in the market which can be used for the purpose of education and intense stimulation. The home library should be looked after well: children should see their parents read, and hear them talk about what they have read and share with each other during family gathering.

TV and Computer: It is obvious that nowadays media is the one of greatest enemies of leisure and the great promoter of idleness that nurtures "brain-death". However, there are programs with educational content which are not only healthy but also educational, such as; programs of geographical findings, scientific, cultural and doctrinal nature. It is also good to select a video portraying human values and virtues, to enable parents and children to view together and share comments afterward, such interactions greatly enhance closeness and parents get to know their children deeper and better as such active involvement in the life of their children would contribute substantially in the formation of their personalities. Children that grow up in families with these practices and values will be equipped with a clear idea of what good media and entertainment is all about, in their teenage life and beyond, they will knowingly select the healthy, good quality and informative media entertainment for themselves and their peers. The possibility of our own children to have a positive influence on their teenage peers is also quite high.

Give your children sports: Give each of your children at least one sports activity, and one hobby, and device methodologies and resources to help them develop it and be good at it. Interest in sports and hobbies should be motivated from a very early age. Sport strengthens the physique and the will, it increases the spirit of sacrifice and the virtue of fortitude; i.e. ability to withstand fear in the face of hardship and not to run away from difficulty: this will better prepare the young person to face life. In training children to be stronger, spiritually and physically, ample opportunities would arise in building friendships and, of course, maintaining good health. Excursions to countryside are good for children: it not only provides them direct contact with nature, as opposed to artificial entertainment, but such outings also toughen them up, by exposing them to experience contradictions in lifestyle, hardships such as extreme tiredness and thirst, instead of a life of exclusive luxury and comfort. Furthermore, physical exercise in groups provides opportunities for children to dialogue, to experience real joy and competitiveness, to acquire the knowledge of oneself and ability, be aware of the boundary of their physical and emotional conditions.

Help them to develop at least one or two favorite sports, such as football, volleyball or basketball, swimming or cycling and skiing etc. and allow them decide which one to select as their key vocation. This would further help sustaining the practice and training of their bodies, and as well as developing the strength of will.

Summer Holidays: Summer holidays should not be long and idle period of days after days of getting up late after playing night long computer-based artificial games. There are many options that a family can choose from, summer holidays should be a time of intense family life: it is a question of having an enjoyable time, by means of varied activities which keep the youth fully occupied. Such activities should be attractive for the children, fostering in them the desire to be with their parents, brothers and sisters. Manual work such as mineral or natural history collections can also be made during the holidays. Parents need to stretch their imagination in order to suggest what activity should be planned, discuss and agree with children of how they are going to make use of this long holiday. Parents could help children engage in activities such as learning to plant flowers, cycling, or to learn a foreign language during a certain time period. Go on excursions as a family, planning them in such a way as to be useful for growing stronger.

To Prepare Children for Courtship

In order to advice a child about courtship and engagement, it is necessary to have exact criteria — to be very precise — both about the connection emerging out of an intimate relationship with opposite sex and the significance of matrimony. A growing child needs to know the moral criteria and the practice of prudence that is necessary to maintain in relevant and healthy relationships with the opposite sex.

Courtship: A very important period to understand that matrimony is a vocation in which some people are destined to marry and some don't. Consequently, matrimony has to be considered as a relationship of two people in love that are prepared to loving each other for life in their marriage. Courtship and the period of engagement is a period in which the couple-to-be begin to learn about the essence of the relationship that leads to marriage, which is a life-time commitment of mutual self-donation of two persons and a way of fulfilling one's life potential. Courtship and engagement must be, precisely because of love, a learning period of self-giving love in which one learns to give oneself to the beloved in preparation for a bright and cheerful family.

Engagement: A good way of preparing for matrimony is to approach it with a sense of responsibility and a willingness to learn the essence of marriage of self-giving love for the good of the beloved. It is necessary to know that long engagement, say over several years, is usually difficult, and if the couple-to-be can avoid delays in marriage, they should not prolong the engagement to an undefined period of years after years. On the other hand, an engagement embarked upon a right moment and well lived by the couple-to-be married is an invaluable guarantee for the future. A well-lived engagement is a time for self abstinence — a time when affection between the engaged couple grows and they get to know each other better, besides the physical attraction, the inner beauty of each of the potential couple. As in every school of love, it should be inspired not by a desire to get, but by a spirit of giving, of understanding, of respect and gentle consideration.

Parents should prepare their children about the danger of "isolation" of the couple-to-be: thinking that the engaged couple is self-sufficient and willfully independent of any temptation of intimate physical contact is an illusion. It would be a mistake to allow the engaged couple-to-be "to stay at home alone" on a regular basis in order to get to know each other well. Quite the contrary, they should learn to open up their circle of relationship to each other's friends and families and continue to fulfill their commitments with families, professional and social duties. The engaged couple will thus be able to learn about each other's personality and different perspectives of their character, habits and views on different aspects of life through the fulfillment of their obligation in different circles. When the engagement is formalized, it is very important that the couple strengthen their ties with their families.

Upright Relationships: The engaged couple-to-be should realize that manifestation of chastity corresponds to those who are preparing for marriage: mutual love, before marriage, is predominantly spiritual. Demonstration of affection, when they are manifestations of love and affection, are always good as long as the intention is not for satisfying one's desire and passion; but to learn to know the beloved in appreciation of the inner beauty, human and moral qualities of the person. The engaged couple-to-be must have a well-formed conscience in their incipient relationship.

Parents should teach their children, long before the pre-teenage period, to face challenges with firmness through practice of the virtues of temperance. Young engaged persons should learn during their engagement, how to distinguish the righteous manifestation of affection of true love from lust and desire which is a direct transgression against chastity, modesty and decency with refinement and clear conscience toward the beloved. Any affection if manifested with untamed passion could be an occasion of great temptation.

It is clear that an engagement needs moments of intimacy, in order to exchange impressions and noble confidence, but intimacy does not mean absolute isolation. It would be good to remember that temptation against chastity, unless one struggles decisively against this passionate inclination, will develop into habitual actions that could easily continue after marriage. Unless the person, especially male, genuinely struggles to uproot this habitual unchaste acts before marriage, it will be extremely difficult to sustain a clean and pure love relationship with one's spouse within marriage. Problems such as extra-marital affairs will possibly appear in the spousal relationship if the desire and acts against chastity are not tackled in the first instance, else it would lead to insurmountable division between married couple. Like all virtues, one must make the serious resolution to grow in the virtue of chastity. Meetings of boys and girls ought to be organized at the right age, so as to foster proper relationships in social life. The best place for such parties is the home, however, troublesome this may be; in this way, the parents come to know the friends of their children, and will be able to give them the appropriate advice.

Loyalty — Fidelity

It is a manifestation of commitment of fulfilling one's promise toward another person. When this is applied to marriage, this commitment is translated into marital fidelity. It is important to educate children about the virtues of responsibility, commitment, fidelity and loyalty from their earlier age so they can familiarize with these values in a natural way.

An engagement is considered to be authentic when the engaged couple-to-be hold the right to each other's affection and commitment in preparation of their perpetual relationship in marriage, instead of going out with another person of opposite sex alone at any time either one or both feel like. A proper formation of marriage also includes the knowledge and understanding of its indissolubility.

Education in Modesty: It is important for women to be aware and modest that relates to her femininity, refinement and elegance. Sooner than later, they will realize that lack of modesty in dress and behavior can be an occasion of great temptation for boys. The essence of education in virtues lies in knowing and practicing "little details" in normal family life. Parents need to explain to children even as young as 2–3 years old the basic difference between boys and girls without going into details of intimacy, but from a simple scientific perspective of physical features and psychology of the two sexes. For example, separation of young children when using bathroom and sleeping area is considered prudent and appropriate. Encourage your children to sleep with pajamas or night clothing for reasons of manner, and ensure that they dress with modesty even when at home — it all begins with the parents. These aspects seem simple and minute and yet they carry great importance in forming sensitivity, refinement and modesty of a person.

Educating Love: If children learn to love at young age, i.e. learn to share things with others and to respect others, this lays a good foundation for understanding human love. Later on, growing children get to learn more about what true love really means which is to bear a little discomfort in order to give oneself to their loved ones and for service of others. If children are equipped with this fundamental concept of what true love is, it will be easier for them to keep away from the trap of sexual hedonism.

Generosity must be lived and practiced at home as well, even though it may seem at times of not making any progress. Children should develop the habit of saving up their pocket money; while on occasions, they should practice giving away some of their money and new toys as alms to the poor and needy. Teach children to be grateful for things they have from an early age, teach them to say "thank you" when someone does something for them, or when receiving a gift or service e.g. from a domestic helper; and say sorry even when they inadvertently commit an error. Practice works of mercy together as a family with the children, this will help them understand the true meaning of solidarity, empathy and sobriety while they would gain first-hand experience from those who suffer from poverty, hunger and loneliness and old people who are abandoned by their own children. It is good for the children to see how their parents do all these work as their role model.

With a loving heart and the will being strengthened through education and training of character, especially in the virtues of fortitude and temperance at early age, children will be in a much better position when exposed to sensuous sentiments promulgated through the media: films, peers, television or social network and internet connections and magazines. The weak one that is normally capricious and has never made any sacrifices for the good of others, will find himself unable to resist any attraction of sensuous nature. Besides, when the time for courtship arrives, if he as a child was brought up with abundant love at home, the experience will serve him, in his later years, as a reference point to strengthen the love of these relationships or to reject infatuations. It is obvious that education of love is primarily focused on mastery of one's character and self-control toward love for others. Thus, human formation and education of human virtues are absolutely essential.

Conclusion

Adolescents, similar to adults, like to know what lies ahead of them and have the ability to reach the goal. They are capable to anticipate the consequences from cause of action they take, whether as a result of good intention, or of disobedience, or negligence. It is therefore, essential to educate children, prior to their teenage, the purpose of life, things that can ignite their interests, stimulate their minds, open their minds and hearts.

When children grow up into their full adulthood, the best bonding between the children and aging parents are those good and memorable moments when they spent time together, those good memories of their childhood, games they played together, places they visited in family trips, the fun they had doing house chores together.

Education and formation of chastity in children involves almost every chapter discussed in this book. The most effective way for parents to impart chastity formation is to start with children at their young age, when there is ample time before children reach their teenage.

A Drug Fight

A 15 year old teenager, Dan, found himself in trouble when he realized that he was bullied by several of his pals who had invited him to a birthday party in one of houses in the nearby town. They tried to get Dan to ingest drugs as a "mandate" of the party. The more he refused, the more he attracted criticism, yelling and screaming that "He is a chicken". A few bigger fellows started shoveling and pulling Dan, someone started to hold down Dan's head pressing him down to bench where the drug was laid. That was the time Dan fought back, he ended up fighting with these pals of his and got his shirt torn-off and ended up with bruises on his face and mouth.

Finally, Dan managed to escape from them and walked his way home. As soon as Dan got home, there were two policemen ringing the door bell at home. When the parents saw Dan and two policemen, the father smelled trouble, but he kept quiet until the police had finished their questioning and report, and left. The father was so angry that he did not bother to ask Dan the reasons and assumed that his son may have been the cause for the fight and so Dan was in trouble. His dad had almost thrown him out of the home had his mother not insisted to hear his son's story first. After an hour or so while everyone was calm, Dan told his story, "Yes, I did fight with these pals of mine because I was trying to do the right thing." His dad stared at him puzzled, Dan continued: "I fought them because I did not want to try the drug that they forced onto me; I struggled to abide to everything you have taught me as a child." Dan's parents burst into tears with strong joyous emotion that their son, Dan, had quietly outgrown their expectations.

The marshmallow test project together with some other examples given earlier taught us the significance of virtues of temperance and fortitude. The story of "Having a heart of gold is not enough" reminds us the similar situation even though the main character, Dick, was kind hearted and generous, he saw it was not right to be with his young mistress, yet he did not have the strength to overcome his passion of sexual attachment with his mistress. What a great lesson? Temperance in self-mastery in one's passion, ability to say "no" to oneself in face of temptation; and fortitude, the gut, courage to forge ahead doing the right thing in face of insurmountable difficulty have become the center piece of this chapter.

There should be a profound unity in our act of chastity by which we live our life and the content which we preach and teach our children. What would be a better gift to our children and the next generations than to help develop in them a virtue of chastity? Imagine a well-lit trail of lanterns along their path of life as good reference point, "blessed are those with purity of heart for they shall see God." It would definitely be much more valuable than the millions of dollars of wealth that we wanted to give it to them!

Chapter 8

A Path to Happiness

On one evening when the city of Hong Kong was celebrating a festive occasion, my wife and I invited some couple friends to have dinner at our home, to enjoy a weekend dinner gathering while watching the pretty fireworks from the window of our living room as part of the program for the evening. The fireworks shooting from the different directions had beautifully lit up the clear sky with different colors and shapes, like thousands of colorful jelly-fishes swimming across the sky above the harbor. It was a moment of delirious joy and excitement in a short 30 minutes performance, our guests had definitely enjoyed the show and the dinner; and they were happy. However, even after the exhilarating excitement was over as the fireworks went silent, leaving a trail of dense smoke in the sky, our guests continued to be enveloped in a short moment of joy and happiness. What makes us truly happy?

What Makes us Truly Happy?

To be happy in the spectrum of one's life is different from experiencing an ecstatic moment or a pleasurable excitement that lasts for a short moment, likens the shooting stars that pop-up into the sky, and disappear into the darkness in a matter of minutes. I think true happiness of a person is proportionate to the amount of love that he, or she, has for the other person, how useful he considers himself in serving the good and bringing joy to others; whether he lives a fulfilling and meaningful life that has a direct co-relationship with the degree of contentment of who he really is; and how satisfied he sees his achievement in family and in work, in fulfilling his destiny as a human person.

In short, to be able to live a fulfilling life, first and foremost, a person should be fully aware of the purpose of his life; he should make good use of his given talents by applying necessary means to fulfill his life objectives with effort, and exercise his personal freedom to do good, and to do the right things at the service of others. Happiness is manifested in joy and peace, which constitutes many different aspects of one's life. "Joy is the immediate consequence of a certain fullness of life. For the individual, this fullness consists above all in knowledge and love." (St. Thomas, Summa Theologiae)

As discussed in the previous chapters, we are living in a world that is filled with a very strong sense of materialism. An ideology that promulgates in every corner of the society and in the mind and heart of its citizens — instead of seeing a person of "who you really are as a fellow person," the value of a person is measured by the exterior manifestation of "what you have, or what things you can afford." This is one of the most important phenomenon, as well as serious problems of our contemporary society that finds its roots in materialism; of looking and treating fellow human beings as objects; for a selfish reason or pleasure. What it says in a plain language is that the value of a human being is measured by the amount of his wealth and material possessions regardless of his personality, quality and values.

A Holiday Trip in Hawaii

My children were between six and nine years old when we went on a holiday trip to Hawaii. We had checked into a hotel-condominium which had access to facilities of the hotel next door. One afternoon, while swimming and playing in the pool, our boys encountered a few boys about their ages and started playing together happily. My wife and I took a walk on the beach when our boys looked for us at the beach because they were hungry. While they were having snacks, our elder boy relayed their interesting conversation with the three American boys of slightly older age. When they were playing at the pool, three American boys cast curious eyesight onto them, one of the boys who was believed to be from Las Vegas asked my son: "Where are you from? How come your English is so good?." My nine year old son replied innocently, "We study in English medium School and we live in Hong Kong.". The boy asked, "Hong Kong? Where is it? We'd never heard of it." After a while, another boy asked: "Where do you live in Hong Kong?" My sons said "We live in an apartment." The three boys seemed to be awed by the answer and asked, "How can you afford to have holiday like this if you live in an apartment?." My sons answered innocently, "We don't know. Our parents brought us here" Then, more questions followed from these American boys: "What does your dad do? My dad works in Las Vegas." Another boy said: "My dad sells cars, we live in California." Later on, my wife and I had the opportunity to explain to our boys that apartment has a different connotation in America than at home. Apartment in the US in general is, more or less, equivalent to government housing estate; whereas, in other places like Hong Kong and United Kingdom, apartment is a generic term for medium-high rise residential buildings, including condominium.

There are obvious reasons why people want to have more material possessions, because they are simply convinced that to possess more material goods would make them safer and happier. Delving into the mentality of consumerism, people are led to believe that the more they possess, the happier they would be. For example, with more money one can afford a better home, children could go to better schools, enjoy better vacation, a larger and better car for the family, etc. Though having material goods and resources for the purpose of serving the need of the family is reasonable and legitimate, whether it makes a person happier is questionable.

An Interview

A friend of mine who is the manager of a recruitment agency asked an applicant in an interview: "What do you want to be in five years time, as your career goal?" The young lady who had graduated from a renowned university replied with enthusiasm: "I want to be a manager, or in a senior position, to be in charge of a team with several people reporting to me." The recruitment manager then asked: "Why do you want to be a manager?" The young applicant replied while rolling her eyes with excitement: "Because I want to buy a brand-new convertible sports car, live in a nice apartment and afford vacations in five-stars luxury hotels." This young lady pulsed for a moment and continued the conversation to the recruitment manager: "yes, that's my career goal, sooner the better, perhaps in three years time." and the recruitment manager nodded with a smile..!

The career dream of this young applicant seems to be legitimate, however, what triggers me, "is that all what she wanted to be? Or to have? We can deduce that this young applicant did not have a clear idea of the difference between "to have" and "to be" as her career goal. Though it is not surprising that this young woman focuses merely on "to have" material possessions as her objective in her career life; yet it is a pity to see the overwhelming desire toward material things as a motivation to work.

Difference of "To Have" and "To Be"

"To have" is more inclined to the exteriority of a person which is normally tangible; whereas, "to be" involves the interiority of a person, normally intangible aspects of a human being, such as, to be honest, to be good, to be happy and to be a responsible husband and father, etc. Below are some examples and analysis of "To Be" objectives in the life of a adolescence. (Please see Table 8.1a and Table 8.1b)

OCD in Consumerism?

We all have material possessions as much as it serves the necessity of our need to do our work and to support our family and our living. However, the point of reference is that when our inclination toward material possessions becomes overwhelmingly obsessive, it overshadows our human nature and life purpose; it blurs our mind and heart that we no longer can see the intangible values of a fellow human; the

Table 8.1.a Who do I want to Become?

	What do I want 'to have' vs. 'to be'	
	In 5 years from today…	As opposed to…
Wealth	• $10,000 in my saving account and iphone-5.	• I read this encyclical to understand what JPII was saying. • I like to use my pocket money to buy food for the poor families. • I like to acquire clean habits.
Relationships	• I have met an attractive girl, she is gorgeous! I want to have her as a girl friend.	• I would like to teach poor kids English during summer vacation. • To study in order to influence my pals with positive attitude.
Health	• I train in the gym to be muscular to attract attention from girls.	• I shall join a football team and help teammates to sharpen our skills through regular training.
Career	• I want to make a lot of money as quick as I can in order to buy a nice car and have good vacation trips.	• I want to be a qualified and conscientious surgeon in order to help and serve people in need.

Table 8.1.b   Who do I want to Become?

E.g. Honest, Hardworking, Courageous, Responsible...

- I need to be more generous and courteous with my friends.
- I treat others with respect and charity.
- I want to learn how to forgive others more readily.
- I should strive to become more responsible and hard-working.
- I want to develop my sense of responsibility and work ethics.
- I want to have a clear sense of purpose in my life that will me give a sense of direction.
- I will live up to my promise and commitment, no matter how difficult it may be.
- When I meet my future wife, I want to give my life to her and work hard for our family and children, so that they will be cared for and be happy.
- If ever I become capable to give alms, or my expertise to help the needy, I will do my best.

---

inner quality and personality of another human being. In many places in the world, consumerism, that promotes the artificial joy and satisfaction of wanting to have more things, is being over-glorified, as if life without continuous glamorous material goods would be dull and unhappy. Without exaggeration, there is a kind of disorder that infiltrates into the lives of many people which I like to name it, "Obsessive Compulsory Disorder" (OCD) in consumerism.

The Handbag of a Nurse

My friend, a medical doctor, once told me after a dinner gathering that one of his young nurses who works at his clinic had recently bought a very expensive handbag of certain luxury brand which was, more or less, equivalent to six months of her salary. I was as surprised as my friend was. The question is why would a young nurse sacrifice several months of her salary to own a such as luxurious and glamorous handbag, and for what purpose? The conversation with my doctor friend continued: "even if she had a wealthy husband who could afford to buy this luxury branded handbag as gift to his wife, the job of a nurse is in the clinic wearing the uniform, where the handbag would be out of place." My friend replied: "I think her husband is a high school teacher!" Though anyone is free to do whatever he or she likes with their money, yet that makes less sense to spend substantial sum, six month salary, on an luxury item that does not mean much at work, what was the motivation any way? Someone reminded me that the nurse may use the handbag during weekends, of course, it would be very useful. Below is another example that I can think to elaborate more on the subject.

Supercars in the Mid-Night

One night, I was woken up by a loud howling noise after midnight. When I looked out of the window, I saw several supercars of the "F" brand, "L" brand and the "P" brand racing uphill generating huge howling sounds from these super-powerful engines in the quiet night of the neighborhood. There could be two reasons: first, regular traffic during the day may not allow these cars to run at such speed, and second, perhaps the owners and drivers of these supercar cars normally don't get up until after mid-day.

Later on, I learned that many of the owners of these supercars are superstars in the film and music industry, or young investment bankers in their mid to late 20s making millions of dollars from the financial markets. Over a decade or two ago, I got to know a foreign exchange trader who owned one of these flashy supercars, he has definitely made a lot more than I did then, he wore expensive outfits, his clothing was branded and expensive, and along with his flashy supercar, he was the icon in the office and on the road. But I came to realize much later that he was out of banking job for years, and with little saving that he had and the lifestyle that he lived, he ended up in working as a janitor in his mid-life in a small discreet housing estate. It is not an uncommon story.

Key Aspects of Life

It is interesting to notice the importance people place in their material possessions, things they want to have; e.g. the handbag of the nurse, or the supercar of the investment banker, because they think that they would be happy once these things are in their possession. They will find out later that it is not the case; they might experience momentary ecstasy, perhaps overjoyed with excitement derived from having nice things, but their thirst for true happiness is not quenched, so they will remain dissatisfied and continue to keep desiring things to fill their emotional void. True happiness indeed cannot be satisfied by material goods alone, because human is not a pure material being, he or she needs more substantial fulfillment of love and life.

There are different roles in the life of a person in which he or she has intuitive responsibility that requires him or her to fulfill, in one way or another. The duty and roles of a married man as a husband in the context of this book, as a father to his children, as a son of his parents, as a co-worker to his colleagues, and as a reliable friend to the social group; the last but not the least, the role as a creature to his Creator for those who has faith. Whereas, the duty and roles of a married woman include as a wife, as a mother, as a daughter, as a housewife and perhaps as a co-worker, as a reliable friend, and as a believer in her faith. That sounds a lot more of added responsibility or obligation onto a man or woman which may sound a bit uncomfortable to some people; but fulfilling these roles well would give a person immense joy, peace and a sense of fulfillment that no material satisfaction could possibly compare.

When a person fulfills his various roles with genuine effort and a rectitude of intention, his righteous intention would bring him the tranquility and peace even though he may not achieve the best outcome from his expectations, his joy and satisfaction would come probably from the mere fact that he tries his best effort with sincerity.

Humility, Sincerity and Simplicity

A genuine humble person is a happy person. Humility is the quality that helps to regulate man's tendency to project himself greater than he truly is; it helps a person to control his inordinate desire for his own excellence and glory. Pride is the real cause of egoism and selfishness, an egoistic person despises everyone else, he is always accompanied by the desire to be the center of attention. Humility is the virtue that opposes pride and the inevitable selfishness that goes with it. Whereas, pride is the origin of all moral evil, "all wickedness has its origins in this particular vice, but self-love is one of its first product." (St. Thomas Acquinas, Summa Theologiae, 177, 4c)

Sincerity is the inner disposition of being truthful to oneself, seeing and recognizing himself as who the person he really is. Sincerity helps a person to regulate the desire of not telling the truth or inclination to hypocrisy, or wanting to act like another person who is not himself. Simplicity is the state and quality of being simple, it is free from complexity; it is opposite to hypocrisy, and duplicity which is understood as deceitfulness in conduct by speaking and acting in two different ways to different people, double-dealing, or making one's external action contradicting one's real intention. Both simplicity and sincerity find their roots in virtue of humility, knowing the truth and reality of who I really am; from an objective and unbiased self-perspective, and from the perspective of the Creator.

In our society today, simplicity seems to carry a negative connotation; "he is a simple 'minded' man" as opposed to "Oh, he is such a sophisticated person." The signs of lacking simplicity and sincerity could be when a person consistently tries to "be" someone else or imitates the lifestyle or action of another person, such as celebrities or famous and successful personalities. This person focuses on the superficiality, of how he appears externally in front of others, he is concerned with how others think of him, and quite often he may fabricate facts merely to justify his appearance to achieve the anticipated visual impact. When a person lives a life of duplicity, in reality, he builds an invisible wall surrounding himself by unnecessary complexity and deceits, his life is untruthful and painful.

Sincerity and simplicity enhance joy and peace. Simplicity, in reality, manifests the inner power of a human mind; for example, an experienced and capable professor who explains a very complex issue or a complicated subject matter in a simple language to his students; in this case, his students would be thankful for having a such great professor and effective teacher. Simplicity also enhances the powerful mind of philosophers who could make complex ideas simple and easy to understand.

A Complicated Man

When a person lives a simple and sincere life, he is inclined to be peaceful and happy; simply because he has no complex unresolved issues within his mind to bother his heart and conscience. However, that is not the case of Jason who craved for luxurious material goods since he was a child. He would spend all his pocket money for a branded sports-shoes, which was almost 10 times the price of a basic pair of sports shoes. Jason had a very different value perception. As an adult, Jason would dress like an senior executive when he was merely a salesman working at a retail shop, and spent most of his income on his appearances. He often lived beyond his means. Jason spent his life daydreaming and had a huge vanity in his mind.

Though dress-to-impress in our modern society is legitimate, it really depends on the extremes of vanity and practicality that swings from one side to the other like a pendulum. Jason did not only live from paycheck to paycheck, he lived on his credit cards, he had a negative balance in his bank account. He enjoyed to shine in front of people and often would tell great stories and dreams that were obviously beyond his ability. One time, he claimed that his small companies were worth hundreds of million dollars each, whereas in reality, they probably were worth less than ten thousands each. Yet he told his foreign business partner that his companies would be publicly listed (IPO) in a matter of few months when, in reality, he had no idea of what it takes for a company to meet the listing requirements of the country. Obviously, his "dreams" were short-lived, all the overwhelming impressive promises that he made were never realized, people who worked with Jason, or close to him, eventually realized that whatever Jason said or promised was not real. Jason always promised things much larger than what they really were, and his promises never come true. It was like Jason lived in a dream or virtual reality all the time, yet he and his actions were real.

Jason managed his small business without knowing the basic principles and criteria that any business needs, such as the difference between account-receivable and profit; he suffered from an illusion that the money which his company received was money for his personal spending. That was how his personal spending would get an upswing, to buy a new car for no reason, or to buy jewelry and expensive watches for his wife when she already had plenty in her safety box while they had no saving for their child's future education.

Jason had little idea of cost structures while he had an unexplainable illusion of equating sales turnover with profits; thus, he thought that the annual sales turnover of the company equivalent to his wealth, the money in his pocket, and he ignored costs, expenses, account-payables and account-receivables, cash flows and financial costs, etc. When friends tried to lend a helping hand to him, or advice him to study accounting and business management, he told them off by saying he was born to be a business genius, and that only college boys needed to study, he as an brilliant entrepreneur did not need to study or learn anything. In reality, Jason had not graduated from his high school, he once told a friend that eventually he would go to college and would graduate from a university sooner than his daughter finished her studies. Obviously, he never did.

When people close to Jason tried to lend a helping hand to his business, Jason was always suspicious that people might possess bad intentions to rob him of his profits; this resulted in people, who had initially wanted to help, losing their original enthusiasm. However, when Jason discovered he needed help, he expected his friends to lend him a large sum of money as easily as probably drawing water from a tap. As if in his mind, the word "help" only meant to give him the money and do not ask questions. When his friends queried the size of the borrowing, or asked for some reasonable collaterals, Jason would be angry and turn away disappointedly making negative comments, or even slanderous comments against his friends. Eventually, Jason declared bankruptcy during his mid-life and he owed substantial money to his debtors. He hid himself in a unknown village where he was nowhere to be found from his debtors for many years.

Yet it appeared that he had not learned from his lessons. After the episode, Jason turned his friends into his business partners. To Jason, his friends were partners or clients, he would make friendships with strangers and befriended them; later on these so-called friends were convinced to buy things from him, or doing business with him. Thus, over the years, Jason lost almost all his friends, genuine friends, including childhood friends because whenever any business opportunity, or deal turned bad, his friends got affected somehow, they were annoyed and left him.

It is a sad but true story, what a lesson learned? I firmly believe that if only Jason had understood the significance of leading a life of sincerity and simplicity, he would not have gone through such a dramatic life and suffered such painful experiences in the whirlpool of ups and downs of our human misery that finds it root in pride. Vanity and vanity; this story brings me back to the discussion of "purity of heart" in Chapter 7, where we discussed that rectitude of intention is essential and important for a simple and sincere person to lead a peaceful and meaningful life.

At times, I am reminded to encourage my own children and young couples of the significance of being *humble* and *sincere* which will enable us to be happy and simple, "Be sincere with oneself, (and with God too) and be honest with other. This will make you simple and happy."

The Pit of Life

When a teenage boy reaches the age of 15, he seemingly experiences his worst period of his life. At 15, he is considered as the pit of his life. Some general symptoms of a teenage boy are often mistaken as rudeness and impolite, here are some clues that speak in silence on behalf of the emotional teenager:

- Teenagers' bodies grow faster than their brain could match.
- They think they are often misunderstood by everyone around them.
- Two long hands almost stretch as far as beyond the knees, and with a poky nose growing large by the day.
- Broader and heavier shoulders grow so fast that they need to rest their upper torso on arm chair, or lying on bench.
- Larger feet and longer legs, often bump into something that produces unwelcoming noise; such as slamming door, or collapsing the whole body in the couch, or breaking things around the house, etc.
- Hormones support the growth and yet excite the temperament, emotion, passion and curiosity, thus the teenager often has the traits of rebellion, wordless and temperamental — often being misunderstood as lack appreciation and disrespect toward parents or elderly.
- Partially adult and partially kid; emotionally unstable. Argumentative and locks himself in the room for hours.
- But mom and dad treat him as the prince or princess he or she used to be; that irritates the teenager as if saying it out loud: "Why can't they make it easy for me, I am already suffering so much?"

Theory of Pain and Pleasure

Pain and Pleasure principle is simply an awareness that nothing comes free; everything has to be acquired through hard work and effort. Thus, children need to know and understand this fundamental idea from their early ages, through actual work and examples from parents before reaching teenage period so that the youth will know and appreciate that it is only after due efforts and difficulties that one gets rewarded. Some illustrations of this simple theory is given below:

1. If I study hard now, I will get to know things and I might have better prospects of job in the future.
2. If I do the right things with good intentions, at times with great difficulty, I will be a happy person.
3. If I make small sacrifices to deter my selfish wants, I can be a better person and could live a clean life.
4. To do good is not always easy, it requires effort and self-denial. But others will benefit from the fruits.
5. If I control my sexual impulse and wait until a proper marriage, I would win a wonderful girl who wishes to marry me, a happy family for life.
6. To love another person is to give away a bit of myself each time and to make the beloved person good and happy.

It is important that teenage children understand the purpose of this dialogue which does not aim at impairing their freedom, or merely an authoritative persuasion to hinder them from getting involved with the opposite sex of their age group. This is to help them understand the truth of the transcendental values of human nature, freedom and responsibility of being a good and useful person; and to be happy and successful, and fruitful in their adult life. Somehow, through family life, children would have observed the essence of the principle of pain and pleasure, if you want to be successful you need to study hard and work hard; or if you want to be good, you need to struggle to exercise self-mastery over passion from early childhood; they will soon realize "there is no free-lunch."

The Golden Key of Life

The best gift parents can give to their children is a happy family, an environment where children see and experience the presence of their parents, the two persons they trust most in their life, loving each other. In a family, children learn how to love and be loved; and learn to experience and practice family values and the necessary human virtues that allow them to grow up to become mature and responsible men and women; and be capable to withstand hardships and the challenges in life, to be generous to other people, understand their needs; and be able to live up to one's commitment and responsibility. Obviously, this is not an easy task for anyone to achieve, however, it is definitely worthwhile to give it a try. The commitment that generates from the married couple reaches out to their beloved children from the day they were born and stays throughout their entire upbringing.

It is obvious that the best thing parents can give to their children is not the millions of dollars in their bank accounts, or the properties inherited from the family; but the ability and disposition to lead a good and meaningful life. It is like passing the golden-key of life that opens the door of genuine happiness in life. Genuine happiness in life also entails to live a life that a person will not regret later; that includes many aspects of Do's and Don'ts. A life without *regrets* is the foundation of true happiness in life that we all try to seek, that includes guiding our young people to navigate through different hurdles anticipated in their life.

Children's Dating

Before reaching the teenager years, a child will naturally have some curiosity of the opposite sex as the child is constantly exposed to ideas and influence from the media, peers, social norms and lifestyle of the celebrities and relatives. Unless the pre-teenage child is well formed with proper values, he or she would easily be confused when engaging in a relation with the opposite sex; and would not know what to do and how to react. Thus, it is better to prepare the child of what to expect from a proper dating. This would help the teenager, especially girl, to anticipate any deviance that could tarnish the nice relationship in her first date and prepare to walk away politely to avoid further progressive acts from her suitor. Here is what I think a useful guide for a decent and proper dating with the opposite sex.

1st Level: Mutual-Communication

1. Eye-to-eye: looking at one another and getting each other's attention; not sensual or provocative look.
2. Voice-to voice: Dialogue of any choice of topic, hobby, interests, sports, books or charitable works, etc.

2nd Level: A Communication of Optimum Physical Contact

3. Hand-to-hand: handshake between friends, or holding hands, but at times human chemistry begins from here.
4. Arm to shoulder: usually expresses "I like you a lot," "I want to take care of you," "I have affection for you" and "we are good friends".
5. Arm to waist: this is the limit of affection, the touch to waist should not arouse passion. If it does, stop right there.
6. Hand to head: a gesture of care and concern that requires level of trust and affection.
7. Hand to arm: holding one another in arms or shoulders, but not touching sensitive parts of the body as a sign of mutual affection.
8. A smack on the cheek is socially polite for greeting or farewell of the dating. That's it, boundary of intimation stops here. It is important for teenage girl to know that observing the limits in intimacy when dating with her male counterpart would send a clear signal of her own personal dignity as a young woman. Not consenting to advances of her male friend will not make her less likeable, nor less attractive; instead she would win the respect of her male friends, and probably his heart too.

Normal Dating Ends Here

9. Mouth to mouth: Kissing is an intimate expression of strong attachment that should be reserved for people sharing special

relationships, and not with any sundry person. It is preferably suitable for engaged or married couple as this intimacy could lead to the next level of passion and desire and potentially light up an inextinguishable fire of passion, especially for the young man.

10. Any step beyond point 8 that involves private sensitive parts on one's body, including mouth to mouth, is intimate and personal; and that should be only reserved for married couple.

Some child psychologists consider that there are three distinctive stages of child development: the first stage is between infancy and 7 years old, the second stage is between 8 and 13 years old; the third stage is between 14 and 18 years old. This grouping slightly varies between boys and girls, it also varies between different races and cultures. The grouping of these three stages serve as guidelines regarding some distinctive features and noticeable behavioral patterns in the overall child development where parents and educators could focus on, and give necessary support they possibly could to help in the proper upbringing of child.

Puberty is considered the second developmental stage since the child's first birth, it is the stage of life during which the boy begins to show physical features of a man, and the girl begins to show some features of a woman. It normally occurs between 11 and 15 years of age, this can vary between races and cultures, usually later for boys than girls. Puberty begins when the pituitary gland at the base of the brain sends out hormone that stimulates the body to speed up the growth. The changes occurring inside the teenage body prepares him or her to be physically capable of human reproduction; of potentially becoming a father or mother. This stage is also known as fertility.

Romantic Love

The youthful romantic love could certainly blind the teenager as discussed in the earlier chapters. An even more interesting aspect is that some areas of the brain are turned off in people who are in love. Three regions of the brain generally used in moral judgment go dim! No wonder normally sensible people seem to fly off to the moon when they're in love, perhaps in a way, what they say literally is true: "I am *deliriously* happy, and I am *crazily* in love." Under this circumstance, teenage boy and girls, driven by this romantic impulse, may fall into the trap of intimate physical contacts that might result in premarital sexual acts and finally, possible pregnancies.

The serious consequences of teenage pregnancy are:

- Babies born to teen mothers are more likely to be born small or die in first year.
- Teenage mother has higher rate of chronic health problems.
- Teenage mother is more inclined to have learning and school problems.
- She can easily get in trouble with the law.
- Higher probability to become teen parents themselves.
- Teens who become parents are more likely to end up poor or on welfare.
- Teen parents tend to have fewer job opportunities.
- They tend to have fewer education opportunities.
- They are less likely to be happy.
- They are less likely to stay married.

In general, teenagers are particularly venerable to these moral errors, if they lack proper formation and support from their families. Many youngsters, due to ignorance and temptation, will fall into the traps of sexuality for pleasure; and this moral error would propagate and repeated like a broken record, years after years, from youth to mature age, it could even propagate to the next generation. Therefore, it is fundamentally important to form the conscience of young people long before their teenage period in order to avoid, or at least minimize these tragic mistakes in life. The best persons to provide this formation of human conscience toward passion and sexuality are the parents themselves. It is good for parents to be aware of key stages in their child's development.

Progression of Sexual Intimacy

Intimate courtship extends gradually as part of a life-long commitment in marriage, and teenagers should be able to grasp this essence that marital love entails that husband and wife love each other freely and completely, detached from any material cause. It is like possessing oneself and one's own future fully and giving oneself to another. That is why some people do not want to get married forever, thus cannot make martial commitments, because they are not free to the extent of possessing themselves and their future; and incapable of committing to something that contravenes their limited understanding of human freedom.

True love involves loving the shortcomings of the beloved. Husband and wife love each other for who they are, but not for what they possess (have). They naturally love the good qualities of their spouse, yet they need to learn to love each other's shortcomings as well. Human Relationships answer the need for persons to love and be loved and come in various forms and degrees. Love — desiring good of the beloved — is the fundamental basis for all true relationships.

While human beings have extraordinary creativity and ability to generate reasons to justify their act, quite often human moral errors are honey-coated, attractively packaged that they blend in well into the modern society in different name tags: lifestyle, modern culture and human rights. For example, nowadays, the practice of contraceptives and abortion are seen as a solution for safe sex, unwanted pregnancies, or for prevention of sex crime, or for sex-liberation lifestyle, and even for health reason. When a person initially sees the news about these propaganda, he or she will unlikely be affected, he could still clearly tell the right from wrong. However, when same messages are propagated repeatedly by the media relentlessly; month after month, year after year, they change people's views substantially, sooner or later, the perception of moral judgment could become blur, the mind would begin to be subconsciously acquainted to these messages; thus the borderline of morality between error and righteousness becomes less clear. Eventually, moral errors would become socially acceptable behavior lifestyle, a "tsunami" of modern society, possibly under the umbrella of "human rights" or any other form of nice sounding slogan. If we take a deeper look into the escalating crime rate of many modern societies, we will see quite a substantial percentage of these crimes can be traced back to its root, which are directly and indirectly related to the crime of passion and sexuality.

These related crimes originating from passion and sexuality are mainly caused by ignorance and lack of proper understanding of human passion and sexuality, nevertheless, in many cases it is due to ill-intention of the perpetrator. When this happens to an individual family, and if the number multiples by hundred-folds and then another hundred-folds, a small domestic problem will eventually become substantial social problems in our societies. While this subject has been discussed at length in Chapter 1, it is clearer now that the call to address and contain this crime of passion and sexuality starting from individual family is becoming even more imminent. Thus, precautionary measures in individual families are essential; beginning from our own home. Parents must take a good look at what else each one of us can do to address this human moral error from within ourselves and family, and help to cease this "structure of sin" from infiltrating into our family life.

Cohabitation

Modern society has been bombarded by new ideologies, one after another, at times with new ideologies intertwined with cultural practices and distorted values. These can be quite very confusing to people. Some ideologies, system of thoughts, attempt to promote new sets of values contradicting the well-established and righteous ones, and quite often, they influence the minds of many people, especially the young individuals. In our modern society, many people commit mistakes mostly due to ignorance or due to the absence of knowledge and awareness of the underlining problems while taking decisions that will only lead to regrets. But, at times, people commit horrible crimes due to selfish reasons while quite often, serious consequences originate from seemingly small mistakes just because the youngster had no idea of the overall consequences and the seriousness of the matter that may leave a lasting scar in one's life and the life of others.

It is not uncommon that young people resort to cohabitation, or so-called living-together, as a lifestyle for discovering sexual compatibility for each other, worse still the socially acceptable lifestyle of "one-night-stand," pre-marital sexual relationship for both passion and curiosity, and/or, for selfish reason, along with the burgeoning of homosexual lifestyles at pre-adolescent age, and of even more perverted behavior such as pedophilias. Such unwarranted behaviors, as far as parents and family activists are concerned, further aggravate morally evil problems such as abortion, marital infidelity, divorce, singled-parenthood, child abuse of all kinds, runaway kids, sex-slavery, youth prostitution and many other related problems and violent crimes. In today's world, subjective morality is an overwhelming ideology, when any moral act is a moving target that subjects to individualistic view, therefore, debates and ingenious manipulation of public opinions, for example, whether abortion is right or wrong, have the ability to anchor a teenager's conviction in life.

Cohabitation is a growing pattern among young adults in almost every country. It must be made clear to our teenage children the truth behind this dangerous practice of socially acceptable lifestyle of cohabitation before and after reaching their teenage years.

Dangers of Cohabitation

In the U.S., cohabitation has increased 11-fold since 1960. Many young people believe that they live together in order to find out whether they are sexually compatible before they decide to marry each other. This is an excuse for the lifestyle that promulgates among teenage and young people that part of the thrill of beginning a married life together is to learn and to explore sex together. However, the reality is to enjoy companionship and sexual relation fantasy without commitment and obligation.

Cohabiting relationships are mostly unstable as statistics shows that over 90% of cohabiting relationships break up in less than five years and the rate of divorce among those who cohabit before marriage is nearly twice that of couples who marry without having lived together.

Men in cohabiting relationships are more likely to be unfaithful than normally married husbands. Cohabitation is considered a loving relationship without the relevant commitment. Women in cohabiting relationships end up contributing majority of the relationship's income; whereas, the poverty rate among children of cohabiting couples is several times greater than for children of married couples. Child abuse is highly common in families where the couple had children without being married. Marriages preceded by cohabiting are more prone to drug and alcohol problems while emotional depression is another potential problem. One scholar summarized the research on cohabitation: *"Cohabitation is bad for men, worse for women, and horrible for children."*

What is Contraception?

In a strict sense, contraception is a deliberate "sterilization" in the sexual act, whether by chemical means, e.g. the pill, or by physical means, e.g. condom or diaphragm. With advancement in science, contraceptives could ensure human sexual act may never be open to life. When the possibility of new life is deliberately excluded in contraception, the sexual act would reduce its significance to an act of mutual masturbation whereby the couple use each other physical bodies to satisfy sexual desire.

Contraceptive mentality underlines the ideology of "happiness merely equates to sexual pleasure" which contradicts chastity.

Contraceptive removes or substantially reduces the possibility of conception in a normal conjugal act, it plainly takes away the responsibility and natural effect of human sexual intercourse. Contraceptive promotes the idea of free-sex and it has also become the ambassador of "safe-sex". Thus, it directly and indirectly encourages pre-marital sexual lifestyle; and extra-marital behavior as well. Under this notion of "safe-sex", the psychological hurdle is removed while young people and adults increase the frequency of their sexual activities that in turn enhances their addiction to sexual pleasures.

Under the influence of the wave in sensuous pleasure, young people may equate self-donation love in a conjugal act to anything that brings pleasure. Thus, there is a tremendous confusion in the minds of many people that sex is a pleasurable game, and the story repeats by itself over and over again. When this pleasurable sex-gaming mentality is extended to adulthood, it would be difficult to remain chaste and retain fidelity in a marriage. When spouses use contraceptive in their conjugal act, it likens to say "I want your body now, not your personhood, to quench the thirst for my sexual desire," then, there will be no communion of persons, the genuine exchange of self-giving love between two persons is absent. Such a sexual act would be reduced to animal mating, similar to basic instinct for instant satisfaction.

Married couples express and renew their pledge to achieve perfect conjugal union. By its very nature, conjugal union is procreative and it is the language of self-giving love within a marriage. The body is the nuptial gift mutually exchanged between the spouses. Any sex outside of marriage demeans the true value of love and sexuality. Only through chastity, purity of heart and body, the husband loves his wife unconditionally in a marriage, such that a couple achieves a meaningful and integral vision of being human and his ultimate destiny of happiness.

A Moment of Passion

I recall a situation that involved an extra-marital affair of a middle-aged man with a successful and wealthy career-woman whom he met at a professional conference. Their encounter soon developed into a passionate affair that this man decided to leave his wife and three lovely daughters for this woman, who according to this man, did not want his money, but his love. The situation of the wife of this man was of course devastating, her attempt of suicide aggravated the children so much that one of the daughters hit her father on his face right in front of the mistress.; while another teenage child was hospitalized due to alcohol intoxication. This man was very dear to his daughters and they used to be such a loving family; a moment of passion and desire had shattered a normal and happy family with the result everyone went in different directions. Later on, this man developed cancer after a few years living with his mistress; a double tragedy.

What Lies Beneath Contraceptive

One reason father–son or mother–daughter need to talk about this intimate and important subject is that there is so much ignorance and misinformation about the subject matter amongst the teenagers and at times even amongst grown-up adults. Ignorance in the area of human love and passion breeds confusion that often leads to disastrous consequences, particularly among the youth. To explain chastity — it is a positive connotation of self-mastering of human sexual passion and practice of abstinence founded on genuine love.

There is plenty of propaganda directly to promote the use of condom as a means to protect oneself from HIV or other sexually transmitted diseases. But in fact, the ultimate purpose of the use of condom is to achieve contraception. As we all know, condom at times fails to be a contraceptive and renders it ineffective in preventing pregnancies, or so called to provide you a "safe sex." Thus, to enable condom manufacturers to continue to earn profits, they will have no choice but to produce products that give absolute guarantee of contraception and to deliver the promise of "safe-sex," as in pills for pregnancy-prevention. To achieve this, some manufacturers have produced condoms which are abortive and are 200% effective as publicized in the companies' marketing propaganda.

Condom may on rare occasions fail to stop the sperms from fertilizing the egg, then how could they be possibly safe in preventing sexually transmitted diseases (STDs) or even the much smaller HIV virus? A normal human sperm measures about 3 microns at the head and the HIV virus about 0.1 microns, which is 1/30 smaller than the head of a human sperm. If human sperm could possibly pass through the latex wall of the condom, then HIV virus will find it too easy to go through the latex wall of the condom. STDs, which includes HIV and HPV infections, cannot be effectively prevented by the use of condoms. In other words, if a person has frequent so-called "safe-sex" with multiple sex-partners thinking that he is safe, in reality the possibility of him getting infected increases dramatically.

More Useful Terms

Though the following terminologies are known to some parents of teenagers, there are parents who need a quick reference either for review or to quote in their mutual dialogues with their adolescent children on the topic of human passion and sexuality. I conclude that it is better to have something rather than nothing in the grip of parents' hands.

Sexuality Human beings have a profound need for relationship and intimacy with others, to get to know and love others and be known and loved. Sexuality is a fundamental essence of human being to differentiate between male and female. Our sexuality is an integral part of our human nature, and it plays an essential and important role in our life, such as gender identification as male and female, the interiority and external expression and communication through the masculinity of man, or femininity of woman — the way we talk, dress, appear, behave, think, feel, and relate to others, etc. Nature advocates that there is no such thing as the existence of a third gender in a substantial way, however, this is opposed by some people that advocate the rights of homosexual union in the modern society.

Sexual union is a unique expression of this longing and need, where a man and a woman are united in the most profound way humanly possible. Sex is by its very nature procreative and unitive. This requires that the human love of a couple for each other should be free, total, faithful (exclusive) and fruitful (open) to life. There exists an unbreakable bond between the unitive and procreative meaning of the conjugal act. Thus, the sexual union between two sexes necessitates in a marital act within the context of marriage in order to provide a stable environment for the growth, education and upbringing of the begotten children, the fruits of the union. Family which is founded on a life-long committed marriage between the couple becomes the vital environment necessary for the flourishing of human life and society.

Sexual acts of humans are on a different order or level from that of animals. For animals, sex is purely for the reproduction of the species and is governed solely by their instincts. The sexual acts of humans are not simply physical but involve the whole of the human person, the physical, psychological, intellectual, emotional and spiritual. Human sexuality has two fundamental elements: love and life; without which there is no true human sexuality, but only animal mating.

Sexual urge or the urge to satisfy sexual desire. Merely letting the sexual desire rule whenever the passion arises is more an animal act than a human act. A human can exercise the given intellect and will freely to choose "to act" or "not to act." One should arrive at a decision to act only after using one's intelligence to analyze if certain action is harmful, or beneficial to oneself and as well as that of others. A failure to think intelligently and properly according to one's conscience before acting intuitively changes a person behavior to more like animal's behavior that is based on instinct.

Sexual freedom is the ability of an individual to freely choose to do the right thing in the expression of his human sexuality. For e.g., when an alcoholic is unable to control his desire to have his next glass of whisky, he is not a free person and is bound by his lust for material things; so much so that, when a person who cannot resist his instantaneous sexual urges or sexual desires is also considered as being not a free person.

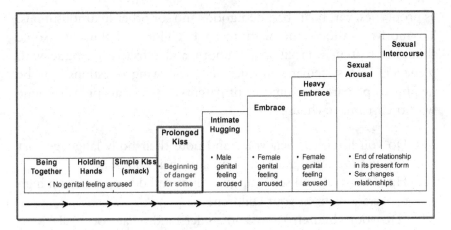

Fig. 8.1.   Progression of Sexual Intimacy

Chastity is a positive and joyful affirmation of what true love is, it often expresses in marital commitment toward the spouse. Through the practice of chastity, the person acknowledges the need and willingness of self-control in thoughts, words and actions in self-mastery of human passion and sexuality. Thus, it helps to avoid lust in our hearts. It is necessary to be chaste before one can love truly. Otherwise lust could be mistaken for love, lust destroys true love — mutual self-donation of two persons within marriage. Above is Fig. 8.1, which shows the level of intimacy between a male and female in a dating that escalates progressively with certain actions appropriate to teenagers, and more intimate acts that are only reserved to married couples. It can be quite embarrassing during a parents–children dialogue, therefore, parents must be tactful in preparing the occasion, use examples of movies and hypothetical situations to help easing the tension and avoid embarrassment.

Give Children a Sense of Purpose in Life

When talking about the purpose of life, most people would relay it to quantifiable achievement such as how much wealth accumulation at certain age, or the material things that a person is able to possess; such as properties, car, boat, branded goods and, or other luxurious items. To motivate a dialogue with teenage children, below are some thoughts that may facilitate a smooth and effective dialogue with teenagers in a systematic manner. The following questions may be helpful to prepare the mindset of parents before starting a dialogue with their teenage children:

1. Do you listen to their voice and note their body language that tells you something about them and their condition?
2. Have you ever you set clear guidelines and do you maintain high expectations from your children?
3. Do your children know and understand what you really want from them?
4. Do your children know why they should be good? Do they have any sense of purpose in their lives, do you know any of it?
5. Do your children know you at all (what kind of a person you are), things you like best, or things you dislike? And why? Do they know a few things that you have great passion of?
6. Do your children know that he or she is important to you? No matter what happens.
7. Do they know you love them for who they are? Not what they can do, or achieve?
8. Do you ever compare their individual talents or achievements? Or try to use them to further encourage your children? Please remember positive stimulation works wonder at times, not negative.
9. Do you know what kind of dreams your children have? See if you have help them achieve their dreams.
10. Do your children trust you at all? Help them to develop a plan for a bright future and healthy relationships with family members and friends..
11. Are your children close to you? Be involved in healthy and intense family life, at school, in their respective community and family activities. Are they aware of the support system (parents, grandparents, teachers and mentor or coach, etc.) that family can provide?

12. Do your teenage children have proper understanding of human sexuality, the danger of cohabitation, teenage pregnancy, responsible parenthood, the evil of abortion and sexual transmittable diseases (STDs)?

13. Have your children been properly formed with the ability to say "No" to peer pressure, temptation to succumb to pleasurable activities of all kinds, incorrect but socially acceptable behavior? This ability originates from the virtues of fortitude and temperance.

14. Have you ever encouraged and educated your teenage children to take healthy and responsible decisions?

15. Are you aware of any house rules in your own home? Such rules should be fair, clear and consistent that applies to everyone, including dad and mom.

16. Do you talk to your teenage children from a high moral ground or at level terms? "My son, you need to listen to me, not only because I am your father, but because what I say is morally correct, and it's good for you, and I love you like no one else in the world."

17. Do you show strong and authoritative language with your children, even though you are well informed and knowledgeable in the subject matter?

18. "If I tell you not to do what I am doing, I am a hypocrite. If I tell you not to do what I have done, I am a humble teacher."

The Evil of Abortion

Abortion is a direct action that terminates the pregnancy before viability, i.e. the fetus is unable to live outside the maternal womb. Consequently, any procedure that causes the removal or death of a fertilized egg is abortion, a pre-mediated murder, and an evil act.

Pregnancy begins at the moment of conception, the marrying between a sperm and an egg, in the process of fertilization. It is essential for pre-teenagers to know the reality of conception and fertilization; the exact moment when human life begins. The period of pregnancy lasts about nine months, during which human conception goes through different stages of development until it is ready for birth. However, it is the same living human being; from conception to birth; from birth to death. There are plenty of scientific discussions on whether a zygote, a fertilized egg, is human or not. But it is simply a matter of common sense that one's personhood starts at the beginning of his own life; is not each one of us today the same being as the one during our conception? Likens the examples of Austin in Chapter 4. Each of us has grown, developed, changed, but our identity, our personhood remains the same and constant all the time, while our body and physical being keep growing and changing all the time, "I am older today than yesterday." We are neither more human or less human this year than last year even though we have "aged" in the last 12 months and physically changed accordingly.

Then, why would some people, even medical professionals and academics, determine that an unborn baby before the 8–12 week of pregnancy be considered as non-human. Is it to facilitate abortion of the baby before 12 weeks, but not the baby older than 12th week? Where do we find this theory and criteria to decide who is human or not at certain days and months? Is it because babies are unable to reason, to cry, to scream and to protest? And we, those who are responsible, have the power to decide if the tiny little creature is to live or not to die!

Obviously, a new born baby can only eat, sleep and cry; he or she is unable to reason, to speak and to protest in the maternal womb. And yet we all know that newly born babies are human persons, not animals, because when properly developed and stimulated in a natural manner under the care of the parents, they will perform human actions — they will be able to reason, to speak, to think and to love, something that little puppies will never be able to do. Many abortions are performed because of the ignorance of the person involved, like the case of the pregnant mother who has very little idea about why abortion is wrong. However, there are also plenty of deceptions.

Some people reduce the malice of abortion to a "psychologically and socially acceptable" convenience. Direct abortion is killing a human life, the murder of an innocent life and thus can never be justified for whatever reason. We can imagine no greater perversion than when a mother would decide to kill her own baby, part of her own life! As Mother Teresa once said: "The greatest destroyer of peace is abortion because if a mother can kill her own baby, what else is left for me to kill you, and you to kill me? There is nothing in between."

Abortion, the deliberate termination of the life of a pre-born human baby, is the killing of an innocent human life which should be seen as seriously as a homicide or a criminal act committed against a well grown human being, such as a toddler, an 8 years boy, or a teenage girl, or an adult. Unfortunately, endless arguments still exists amongst scientists, medical practitioners and state governments and in the court of law as at how many days or weeks old of the living fetus should be considered as a human person or not; leaving the core issue, i.e. human moral responsibility in killing of our own kind, unattended.

Besides ending the baby's life, it damages the mother's own life in various ways. In addition to physical risks during the abortion itself, the mother risks experiencing post abortion distress syndrome (this includes guilty feeling, stress, flashbacks, etc) and an increased incidence of breast cancer (which is also an inherent risk with oral contraceptives). No one in the right mind would plan an abortion when he or she engages in contraceptive sexual intercourse, but many see abortion as an option in the event of contraceptive failure. Contraceptive sexual intercourse gives rise to a contraceptive mentality that views abortion as an justifiable act and a convenient solution to not having to bear the responsibility of a unwanted new life.

Perhaps, youngsters before they get entangled by the problem of passion and sexuality should understand the story of life, how human life comes about, how we could help to contribute an environment, or culture that would enable more people to respect and treasure the baby's life, by asking the first question. "Who is that little person in an embryo, or the fetus? How must he or she be protected and cherished? How precious is a human life, my dear, do you know?

Discovering Life

The value of life and love is naturally discoverable by a rational mind. Human life has an intrinsic value that is precious and is always worth promoting and protecting. The various forms of human relationship are answer to human need, the need to love and be loved is inscribed in our nature as human being, male and female, a call to share and to give of oneself in marriage is one that is particularly close to the hearts of many people. We should not perceive others as objects of mere pleasure, or as objects for another person's gratification, nor a means to satisfy any form of sexual desire, it is a serious violation of human dignity. Lust is counterfeit love, while true human love is always self-giving for the good of the other, lust is selfish act for self-gratification at the expense of other. Love gives while lust takes. Marriage is where a couple publicly pledge their loving commitment for life with free will, total and unconditional love, faithfulness, exclusiveness and fruit-fulness to each other. Chastity involves self-control and self-mastery, it requires the cooperation of the virtues of modesty, temperance, self-respect and respect for others.

Below is a short reminder that aims to provoke the thoughts of young people of their inescapable responsibility of the importance of human life:

How can I Respect Life in making choices?

I must Promote, Protect and Cherish:
(*Response*)
Human life is a gift.
Human life is precious.
The Embryo, no matter how small, is a human life.
The Fetus is a human.
Adoption instead of abortion.
Absolute Respect for life.

A Story of a 12 Weeks Old Baby in Mother's Womb

A sequential development of a little human life from an embryo at the moment of conception to a fetus within the womb of a mother, a tiny human baby is living and growing pending on the mother's love, nutrition and care.

Your heartbeat begins approximately on the 15th day.
By the 20th day of the conception, your entire nervous system is being gradually constructed.

At 45th day, your skeleton is complete, you movement shows the signs of reflexes.

Electrical brainwaves have been recorded as early from 42nd day onward..

By the 8th week, your brain and entire body systems have begun to function normally. If your daddy tickles your nose, you will flex your head backwards away from the stimulus.

At 9 to 10 weeks, you squint, swallow, move your tongue and if I stroke your palm, you will close your little fingers and make a tiny fist.

You suck your thumb vigorously and breathe amniotic fluid to develop the organs of respiration at 11 weeks.

Your fingernails are present by 12th week, your eyelashes by 16th week.
By 12th week in the womb of your mother, you weigh about 30–40 grams and will be approximately 7–8 cm long. "My baby, your entire body would fit comfortably in the palm of my hand."

Conclusion

In life, we are always attracted to do what we inclined to do, but there are necessary choices in different aspects in life, it is up to a person to make that right choice or otherwise. A teenager needs to know that whatever he or she does in life, he must act with responsibility, otherwise he would not only end up paying a heavy price, others may end up paying the price too. One of the reference point of genuine happiness of a person is to lead a righteous life and try to avoid doing things that he would regret later in life.

Making the Right Choice

A child's upbringing involves the risk of letting him make mistakes, after all, he cannot hold his parents' hands forever. Some day, he will have to stand on his own and take responsibility for his own actions. The challenge is, of course, whether parents would instill the proper notion of true human freedom into the child's heart and mind, so when they reach the age of responsibility, say teenage period and beyond, they would be in a position to knowingly choose and do the right things in life, and to choose to do good. This presents a substantial challenge in balancing between letting the child to try out his freedom and, or keeping the child away from any "social contamination" by sheltering the child in a "green house" wherein the child is totally free from external influence; only later on in life the green house effect of child protection would be subject to test when the child reaches her teenage years and beyond. Human is a rational being with intelligence and will; freedom and conscience. After going through all the previous chapters, we should acknowledge that love desires the good of the beloved person through the act of giving oneself to the other, thus love is more than an emotion or feeling that is merely driven by momentary impulse of seeking pleasure and satisfaction of desire.

A Coat in the Winter

An incidence reminds me of this self-giving love of a teenager in exercising solidarity in his young life. Joseph is 19 year old and lives abroad away from his parents for university studies. On a freezing cold winter night, while he experienced one of the coldest winter days since his arrival to this coastal town, he walked along the path that normally would take him from school to home. On the way, he saw a man probably in his mid-40s squatting at the street corner and trying to braise himself from the fierce wind by wrapping himself by a thin-blanket full of holes. Joseph saw this man in grief and was touched by the scene; without much further thoughts, he took off his only over-coat on him and gave it to the man and said: "this is for you, keep it." Probably because the incidence occurred so fast that the middle-aged man who was still squatting on the road side did not know what to say; he hesitated for a moment, then said with a trembling voice: "thank you" Joseph soon realized that he was only wearing a thin sweater that his mother bought for him, he suddenly felt the pinch of the freezing wind from the sea, he decided to run all the way home in order to keep his body warm. Though he did not have the overcoat any longer with him, Joseph felt happy that he could help someone during distress and felt good that evening.

A life With no Regrets?

To be able to say sincerely that "I have no regrets" at the evening of one's life is such a blessing, because there are always things that we would feel that "Oh, I should have done this, or I should have done that." Or we would say: "if ever I knew that, I would not have done that to him or her...!" It is highly possible that there might be plenty of remorse when a person gets to the evening of his life, he or she would have a lot more reflection and hopefully not many regrets!

An Aged Man Says

An aged man lying in his sick bed said to his wife softly while holding her hand: "My dear, what a wonderful life I have been with you for almost half-a-century? The lovely children we have raised together, and the happy moments we shared and the hard times we have overcome together. Our children are good people, aren't they? And the grandchildren, they are all good, lovely and cute little ones." "We were not wealthy, but we had never let our children go hungry, and we have a lovely home, right?" "And you, my love, thank you for being my loving wife; and all these years you have been patient with me and bore my defects, you have made me a better man indeed!" Then the aged man sighs quietly and continues: "Darling, I have so much good memories, and I have no regrets!" What a great reflection of one's life? How wonderful it is to be readily closing the chapter of life like this man at his mature years of life having lived a wonderful life with a loving family with good children and grandchildren; and be able to say, "I have no regret." Perhaps, this loving statement of genuine love and friendship between a husband and his wife would serve as a good reminder to married couples; particularly during conflicts, or when one is at emotional crossroad in life; or when one encounters marital problems, such as the mid-life crisis; momentary infidelity of one party, or other types of challenges in marital relationships. This brings me to the thought "We may not have it all together, but together we have it all."

The mere fact that I am able to finish this book "Mirror of Love" at the closing of the "Year of Faith" means a lot to me. This book also serves as a reminder that we all have choices to make; preferably these choices are directed to seeking the good and righteousness in life, to do good at the service of others; beginning from those who are closest to us, the spouse and children. "Mirror of Love" is a reflection of our genuine inner being as person, whether we see a reflection of "self-love," or a reflection of "love for others" is in fact a fundamental choice of ours.

Additional Readings

- Abortion Statistics and Other Data by Wm. Robert Hohnston, 18th February 2007.
- Abortion the Abominable Crime by Fr. Joseph Giaime, SDB, 9th February 1976.
- Apostolic Exhortation, Familiaris Consortio of Pope John Paul II to the Episcopate, to the Clergy and to the Faithful of the whole Catholic Church on the role of the Christian Family in the modern world, 22nd November 1981.
- Centesimus Annus by John Paul II, On the 100th Anniversary of Rerum Novarum, Published in 1991.
- Character Building, A Guide for Parents & Teachers by David Isaacs, Published in 2001 by Four Courts Press.
- Christian Philosophy by Joseph M. de Torre, Published in 1980 by Vera-Reyes.
- Compass: A Handbook on Parent Leadership by James B. Stenson, Published in 2003 by Scepter Publishers, Inc.
- Covenanted Happiness, Love & Commitment in Marriage by Cormac Burke, 1990.
- Demographic Statistics Section, Census and Statistics Department, 26th July 2007.
- Encyclical Letter: Caritas In Veritate of the Supreme Pontiff, the Solemnity of the Holy Apostles Peter and Paul, by Emeritus Benedict XVI, in 2009 in Rome.
- Encyclical Letter: Deus Caritas Est of the Supreme Pontiff, the Solemnity of the Nativity of the Lord, by Emeritus Benedict XVI, in 2005 in Rome.
- Encyclical Redemptor Hominis of John Paul II, 4th March 1979, the 1st Sunday of Lent.
- Fides Et Ratio to the Bishops of the Catholic Church on the relationship between Faith and Reason, the Feast of the Triumph of the Cross, by John Paul II, 14th September 1998 in Rome.
- God & Children by Jesus Urteage, Published in 1973 by Sinag-Tala Publishers.
- Gratissimam Sane, Letter to Families from Pope John Paul II, 1994 Year of the Family, 2nd February 1994.
- Humanae Vitae, Encyclical of Pope Paul VI, 25th July 1968.
- In Conversation with God, by Francisco Fernandez, Published by Scepter.
- John Paul II on the Origin of the Crisis in Marriage, Address to Roman Rota, 30th January 2003.

- Letter to Women by John Paul II, Published in 1995 by USCCB Publishing.
- Lifeline: The Religious Upbringing of Your Children by James B. Stenson, Published in 1997 by Scepter Publishers, Inc.
- Love: A Fruit Always in Season by Mother Teresa (Edited by Dorothy Hunt), Published in 1987 by Ignatius Press.
- Marriage a Path to Sanctity by Javier Abad Eugenio Fenoy, October 1988.
- Mother's Choice, Annual Report 2005–2006, Published in 2006 in Hong Kong by Mother's Choice.
- Novo Millennio Ineunte by John Paul II, The Great Jubilee of the Year 2000.
- On The Family, St. Josemaria Escriva, 1972.
- Pastoral Constitution on the Church in the Modern World, Gaudium Et Spes, Promulgated by his Holiness, Pope Paul VI, 7th December 1965.
- Preparing for Adolescence, A Planning Guide for Parents by James B. Stenson, 1st March 1990.
- Reference made to a project study on human brain in relationship to its emotion conducted by Dr. H. Fisher, an anthropologist at Rutgers University in New Jersey, Dr. Arthur Aron, a psychologist at the State University of New York, and Dr. L. Brown, a professor of neurology of Albert Einstein college of Medicine, Published on 31st May 2005, *New York Times*.
- Successful Fathers: The Subtle but Powerful Ways Fathers Mold Their Children's Characters by James B. Stenson, Published in 2001 by Scepter Publishers, Inc.
- The Family Planning Association of Hong Kong, Highlights, Published in 2006 by The Family Planning Association of Hong Kong.
- The Ignatius Holy Bible by Catholic Biblical Association of Great B, Published in 1994 by Ignatius Press.
- The Navarre Bible: Pentateuch by University of Navarre, Published in 1999 by Scepter Publishers, Inc.
- The Summa Theologiae of St. Thomas Aquinas by Thomas Aquinas, Published in 2009 by CreateSpace Independent Publishing Platform.
- The Theology of The Body — Human Love in the Divine Plan by John Paul II, Published in 1997 in the USA by Pauline Books & Media.
- The Truth and Meaning of Human Sexuality by Alfonso Card. L Pez Trujillo, President of the Pontifical Council for the Family, 21st November 1995.
- Theology by Fulton J. Sheen, Published in 1981 by Servant Books.
- Three to Get Married by Fulton J. Sheen, Published in 1996 by Scepter Publishers, Inc.
- Upbringing: A Discussion Handbook for Parents of Young Children by James B. Stenson, Published in 1992 by Scepter Publishers, Inc.
- Veritatis Splendor, Feast of the Transfiguration of the Lord, by John Paul II, 1993 in Rome.

Appendixes

Data on Family Structure

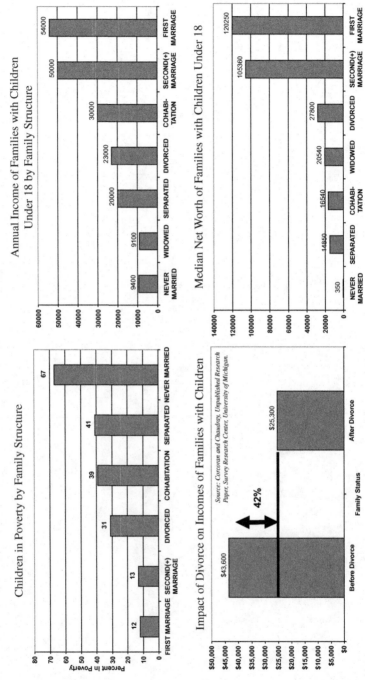

Annual Income of Families with Children Under 18 by Family Structure

Median Net Worth of Families with Children Under 18

Children in Poverty by Family Structure

Impact of Divorce on Incomes of Families with Children

Source: Corcoran and Chaudry, Unpublished Research Paper, Survey Research Center, University of Michigan.

Emotional Disorders: Children, UK by Family Structure

Married — 3.5
Cohabiting — 4.4
Lone Parent - Always Single — 5.1
Lone Parent - Widowed Divorced Separated — 7.6

% of Children with the Disorder

Source: Meltzer, H., et al., Mental Health of Children and Adolescents in Great Britain, London: The Stationery Office.

In UK, a Child whose Biological Mother Cohabits was 73 Times more likely to suffer Fatal Abuse than a Child with Married Parents

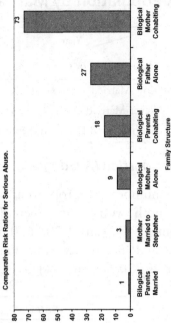

Comparative Risk Ratios for Serious Abuse.

Bilogical Parents Married — 1
Mother Married to Stepfather — 3
Biological Mother Alone — 9
Biological Parents Cohabiting — 18
Biological Father Alone — 27
Biological Mother Cohabiting — 73

Family Structure

Source: Robert Whelan, Broken Homes and Broken Children.

Married People are More than Twice as Likely to be Happy

Percent Who are "Very Happy"

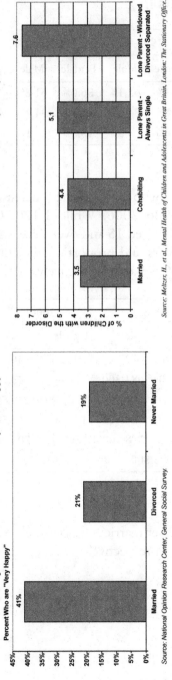

Married — 41%
Divorced — 21%
Never Married — 19%

Source: National Opinion Research Center, General Social Survey.

In UK, a Child whose Biological Mother Cohabits was 33 Times more likely to suffer Serious Abuse than a Child with Married Parents

Comparative Risk Ratios for Serious Abuse.

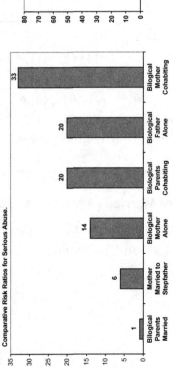

Bilogical Parents Married — 1
Mother Married to Stepfather — 6
Biological Mother Alone — 14
Biological Parents Cohabiting — 20
Biological Father Alone — 20
Biological Mother Cohabiting — 33

Family Structure

Source: Robert Whelan, Broken Homes and Broken Children.

HK Population by Marital Status in %

Year — Marital Status (%)	1996 Female	Male	2006 Female	Male
Now Married	58.7%	62.1%	56.0%	61.8%
Never Married	29.1%	34.4%	30.5%	34.1%
Widowed and Divorced/Separated	12.2%	3.5%	13.5%	4.1%

Now Married (Aged 15 and above)

The number and proportion of persons who were married increased for both women and men during 1986–2006. While 1,120,100 women (48%) and 1,209,600 men (52%) aged 15 and over were married in 1986, the corresponding numbers and proportions in 2006 were 1,730,300 (50.4%) and 1,702,000 (49.6%) respectively.

Year — Age Group	1986 Female	Male	1996 Female	Male	2006 Female	Male
15–29	214,900	112,900	163,300	73,200	98,200	40,300
30–44	468,900	491,900	750,100	684,300	719,800	525,700
45–64	365,300	461,600	473,500	594,100	723,500	827,500
65 and above	71,100	143,200	130,200	226,600	188,800	308,500
Sub-total	1,120,100	1,209,600	1,517,100	1,578,200	1,730,300	1,702,000
Total	2,329,700		3,095,300		3,432,300	

Never Married (Aged 15 and above)

During 1986 to 2006, the number of never married persons increased by 51.4% and 10.9% for women and men respectively.

| Year | 1986 | | 1996 | | 2006 | |
Age Group	Female	Male	Female	Male	Female	Male
15–29	546,600	685,700	565,800	621,900	634,100	624,800
30–44	54,900	126,900	158,900	209,300	230,800	243,000
45–64	8,700	29,600	18,000	32,100	69,100	57,200
65 and over	11,900	4,900	10,800	11,800	7,700	14,600
Sub-total	622,100	847,100	753,500	875,100	941,700	939,600
Total	1,469,200		1,628,600		1,881,300	

Widowed and Divorced/Separated (Aged 15 and above)

The number of widowed and divorced/separated persons increased from 346,700 in 1986 to 529,500 in 2006 and their proportion in the population also increased in recent years.

| Year | 1986 | | 1996 | | 2006 | |
Age Group	Female	Male	Female	Male	Female	Male
15–29	2,500	1,400	1,700	900	3,200	1,400
30–44	16,400	9,800	31,800	13,400	55,300	17,500
45–64	88,100	26,700	80,300	25,700	133,900	41,100
65 and over	167,100	34,700	201,700	49,000	224,900	51,800
Sub-total	274,100	72,600	315,900	89,000	417,300	111,800
Total	346,700		404,900		529,500	

Population Aged 15 and above by Marital Status and Gender

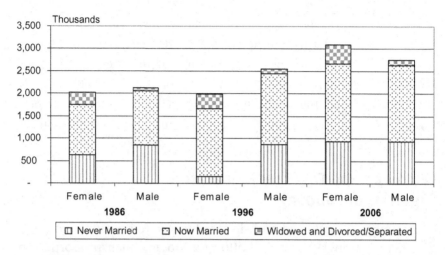

Median Age at First Marriage

As increasingly more women and men stayed longer in education and started to work late, the median age at first marriage rose steadily for both women and men during the period 1981 to 2006. The median age at first marriage for women was 23.9 in 1981 and 28.2 in 2006 while that for men was 27.0 in 1981 and 31.2 in 2006. The increase in the median age at first marriage for both women and men indicated a trend of late marriages.

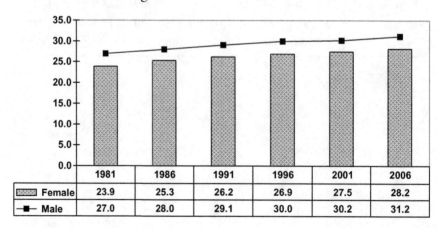

	1981	1986	1991	1996	2001	2006
Female	23.9	25.3	26.2	26.9	27.5	28.2
Male	27.0	28.0	29.1	30.0	30.2	31.2

Single Parents

The number of female single parents rose markedly from 23,059 in 1991 to 57,613 in 2006, while that of male single parents rose less significantly, from 11,479 in 1991 to 14,713 in 2006.

Year / Age Group	1991 Female	1991 Male	1996 Female	1996 Male	2001 Female	2001 Male	2006 Female	2006 Male
15–29	1,152	627	1,283	477	1,879	692	1,769	389
30–39	8,836	3,388	12,386	3,775	17,042	3,741	17,700	3,468
40–49	8,727	4,323	14,109	5,235	22,642	6,072	31,210	6,984
50–59	3,748	2,371	2,277	1,775	3,310	2,127	6,521	3,030
60 and over	596	770	347	645	199	756	413	842
Sub-total	23,059	11,479	30,402	11,907	45,072	13,388	57,613	14,713
Total	34,538		42,309		58,460		72,326	

Total No. of Single Parents

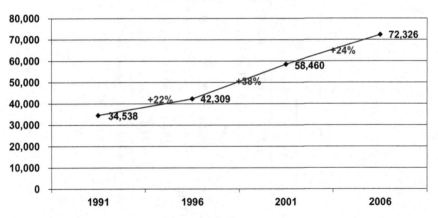

Persons Arrested for Crime by Type of Offence and Gender

The proportion of female offenders committing crime was lower than male offenders. There was a rather notable increase in both women and men arrested for sexual offences over the past years.

Year	2004			2005			2006		
Type of Offence/gender	Female	Male	Sub-total	Female	Male	Sub-total	Female	Male	Sub-total
Violent Crimes	1,274	8,037	9,311	1,440	7,899	9,339	1,672	8,680	10,352
Burglary and Theft	5,482	11,361	16,843	5,548	10,188	15,736	5,505	9,945	15,450
Sexual Offences*	402	2,484	2,886	814	2,843	3,657	633	2,495	3,128
Narcotics Offences	507	2,205	2,712	391	1,833	2,224	454	2,168	2,622
Serious Immigration Offences	220	379	599	294	385	679	274	510	784
Misc. Crimes	2,271	10,209	12,480	2,278	9,147	11,425	2,369	9,509	11,878
Total	10,156	34,675	44,831	10,765	32,295	43,060	10,907	33,307	44,214

* Sexual offences including rape, indecent assault, unlawful sexual intercourse, keeping vice establishment, procuration, abduction of female, etc.

Total No. of Offences 2004–06 *(By Type)*

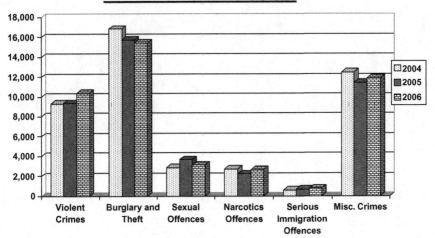

Year 2006 Type of Offence in %

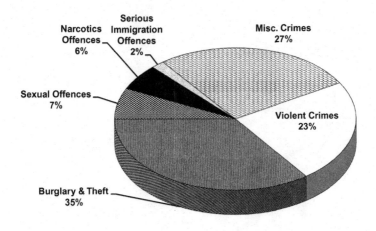

Printed in the United States
By Bookmasters